COMPUTING AND DIGITAL LEARNING FOR PRIMARY TEACHERS

Whether they are new or experienced, teachers are expected to plan and deliver high-quality computing lessons to their pupils. *Computing and Digital Learning for Primary Teachers* provides an accessible introduction to teaching computing effectively and for deeper understanding in the primary classroom.

Filled with practical resources to support lesson design, long-term planning, and assessment, readers will benefit from building their subject knowledge and learning to create engaging lessons for their pupils. Chapters explore:

- Supporting computational thinking and problem-solving to teach our pupils how to solve problems logically and systematically.
- Developing pupils' digital literacy and use of IT, creating exciting opportunities for children's digital self-expression through film, animation, and 3D design.
- Managing technology in our schools, such as setting up and maintaining a virtual learning environment (VLE).
- Cross-curriculum links with STEAM and engineering, allowing children to solve real-world problems by combining their digital literacy with their knowledge of maths, science, and technology.
- Cost-effective and accessible ways of introducing physical computing and robotics to children.
- Safe and responsible uses of artificial intelligence (AI) in our primary schools.

This essential resource provides a highly practical guide to delivering effective computing lessons in the primary classroom and is a must read for anyone who wishes to become a more confident and knowledgeable computing teacher.

Owen Dobbing is an experienced educator, with 10+ years of experience in teaching and leading the development of technology in schools. He is also a member of several Computing at School (CAS) hubs and of the National Centre for Computing Education (NCCE) and STEM Learning. He is currently Head of Computing and Digital Learning at a school in London.

COMPUTING AND DIGITAL LEARNING FOR PRIMARY TEACHERS

Owen Dobbing

LONDON AND NEW YORK

Designed cover image: © Getty Images

First published 2025
by Routledge
4 Park Square, Milton Park, Abingdon, Oxon OX14 4RN

and by Routledge
605 Third Avenue, New York, NY 10158

Routledge is an imprint of the Taylor & Francis Group, an informa business

© 2025 Owen Dobbing

The right of Owen Dobbing to be identified as author of this work has been asserted in accordance with sections 77 and 78 of the Copyright, Designs and Patents Act 1988.

All rights reserved. No part of this book may be reprinted or reproduced or utilised in any form or by any electronic, mechanical, or other means, now known or hereafter invented, including photocopying and recording, or in any information storage or retrieval system, without permission in writing from the publishers.

Trademark notice: Product or corporate names may be trademarks or registered trademarks, and are used only for identification and explanation without intent to infringe.

British Library Cataloguing-in-Publication Data
A catalogue record for this book is available from the British Library

ISBN: 978-1-032-82017-0 (hbk)
ISBN: 978-1-032-82014-9 (pbk)
ISBN: 978-1-003-50255-5 (ebk)

DOI: 10.4324/9781003502555

Typeset in Interstate
by codeMantra

This book is dedicated to my wonderful wife and my lovely daughter, Emily

CONTENTS

	Preface	ix
1	What is computing?	1
2	Computational thinking and problem-solving	6
3	Computing concepts	10
4	Computing schemes of work	31
5	Teaching effective computing lessons	37
6	Teaching computer science	51
7	Teaching information technology	81
8	Teaching digital literacy	95
9	Computing and ICT in early years	105
10	Robotics	112
11	Physical computing	119
12	'Unplugged' activities	126
13	Debugging	131
14	Inclusion	136
15	STEAM	142
16	Green opportunities	145
17	Evidencing and feedback	150

viii *Contents*

18 Assessment and progression 155

19 E-safety and digital citizenship 164

20 Leading computing and digital learning 177

21 Artificial intelligence 188

22 Computing CPD 193

23 Computing and other subjects 197

24 The future of computing 220

Index 227

PREFACE

In computing, children will learn skills that enable them to understand and shape the modern world. They will learn new ways to express themselves, through programming, digital design, filmmaking, animation, and 3D design.

For many children, the learning that takes place in computing lessons will inspire life-long interests. Some children will continue their computing studies into secondary school, further education, and rewarding careers.

Computing can be a joy to teach. Teachers explore technology with children, guiding them through creative expression and problem-solving. Children will harness the power of computers to accomplish things, amazing teachers and themselves!

Computing can also be a challenging subject to plan and teach. Compared to other subjects, resources and thinking for teaching computing are still developing. Many teachers were not taught computing when they were at school and are now required to teach concepts that are unfamiliar.

This book is written to support teachers, enabling them to deliver high-quality and effective computing lessons. It offers teachers a solid understanding of the subject of computing, its rationale, and requirements. It also contains descriptions of some of the best resources available for schools, matching them to computing objectives and lesson activities.

The book can be read all the way through, moving from explanations of the three strands of computing to discussion of more specific fields of computing. Readers can also use the book as a reference text, reading about topics as they are required.

1 What is computing?

National curriculum 2014

In 2014, computing was introduced as a subject into primary and secondary schools in England.

The opening statement of the computing curriculum sets out the aim:

A high-quality Computing education equips pupils to use computational thinking and creativity to understand and change the world.

The introduction of computing as a subject was a timely response to the need for more young people to develop the skills and interests that would meet the challenges and opportunities of the 21st century.

Three strands of computing

Under the national curriculum, there are three strands of computing: **computer science**, **information technology**, and **digital literacy**. It is important that schools give appropriate weight to all three strands.

Computer science is explained in the national curriculum accordingly:

The core of Computing is **computer science**, in which pupils are taught the principles of information and computing, how digital systems work and how to put this knowledge to use using programming.

The 'principles' mentioned here refer to children being able to explain how technology works. Children should be taught to break tasks down and explain them using algorithms – step-by-step instructions for achieving a desired result. Children can then express these algorithms through being taught to create computer programs.

Computer science helps children to understand the technology around them by breaking process down and thinking about what triggers processes and what the outcomes are. Through doing this, children start to think about their own ideas for things that could work, whether new programs or physical systems.

In the national curriculum, **information technology** is defined as,

Equipping pupils to create programs, systems and a range of content.

DOI: 10.4324/9781003502555-1

2 *What is computing?*

Table 1.1 Key stage 1 computing objectives organised by strand

Computer science	• Understand what algorithms are; how they are implemented on digital devices; and that programs execute by following precise and unambiguous instructions • Create and debug simple programs • Use logical reasoning to predict the behaviour of programs
Information technology	• Use technology purposefully to create, organise, store, manipulate, and retrieve digital content
Digital literacy	• Recognise common uses of information technology beyond school • Use technology safely and respectfully, keeping personal information private; identify where to go for help and support when they have concerns about content or contact on the internet or other online technologies

Information technology is usually explained as the content of ICT teaching before 2014. This includes children learning to use software, programs, and equipment and systems to create work. This could involve writing a blog, editing photographs, creating films, animations, and programs.

In the national curriculum, **digital literacy** is defined as teaching pupils to,

> Use, and express themselves and develop ideas through information and communication technology ... as active participants in a digital world.

Digital literacy is usually interpreted by schools as teaching pupils to use technology safely, as responsible digital citizens who understand the consequences of what they do with technology.

Objectives by strand

Although the national curriculum does not explicitly state which objectives belong to which strand, they do seem grouped together as strands in the list of objectives for each year group.

In Table 1.1, the objectives for key stage 1 are organised by strand.

It is worth noting that some objectives have a connection to more than one strand. The objective "Create and debugg programs" involves computer science but also involves using computers creatively and can overlap into the information technology strand.

In Table 1.2, the objectives for key stage 2 are organised by strand.

As with the key stage 1 objectives, we can see several key stage 2 objectives with the potential to overlap into other strands.

The objective "Design and create a range of programs, systems, and content that accomplish specific goals" involves children understanding how systems work through computer science. It also involves them using technology creatively, using IT to express their own ideas.

The objective "Use search appreciate effectively; understand how results are selected and ranked and be discerning in evaluating digital content" involves children using and understanding search engines, while being discerning about the information generated. This could be said to involve computer science, information technology, and digital literacy.

What is computing? 3

Table 1.2 Key stage 2 computing objectives organised by strand

Computer science	• Design and create a range of programs, systems, and content that accomplish specific goals, including controlling or simulating physical systems; solve problems by decomposing them into smaller parts • Use sequence, selection, and repetition on programs; work with variables and various forms of input and output • Use logical reasoning to predict how some simple algorithms work and detect and correct errors in algorithms and programs • Understand computer networks including the internet; how they can provide multiple services, such as the World Wide Web; and the opportunities they offer for communication and collaboration
Information technology	• Use search appreciate effectively; understand how results are selected and ranked and be discerning in evaluating digital content • Select, use, and combine a variety of software (including internet services) on a range of digital devices to design and create a range of programs, systems, and content that accomplish goals, including collecting, analysing, evaluating, and presenting data and information
Digital literacy	• Use technology safely, respectfully, and responsibly; recognise acceptable/unacceptable behaviour; identify a range of ways to report concerns about content and contact

Overlap between strands in any subject is to be expected. In maths, for example, children are required to use calculation skills in other areas of maths, such as when calculating the size of angles in geometry.

In any subject, including computing, it is useful to think of subjects in terms of strands to ensure that children's exposure to a subject is balanced across more than one discipline.

Computing by key stage

Under the national curriculum, subjects, such as maths, science, and English, have objectives for children in each year group. Subjects, such as history, music, and computing, have objectives for each key stage.

For computing, this presents challenges and opportunities.

Here is one of the national curriculum requirements for computing at key stage 2:

Pupils should be taught to use sequence, selection and repetition in programs; work with variables and various forms of input and output.

This requirement for key stage 2 contains several topics: sequence, selection, repetition, variables, input, and output. All these topics require thorough discussion over several lessons.

A challenge here is that the computing curriculum doesn't specify the difference between years 3 and 6 learning (both in key stage 2). Should year 3 be learning about variables? If so, this would look different than year 6 work on variables.

Many schools and schemes of work teach more abstract concepts later in the key stage. Variables, for example, are sometimes saved until year 5 or 6, with simple concepts, such as sequence, repetition, and selection, being taught earlier on.

4   What is computing?

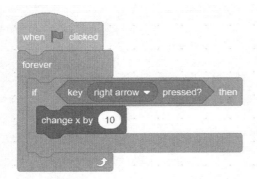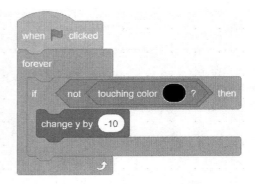

Figure 1.1 An image of Scratch programming showing selection in years 3 and 6. Taken from Scratch, owned by the Scratch Foundation, screenshots are used under CC BY NC 2.0 DEED.

Another approach is a 'spiral' approach, where ideas are covered again and again across year groups, with increasing complexity each time. This more closely resembles the approach taken in 'core' subjects. In maths, division, for example, is taught as early as years 1 and 2. It is not saved until later years, even though it is arguably more abstract than other operations.

In computing, we can teach topics at varying levels of complexity. Selection in year 3 might be as simple as 'if touching' in Scratch, whereas in year 6, children might be using selection with more complicated, Boolean logic (and, not, or). Likewise, children could be introduced to variables in year 3 or 4 in terms of a score in a game changing so that by the time they are in years 5 and 6, they are confident at creating and using their own variables in more sophisticated ways.

As with some other subjects under the national curriculum, schools have flexibility to decide when they teach topics within the requirements for each key stage. In Chapter 4, we will explore how the requirements set out in the national curriculum can be taught via a scheme of work. In Chapter 18, we will look at an interpretation of learning objectives derived from the requirements of the national curriculum.

It is also worth considering how some computing objectives can be achieved or embedded through teaching in other subjects. This is the topic of Chapter 23. As we will see, relationships and health education mention E-safety objectives that complement the objectives required for computing. Design and technology and geography also mention use of digital tools, making it possible to use computing skills in these subjects. In Chapter 23, we will see the potential for use of skills taught in computing in subjects across the curriculum, just as skills taught in English and maths are applied and developed in other subjects.

> **PAUSE AND REFLECT...**
>
> There are three strands to computing under the national curriculum: computer science, information technology, and digital literacy. Requirements are set out according to key stage.
>
> - How can schools ensure that each strand is covered sufficiently?
> - Should schools divide key stage requirements between year groups, or should requirements be taught at different levels of complexity within key stages?

What is computing? 5

Conclusion

The objectives set out by the computing national curriculum provide the framework for children's use of technology in primary school. By receiving a computing education that gives appropriate weight to all three strands of computing, children learn to be creators of technology, as well as users. They learn to use technology effectively, safely, and critically, and they learn exciting and modern forms of self-expression.

Reference

Computing Programs of Study: Key stages 1 and 2, National Curriculum of England, Department for Education, 2013.

2 Computational thinking and problem-solving

What is computational thinking?

Computational thinking is a term used to describe a logical way of approaching problems. It has applications to solving problems in computing and other subjects.

The opening line of the national curriculum for computing[1] states:

A high-quality Computing education equips pupils to use computational thinking and creativity to understand and change the world.

There is a requirement that children learn to approach problems in a logical way, alongside applying their creativity.

There is no single definition of what constitutes computational thinking. Most definitions contain the following terms:

1. **Decomposing** the problem (breaking it down)
2. **Pattern spotting** (within the problem, or between problems)
3. **Abstraction** (ruling out unimportant information)
4. **Algorithm design** (creating a set of step-by-step instructions to solve the problem)

A fifth stage, **Debugging,** is sometimes included, which is where children test and improve their algorithms.

Other aspects of computational thinking include:

- **Generalisation** – using an approach in this problem that works in a previous problem
- **Tinkering** – trying out the equipment and software to see what it is capable of
- **Persevering** – knowing what to do if an approach fails, including trying a different approach

Computational thinking can be taught to children as an example of **meta-thinking** (thinking about thinking). The more that the teacher models using the above terms and applying them to a problem, the more children will start to emulate this.

Some classrooms have 'thinking stations', where children can walk away from the work and go and sit, write notes, and chat through problems. Again, this is all about teaching children to think about and be aware of the thinking process itself.

Computational thinking need not be limited to computing. When children write a story in English, they **decompose** the problem by creating characters, a setting, a plot outline, etc.

DOI: 10.4324/9781003502555-2

Computational thinking and problem-solving 7

They engage in **pattern spotting**, using 'story mountains' for the plot of their story, recognising that most stories start with a setting description, build up tension, have some kind of problem, resolution, and an ending. When writing dialogue, children might follow the pattern: speech → action → speech → action.

In sports, children break down the game into stages and come up with strategies, or **algorithms**, for each stage. They will create 'plays' for different types of scenarios in sports games, recognising patterns and knowing how to respond to these.

Chess is a good activity to develop children's thinking. At a beginner level, children learn the moves of the pieces and the rules of the game. At a slightly higher level, children will learn patterns of openings, counters, tactics, and checkmates. There is a strong case that through playing chess, children learn skills that are transferrable elsewhere, including planning, pattern spotting, and strategy. Chess is also great fun and a good way to make friends!

The more the computational thinking terms are used, the stronger children's meta-thinking becomes, giving them strategies with which to independently work on problems in any context.

Computational thinking is linked to the idea of **growth mindset**, which is gaining recognition in schools. Growth mindset refers to children understanding the importance of working at something in order to master it. It includes children accepting that mistakes and failure are a necessary part of the path to success.

When children in lessons explain that they are stuck, they can be reminded that stuck is good, as it means that you are thinking, provided you have strategies for getting unstuck. Of course, this is of high importance when it comes to debugging – covered in Chapter 12. It is really important that children see debugging as part of the creative process and not an annoying last thought.

With computational thinking, we aim to give children a pathway to solve problems independently, logically, and successfully, as they will hopefully do in their workplaces.

Computational thinking needs to be taught, practised, and modelled, ideally across the whole school in different subjects, and with common language and terminology. It is a worthwhile investment and a key part of empowering children so that they can solve problems independent of the teacher.

Teaching computational thinking

As with any requirement for children to work in a certain way, the best way to ensure computational thinking is by the teacher **modelling** and **scaffolding** it.

The teacher can **model** computational thinking in computing lessons and in other lessons across the curriculum. The more that the teacher uses language like 'decompose the problem', 'spot patterns', and 'algorithm', the more useful these ideas are going to become for children when they solve their own problems. As mentioned above, use of this language develops children's growth mindset. They realise that success is achieved through addressing each aspect of a task, and they learn strategies to help them with this.

The modelling of computational thinking can be used in all subjects where creativity is required. In English lessons, children will plan a story before writing it. They will decompose the story into elements (antagonist, protagonist, opening, build-up, etc.), tackling each part in

8 *Computational thinking and problem-solving*

turn. They will look for patterns – 'what do openings to stories usually contain?' They will use abstraction to rule out irrelevant information to the story. The story itself is their algorithm, the solution that they wrote to the problem of conveying the idea in their head.

In PE, children might learn to decompose a particular movement or play, such as taking a penalty. In maths, they might learn how to start solving a worded problem. In science, children might follow an algorithm for performing an experiment safely. These are all great opportunities to use the language of computational thinking.

As computational thinking is expressly mentioned in the computing curriculum, the teaching of computational thinking skills might take place within computing lessons. The teacher will model using computational thinking when approaching a computing task or problem. In doing this, the teacher will make clear use of the language relating to computational thinking.

For example, children may be tasked with programming a quiz about a topic. The teacher might lead a class discussion about this, modelling the process of planning out the task, writing algorithms for different aspects, and using these algorithms to create code.

This leads to the second aspect of teaching computational thinking, **scaffolding**. This is where we help children to organise their thinking and their work. We do this by providing them with prompts, planning sheets, half-completed examples, and visual indicators of what they should include in their work.

Scaffolding could be used in the quiz activity mentioned above. The teacher could provide children with a planning sheet, containing prompts to help them decompose the task, such as 'what happens when the green flag is pressed?', 'which questions will be asked?', and 'which answers will be accepted?' This scaffolding can be adapted to meet the learning objectives of the lesson, asking children to think about the topic being practised and giving them examples of structures not being taught.

Children who had programmed quizzes before can be prompted to use generalisation at this stage; they will use a similar algorithm for this game as worked in a previous one.

Abstraction is also key and can be prompted through scaffolding at this stage. Children need to define the limits of the problem they are trying to solve; they might only need to create three questions to be answered, so do not need to spend time thinking about more.

As well as making use of computational thinking within creative activities in computing, it can also be worth teaching this approach explicitly.

There are some great tasks with which children can learn about these skills. An example is the 'straw tower', where children are asked to make a tower out of straws to support the greatest weight or reach the highest height. A 'brute force' approach would be children beginning to connect the straws immediately, before realising that the tower topples over, and they try again. Children who had been taught about computational thinking might take a moment to think, sketch out ideas for the base, shape of the sides and platform for the top, listening to each other's ideas. They would talk about the types of shapes they have seen in construction (pattern spotting). They might even decide that they are not going to go beyond a certain height, as they have the goal of having the tower stand up (abstraction). They would then write or verbally give instructions for building the tower (algorithm design). The more that children practise these physical activities, the more confident they become at using computational thinking skills to approach problems.

PAUSE AND REFLECT...

The national curriculum for computing requires teaching children to use computational thinking.

- How often do we teach children *how* to think and solve problems?
- Are there any other types of *meta-thinking* that we should do with children?
- What kinds of activities could help children establish a thinking process?
- How could teaching children to use computational thinking benefit them in other subjects?

Conclusion

Children should be taught to think about thinking and their approach to solving problems from early years onwards. Schools should focus on the process as well as the outcome. This has the added benefit of children shifting their view away from success or failure, towards evaluation of their work.

Children often struggle to start writing a story or start tackling a maths problem. However, when the teacher engages with these children and asks questions such as 'who are your characters going to be?', 'what do they look like?', 'what are the important words in this maths problem?', and 'what do we usually do in a science experiment?', most children can begin the task with confidence. In these cases, the teacher is helping children to use computational thinking, although the children may have started the task without being aware that they need to do this.

The same can be true with computing problems. It is common for computing lessons to consist of the teacher leading a class discussion and modelling the work, before the children attempt the task themselves. This can lead to good outcomes, but it bypasses the thinking and planning stages of the task, meaning children will become stuck when they must solve a problem on their own. Whether they are writing a program, creating a website, or shooting a film, children should always have the chance to plan it out and to have this planning to fall back on if they are stuck.

Note

1 Computing programmes of study: key stages 1 and 2, National curriculum in England, Department for Education, 2013

Reference

Computing Programs of Study: Key stages 1 and 2, National Curriculum of England, Department for Education, 2013.

3 Computing concepts

The vocabulary of computing

It is important that teachers and children are clear about the terminology relating to computing.

The vocabulary covered in this chapter is mostly taken from the curriculum requirements of the key stages 1 and 2 national curriculum, with some additional useful terminology explained.

'Algorithm'

An algorithm is a set of instructions for accomplishing a specific task.

Examples of algorithms include recipes and Lego instructions. The teacher's instructions to children as they come into the classroom constitutes an algorithm (bonus points to teachers who use conditions in their algorithms – i.e. 'if your shoes are muddy, take them off!')

A computer program is also an algorithm, written in a language the computer can understand and follow.

When we are planning out what we want to happen, we write an algorithm (step-by-step instructions) to accomplish the task. This algorithm can be written in sentences, as a flow chart, or using **pseudo-code** (short-hand language that resembles a computer program). When children are happy with their algorithm, they start creating their program.

Use of pseudo-code by children when they are planning their ideas for programs is important for several reasons. First, it can save children time if they realise they do not have to write their ideas in full sentences. Second, it means children think like programmers, using loops, making the program wait until something happens, etc. Third, it makes writing their programs much easier and quicker, as they have already mapped out what they need to include, in precise programming terms.

'Program'

A program is a set of instructions (an algorithm) written in a language that a computer can understand and execute.

Programming languages include **Scratch Junior**, **Scratch**, **Snap**, **Logo**, **Python**, **Java**, **C**, and many more.

DOI: 10.4324/9781003502555-3

Computing concepts 11

Computer programs each have their own **syntax**. The term 'syntax' refers to the rules of a language. In English, a name must have a capital letter at the start, or the reader gets confused and notices an error. As humans, we can overcome this error and put it down to a mistake by the writer, before carrying on reading. A computer cannot overcome a syntax error, and the program will usually stop running, reporting the error.

In Scratch and other block-based programming languages, children can compose and run several **scripts** at the same time. When programming a maze game, they might have several 'when green flag pressed' event blocks, each with a script for a different part of the game. While we should eventually guide children towards having fewer, or one script of commands, eventually using functions to run useful code, children can initially use multiple scripts when they are programming. By doing this, children are **modularising** the task, which supports the idea of decomposing a task and makes finding errors a lot easier.

'Condition' (selection)

'Selection' is the term used by the national curriculum for teaching conditional structures to children.

Children usually grasp this concept quickly as they are used to the terms 'if' and 'otherwise' (particularly from conversations with parents). Computers use the term 'else', instead of otherwise.

According to the national curriculum, children do not have to use selection in programs until key stage 2. However, some of the programs and devices that children will look at in key stage 1 will allow them to consider conditions. The popular app **Kodables** features coloured blocks that cause the character to change direction. Even the fantastic **Duplo Coding Express** features coloured blocks that can be placed on the track and make the train hoot, stop, etc., if the train goes over them. The focus when teaching program reading and creation at key stage 1 should be children reading programs accurately and becoming proficient at stating how devices will move/change direction, etc. However, teachers need not shy away from using conditional language such as 'if' or 'when' with younger children.

In years 3 and 4, children should start considering decisions that a computer has to make. The term 'selection' is used because the computer selects one path to follow if something is 'true' or follows the other path if it is 'false'. A good way to teach selection to children is to pose questions that the computer asks, for example, 'has the right arrow been pressed?' which can be shortened to 'right arrow pressed?' This helps children to draw two outcomes for each decision and they end up with a decision tree. With the example of the right arrow, if the right arrow has not been pressed, the children may want the computer to ask this question again and again, bringing in a forever loop.

The software **Flowol 4** illustrates this well, as whenever a diamond-shaped question (a condition) is posed, there are two lines coming out of it, 'yes' and 'no'. The 'no' line often just feeds straight back into the question, such as for the traffic light button, which continually asks itself if it has been pressed. Flowol 4 is ideal for use with year 6, as the challenges get complex quickly, but children in year 5 could cope with most of the challenges too.

When children have decided on the questions they want to ask in their algorithm, they will be ready to put this into the form of a program. In Scratch, they will use an 'if' block

12 Computing concepts

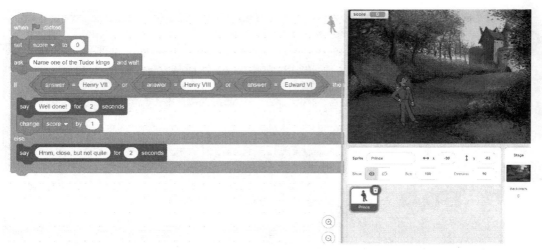

Figure 3.1 A screenshot of a 'quiz game' created in Scratch. This versatile idea for a project uses conditional logic, along with green 'operator' blocks to improve the user experience. Taken from Scratch, owned by the Scratch Foundation, screenshots are used under CC BY NC 2.0 DEED.

and insert a light blue sensing block into the hexagonal space. They may also add in a green operator block, to say what happens if a condition is not met, or if one condition or another is met. Using an 'if/else' block in Scratch allows them to say what happens otherwise, or if the answer to the question is 'no'.

One of the best ways to teach years 3 and 4 children about conditional programming is by having them plan and make a 'quiz game'. Children plan out the questions they want the computer to ask and the responses it gives if the user inputs the correct answer. This is a great project, as it can allow programming to be used for learning in other subjects and make a great cross-curricular project. From the point of view of teaching computing, the potential to extend children on this project is enormous. Children could use green operator blocks, as shown in Figure 3.1. They could add a score by creating a score variable, and they could even use several 'if/else' blocks inside each other. Doing this, they are learning to eventually use 'elif' in text-based programming, where lots of possibilities can be considered by the computer.

As children progress with their understanding of conditionals, they will learn to use different Boolean logic with conditions, so that things can happen if something is **not** true, if something **and** something are true, or if something **or** something is true.

Children can also progress to use 'branching', or 'nested' conditionals to check if lots of things are true. This leads to them using an 'if, elif, else' structure when they start text-based programming in key stage 3.

'Loops' (known as 'repetition', 'iteration')

The concept of loops, referred to as 'repetition' in the national curriculum, is the other significant chunk of programming logic that children need to be taught at primary school.

Computing concepts 13

Use of repetition or loops is closely related to pattern spotting, the second aspect of computational thinking, covered in Chapter 2. When children realise that the same thing, or set of actions is happening more than once, they should be able to suggest that they could just tell the computer to repeat it x times. For example, the algorithm 'red, blue, yellow, red, blue, yellow' can be shortened to 'red, blue, yellow × 2'.

Looping instructions like this is important for several reasons:

1) Using repetition allows for much quicker programming
2) Programs using repetition become neater, better organised, and easier to debug.
3) Computers run more quickly when programs are written more efficiently (only noticeable with very long programs!)

An interesting activity to carry out with children is to give them examples of code that uses loops and doesn't use loops to achieve the same outcome. Get them to match up the same outcomes and discuss why loops have been used!

Nested loops are loops within loops. Nested loops are not necessary to cover until key stage 3, but some children will be able to grasp the concept. A good example of this is in drawing patterns made from shapes. The algorithm ('forward, turn right 90 (repeat ×4) repeat ×10)') will draw 10 squares.

According to the national curriculum, children should start using repetition in their programs from key stage 2. Most children in key stage 1 will encounter repeat loops if they do any programming on a screen. Characters in Scratch Junior, for example, are a lot easier to control if a numerical loop is used. Even when teaching children to compose algorithms for Beebots, they can be encouraged to look for repetition or patterns and to group these into a loop if they are capable.

An **iteration** is an instance of something happening. We saw earlier that programs follow instructions in sequence, moving onto the next instruction when the previous one is complete. If we tell the computer to repeat an instruction three times, there are three iterations of that command before the computer moves onto the next part of the program.

A great way to teach children about loops is to link them to music or dancing. Children can be given children lyrics from pop songs and asked to re-write the lyrics using loops. Making programming about something familiar, such as music, is a way to engage children and help them understand the value of repetition.

Asking children to map out dance routines is another great way to teach them about loops. They can come up with their own dance routine or map out an existing one. The website **Code.org** has a digital, coding-based version of this, where children program a sprite to dance.

As children develop their understanding of using loops to repeat single instructions, they progress to looking for patterns of instructions. Once children identify that there is a pattern, they can repeat several instructions instead of just one.

Teaching children to draw shapes is an excellent way for them to practise spotting patterns and using loops in programming. Asking them to start by coming up with algorithms for simple shapes, such as a square, will enable them to spot patterns in an algorithm such as 'forward 70, turn 90 degrees, forward 70, turn 90 degrees, forward 70, turn 90 degrees,

14 *Computing concepts*

forward 70, turn 90 degrees'. To use a loop and repeat iterations of code, children need to spot the part that is repeating. In this case, it is '(forward 70, turn 90 degrees) × 4'.

When creating shapes in Scratch in this way, it is important that children know that they are turning the **exterior angle** of the shape. Most children at first will suggest the algorithm '(forward 70, turn 60 degrees) × 3' for an equilateral triangle, as the interior angle is 60 degrees. However, modelling this practically to children shows them that the cursor is turning the exterior angle, not the interior angle. This is a great mathematical investigation for Year 5/6, who may benefit from knowing the formula for finding the exterior angle of a shape, which is 360 degrees divided by the number of sides.

There are so many potential activities to practise drawing shapes in this way. Here are some possibilities:

Scratch – Children get a real thrill out of creating shapes in Scratch, having formulated an algorithm and used a repeat loop to make their program efficiently structured. This can make a great mathematical/computational display or be taken further by the children if they chose to create a pattern out of these shapes. Of course, once the children have the program for a shape, they can 'make a block' in Scratch called the name of this shape and then re-use this code again and again. This is called making a function (see below).

Robotics – Robotics is a great area for children to practise repetition of instructions, as through watching a robot repeat tasks, they really see the value of using repetition in their programs. Two of the best on-screen resources available are **VexcodeVR** and **Gearsbot**, the latter a Singaporean website set up to simulate robotics. The website features challenges such as robots retrieving blocks, or navigating mazes, and is a perfect way for children to think of algorithms that repeat instructions. The website is free and simulates all of the activities that expensive robot sets would achieve. See the chapter on robotics for more ideas.

'Subroutines' – functions, procedures, and parameters

Functions and procedures are both types of **subroutines**. A subroutine is a small section of code that runs within a program. Subroutines (including functions and procedures) can be thought of as being 'mini programs within a program'.

There is a distinction between a function and a procedure, outlined below:

A **procedure** is a block of code that is created once and then named. This code can then be repeated as often as necessary, saving typing in the code again.

A **function** is like a procedure, but when a function is run, it returns a value.

A **parameter** is where we can feed arguments which are values that we feed (often numerical) into a function we have created.

Blocks of code that children create can be safely referred to as functions, without worrying too much about the distinction between functions and procedures.

Teaching functions and procedures is not required under the English national curriculum until key stage 3. They are included in this book as an extension for children who are ready for new ways to structure code more efficiently. Children as young as year 4 can be taught to create their own blocks of code in Scratch to enable them to repeat patterns of shapes. If anything, this makes the programming easier for them.

Computing concepts 15

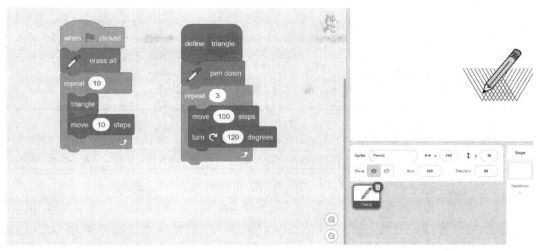

Figure 3.2 A screenshot of code from Scratch that shows how code can be organised into a subroutine, through 'making a block'. This could be referred to with children as a 'function'. Taken from Scratch, owned by the Scratch Foundation, screenshots are used under CC BY NC 2.0 DEED.

Fairly while learning to code in Scratch, children will learn to (and need to) use **broadcasts** to make one sprite give instructions to another sprite. Broadcasts are similar to procedures, in that the program contains a single line of code, a named command, that starts a sequence of other commands. Broadcasts can be introduced at key stage 2 and are a good stepping-stone to the more abstract concept of procedures.

In Scratch, children can create their own blocks (the pink blocks of code). Creating and naming a block of code is called 'defining' a function. Including the function in the program so that the computer carries out the instructions contained in it is called 'calling' a function.

On the website **code.org**, there is a great video analogising this to plays in sports, where the coach says 'attack' and the team knows what to do. A good example of a function is the idea of the teacher saying, "tidy up" and the class knowing the actions to perform.

As well as creating blocks of code in Scratch, children are able to create subroutines in Flowol 4 when they solve the problems there. This helps them to organise their programs and should save them time in some of the problems.

A **parameter** is where we feed information into a function or procedure. The command 'go forward' is a procedure, as it is a command for the robot's wheels to turn one way for a certain duration. If we gave the command, 'go forward (3)', the '(3)' would be a parameter.

Once children have mastered creating their own blocks (functions), the next step for them is to create functions that use **parameters**. This is a big jump in terms of understanding and should only be taught to the most able children. Parameters are included in this book for the sake of teacher understanding and for the most capable children.

16 *Computing concepts*

'Variable'

A variable is a value that can change. Very often, variables are numerical values, such as 'score' or 'lives'. We can program 'score' to increase when a sprite touches an item in a game, or another even occurs.

Variables can also be other forms of information that can change in a program. For example, in Scratch, 'answer' is a variable which is set to the answer to the question asked using a light blue 'ask' block

'X position' and 'Y position' are variables, as they are values that change depending on the position of a sprite. They are incredibly useful variables that allow other parts of the program to know the position of a sprite.

When children start programming using **Python**, they must create and name their own variables before writing code to control them or make the program respond to them. In Python, variables cannot start with a capital letter and must be all one word or two words separated by an underscore. Most key stage 2 children will not program using Python, as block-based languages are more than sufficient and allow children to focus on logic instead of syntax.

Variables are used in science, and it is good for children to make this connection. To run a fair test in a scientific experiment, children must only change one variable, such as the temperature, so that they can see the effect that this has in their experiment. They term 'variable' helpfully contains the word 'vary', so children can easily remember that a variable is something that can vary, or change.

'Events'

It is important for children to consider what causes computers to start running programs. In **Scratch** and other block-based languages, this is referred to as an 'event'. Another word for an event is an 'input' (see input and output below).

When children are doing on-screen programming, the event will very often be 'when the green flag is pressed', 'when the sprite is clicked', or 'when a key is pressed'. Other events could be 'when the sprite is close to another sprite', 'when the sprite touches another colour', or 'when a variable = an amount'. Broadcasts can also be used as events, such as 'when the sprite receives 'happy''.

Helpfully, even simple block-based programming languages reinforce the concept of events. In **Scratch Junior** on the iPad, children quickly learn that their scripts need to start with an event, usually the green flag to start with. Even tools such as the excellent **Duplo Coding Express** sets start children thinking about the event (coloured tile) that will cause an action, or several actions to happen.

By the time children start learning to program in Scratch, or other block-based languages, they should be familiar with an event (input) and an action (output). This logical way of structuring their programs prepares them well for decomposing programming tasks into their futures.

One of the clearest examples of event-based programming is in the excellent **App Lab**, within **code.org**. Although this environment looks complex, children can create simple apps

Computing concepts   17

using the **on event...** block together with the **set screen** block. With this structure, children can create simple apps that change screen when buttons are pressed.

App Lab can be used for the brilliant **Apps for Good** project, which is covered in Chapter 16.

'Sequence'

It can be interesting to explore how differences in sequence in children's code can affect their programs. 'Sequence' refers to the order in which commands exist in their program. It is important to teach children that computers follow commands in exactly the order they are given, sometimes with unexpected results!

One of the mistakes that nearly all young programmers make is forgetting to put 'wait' commands in their programs. **Flowol 4** illustrates this well. In certain 'mimics' (scenarios), children are required to program things like traffic lights. Nearly all will tell the traffic lights to change colour, without putting a 'wait' command in. They will then see only one colour of the traffic light. This leads to class discussion of how quickly computers carry out instructions and that they do not pause to allow humans to keep up! Similar things happen when children animate characters in Scratch.

Another example of a sequencing mistake is when children have to choose whether to use the 'play sound' block in Scratch, or the 'play sound until done'. Both can be useful; the second will not start the next instruction in the sequence until the sound has been played. This might not work in a game, as children might want the sound to play while the next instruction in their code happens.

Loops are an important aspect of sequencing. When children program characters to move, they will say, 'if right arrow is pressed, move right'. What needs to be explained to them here is that this command has now been followed by the computer and the computer has moved on down the sequence. To make the arrow key work as desired, the computer needs to be told to do this forever, or until something happens.

The above examples of exploration of sequence are likely to be explored with key stage 2 children. Sequence is also often explored at key stage 1, when children are learning about simpler instructions.

'Script'

A script is a sequence of code. Children will encounter this term in block-based languages such as Scratch. In block-based languages, they can create several separate scripts, which helpfully can run simultaneously. Creating separate scripts can help children organise their ideas and create their code. The alternative, putting all the commands into one long script, makes spotting bugs harder, especially if small screens are used in schools.

Separating code into different scripts allows the children to eventually develop their programming by creating 'functions'. To create a function, children would create a 'custom' block and name it, before adding the code from separate scripts to this block. It might look a bit amateurish to have lots of scripts running, and some programmers might prefer to give all commands in the same script, but for less confident programmers, having separate scripts can help them organise and construct their ideas.

18   *Computing concepts*

'Pseudo-code'

Pseudo-code refers to instructions written using the language of coding, but which is not quite code that a computer can follow.

Children can use pseudo-code from an early age without realising, if they are encouraged to use words like 'if', 'until', 'repeat', 'wait', and 'when'. These are all 'computing terms' and should be displayed prominently to children, as well as modelled by the teacher. When using this language, the teacher should make it clear to children that we are using 'computer talk', or a similar expression, to help children to see that we use a certain type of language when formulating instructions for computers.

As children learn to write, they will naturally start to use these terms in their written algorithms.

Older children will write pseudo code that more closely resembles a computer program. It is not uncommon to see children even drawing out ideas using Scratch-like blocks of programming.

When children start text-based programming (most likely in year 7 or 8), they will write text that closely resembles Python, or whichever text-based language that they are learning. They will miss out the colons, brackets and some of the other syntax that they would include in their program, but other than this, what they write down as ideas will closely resemble code.

'Axis'

As soon as children start programming sprites to move on screen, they will be required to instruct the computer on which axis to move their sprites along. This can cause problems, since children are usually taught about the 'x' and 'y' axis and negative numbers in years 5 and 6, later they will use these concepts in computing. This does not have to cause major issues. If well scaffolded, children can cope with understanding that a character moving up and down moves on the 'y' axis and moving left and right moves on the 'x' axis.

Scaffolding and supporting the concepts of 'x' and 'y' axis can include using printed sheets of paper with axis drawn upon them, for children to move physical representations of sprites around on.

Children can also be provided with examples of code to modify. Providing code such as in the examples below offers children an excellent opportunity for pattern spotting, as they realise that the algorithms for moving in different directions are almost identical. When they are coding, they can create code for one direction and then 'duplicate' it (right click and select 'duplicate'), before changing the values. This is extremely good practice and reflects how programmers work.

It is worth noting that nowadays, children do not have to use axes in their programming. Alternatives exist, particularly in the field of robotics. These include using **Lego Mindstorms/EV3/Spike Prime**, **Sphero** robots, and even **VexCode VR** and **Gearsbot** (all covered in Chapter 10). None of these platforms use 'x' or 'y' axis; the robots move using conventional 'forward'/'backwards', etc., commands. Using **Kodu** is an alternative for on-screen programming that also does not use 'x' or 'y' axis.

Computing concepts 19

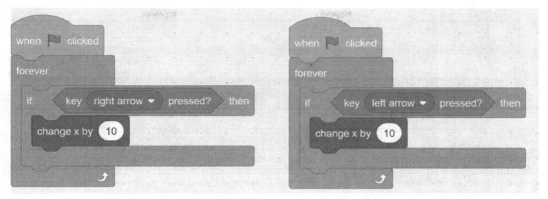

Figure 3.3 A screenshot of code from Scratch showing code that children can modify to control the direction of a sprite. Screenshot by the author. Taken from Scratch, owned by the Scratch Foundation, screenshots are used under CC BY NC 2.0 DEED.

> **PAUSE AND REFLECT…**
>
> According to the national curriculum, children should recognise, understand, and be able to use sequence, selection, repetition, and variables. These are the building blocks of programming.
>
> - What small activities can we give children to ensure that they remain familiar with these concepts?
> - How can we balance children's reading of code to spot coding concepts, with writing their own code?

'Computer'

'What is a computer?' 'What do computers do?' 'Where are computers?' These are all questions that can stimulate interesting and valuable discussion among children at all ages. The questions could be answered at all levels, from early years to degree level. The important thing is that children start to think about how the world around them works and consider that the technological outcomes they see have causes and controllable outcomes.

A possible answer to the question 'What is a computer?' is that a computer is a device that receives instructions from a user and performs actions based on its program. Computers contain switches that can be on or off. Programs tell the computer which switches to turn on or off, computers therefore need memory to remember these instructions. Modern computers have billions of switches in their processors, which act like the brain of a computer. A light switch is not a computer, as it is only a single switch with no memory, although this is a good distinction to explore.

At primary level, children should start thinking about their own ideas for **inputs** (information that could go into a computer) and **outputs** (what they see the computer do). Programs

20 Computing concepts

determine how the computer responds to inputs and how it controls outputs. Discussions with children about computers and devices in the world around them will help them to think about their own ideas for controlling inputs and outputs.

Children are often surprised by the fact that there are computers all around them, in their cars, in their cookers, in everyday equipment such as automatic doors. Digital watches from the 1990's were more powerful than the computer that sent Apollo 11 to the Moon, so imagine how much more powerful iPads and modern computers are! **Moore's law** states that processing power roughly doubles every year; and this trend has led to exponential growth in processing power. Whether this trend will continue is unknown. **Quantum computing** may allow for even more powerful computers that can solve some of mankind's deepest mysteries. Quantum computers contain 'switches' that can be on, off, or on/off at the same time, vastly increasing the number of possible calculations possible.

It is not suggested that discussion of Moore's law or quantum computing takes place in primary school (although it might!). Children should start to talk about how computers control some of the processes they witness in the world around them. This may, in turn, lead to further discussion about the nature, limitations, and future of computers.

'Boolean statement'

Boolean logic, named after the English mathematician **George Boole**, refers **to statements that are evaluated as true or false**. Computers use conditions to check to see whether statements are true or false all the time, such as 'if the space key is pressed, jump, otherwise do nothing'.

Boolean logic can incorporate the statements 'and', 'not', or 'or'. In block-based languages such as Scratch, this type of logic is available by using the green 'operator' blocks.

Under the national curriculum, using a full range Boolean logic is not required until key stage 3. The logic that teachers and children will most likely want to start using at key stage 2 is the 'not' logic. For example, if they were making a game which required a sprite to fall (simulating gravity), their algorithm might read 'if not touching the ground colour, then change y

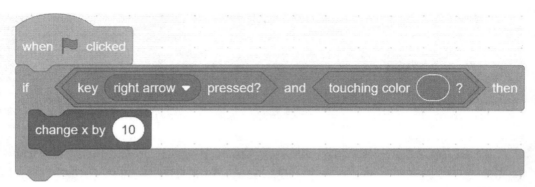

Figure 3.4 A screenshot of code from Scratch, showing 'if' blocks with an 'and' operator. Screenshot taken by the author. Taken from Scratch, owned by the Scratch Foundation, screenshots are used under CC BY NC 2.0 DEED.

by 10'. Children programming robots may wish to include programming such as 'if not close to an object, then drive forward'.

This is about as far as I would stretch most children at key stage 2. The most capable children might use the 'or' or 'not' blocks in block-based programming. Teachers might not initiate conversations about the range of logical statements under Boolean logic. Explaining that computers use conditions to do something 'if' something else is true is enough at key stage 2 and prepares them well for the next stage of their computing education.

'Operators' and expressions

In most block-based programming languages such as Scratch, operators are the green blocks. These determine what type of action is to be performed.

There are three types of operators, all of which are useful at key stage 2. These are:

Mathematical operators

These tell the computer to perform a mathematical function to a value, including '+', '−', 'times' '(*)', or 'divide' ('/'). Additional mathematical operators include the 'mod' operator, which returns the remainder after a division.

Children can make simple programs to return mathematical values, including 'times table practise' programs, mathematical quizzes, or doubling programs. All of these let children see how quickly computers can perform calculations!

Comparison operators

These operators tell the computer to check a value compared to another value. This includes 'more than', 'less than', and 'equal to'. Children will use these operators frequently, as they check to see if the position of a sprite on the screen is less than a certain amount (i.e., if the sprite has fallen too low!). Children will also use comparison operators to check other variables, with algorithms and code such as 'if the score > 100, you win'.

Logical operators

As explained in the section on Boolean statements, these are the statements that computers can use to evaluate whether something is true or false. This includes 'not', 'and', or 'or' statements. The most useful logical operator at key stage 2 is the 'not' block, which children can use in programs without too much trouble, such as saying 'if the answer is not ...'. The 'and' and 'or' operators require slightly a higher level of thinking which most children will be ready for at key stage 3.

'Pixel'

Pixels are the tiny lights that make up a computer screen. Each pixel can be set to any one of millions of colours, making up an overall image. Understanding pixels is important at key stage 2, as most on-screen programming languages use pixels as reference for movement.

22 *Computing concepts*

'Move 10' in Scratch, means move ten pixels to the right. It is therefore, worth a discussion about what this means, and that moving ten pixels across on the screen is a fairly tiny movement!

Children who use **Microbits** or other physical equipment in school will be able to write programs to turn the individual lights on or off or create pictures by turning combinations of lights on or off. This is a perfect introduction to pixels and how they make up images on screens. On a Microbit, there are 20 lights (pixels) that make up the overall picture. The picture is therefore low resolution (low quality). Modern computer screens have ranges such as 1024 × 800 pixels (1024 across and 800 up), resulting in millions of pixels and a high-resolution image on the screen. Children with good eyesight can see the individual, square pixels on a screen, although be careful of eye strain if looking for too long!

'Debug'

The term 'debugging' is often attributed to **Admiral Grace Hopper**, whose team discovered a moth inside a computer. Grace Hopper then remarked that her team were 'debugging the system' to make it function again. The term 'bug' was, in fact, used much earlier by **Thomas Edison** to describe problems with mechanical engineering.

Debugging is a crucial part of programming, with programmers often spending longer debugging than writing the programs in the first place. Debugging is often regarded as one of the stages of computational thinking. It also has comparisons with the engineering cycle: 'define the problem, imagine solutions, decide on a solution, build, test, improve'. As stated earlier, 'growth mindset' is rightly gaining prominence in schools, that is teaching children that failure is part of success.

Teaching children to debug effectively and independently is a crucial part of teaching computing. Children should expect there to be errors when they run their programs and should know a logical, independent process to follow when their program does not work. Failing to make this process explicit to children will result in unnecessary frustration and 'hands up' across the whole classroom, derailing the teacher's plans for the lesson!

For children to debug successfully, they need to do several other things as they code:

1) Children need to decompose problems and test them step by step. By doing this, they will know where bugs are, as opposed to having to look for bugs in the entire program when they have finished.
2) Children need to have a logical approach to debugging, which they are familiar with. This could be as follows: (1) Run the program and observe the behaviour. (2) Locate which part of the code might be wrong. (3) Change and retest.
3) Know about different types of bugs. These include numbers being wrong, missing commands, incorrect sequence, wrong structure (missing loops, commands outside of conditionals, etc.)

If these steps to debugging are prominently displayed in the classroom and children have plenty of practise, debugging will become as much a part of the lesson as coding.

There are some good activities to practise debugging. One of the best is where the teacher creates a program which contains one or more errors and shares this with the class. This can

Computing concepts   23

be done via Scratch, by giving the children a link to a project created. Depending on the age group taught, the code and the bug can be easier or harder to read and spot!

Debugging is explored in more depth in Chapter 13.

'Input'/'Output'

An 'input' is the term used for information entering a computer. This is often through signals from a physical device, such as a keyboard or a mouse, or through a sensor, such as a distance sensor on automatic doors.

An 'output' is information coming out of the computer to cause the action that a computer takes, very often, something that a user sees happen. Examples of outputs are motors turning, lights flashing, a document printing, or a speaker making a sound.

The basic premise of how computers work is 'input → process → output'. A computer receives data from an input. The computer's program tells it what to do when it receives this data, with the result of an output.

Some great conversations can be had with children around this premise. Once they understand this premise, they start to make sense of how technology around them works. Teachers can start with the input, i.e. 'What happens when we press the letter 'I' on the keyboard?', or the output, such as 'Why do the automatic doors open?' Encouraging children to be as specific as they can with the explanations helps deepen their understanding. For example, instead of accepting 'the letter I appears on the screen' as an answer for the first question above, asking pupils to refer to the pixels (tiny lights that make up the screen) illuminating leads to a higher level of discussion and thinking about how technology works.

When it comes to physical computing and robotics (see the relevant chapters), discussion of input and output is fundamental to children being able to control and design their own devices.

Even for screen programming, discussion of input and output is important. In Scratch and other block-based environments, children are usually encouraged to think about 'events' that will cause sections of their code to run. The teacher helping them to structure their planning as 'input' (event) and 'output' (behaviour) is a logical and beneficial way for them to plan their programs.

'Network'

Children at key stage 2 are required to understand computer networks, including the internet.

A network is created when computers are linked together. This can be done wirelessly or using wired connections. Most computer networks are a combination of wired and wireless networks.

All information on the internet is stored on computers, grouped together into banks of many together called **servers**. Big companies have hundreds of servers grouped together in buildings called **data centres**. Each of these servers has an IP address, similar to a postal address.

Each computer or mobile device also has a unique IP address. When you request information from the internet, the request travels through the network cable from the back of the

24 *Computing concepts*

computer, through a switch and then through a cable that leaves the school. This cable connects to the 'internet', which is the name given for the network of cables that extend across the world. Cables are linked together via junctions called 'routers' so that information can take many different paths. Information is broken down into 'packets' that are reassembled when they have travelled from one device to another.

The above may sound confusing at first, but there are a lot of materials available online to help teach this. Children could start by watching simple videos explaining this process (available via YouTube) and then complete activities such as labelling diagrams with terms including 'router' and 'server'.

To help teach the concept of a network, a great activity is to have the children create a network using themselves, where they each take on the role of one of the above components. Children then pass 'packets' of data around the network to explore and understand the journey that information takes.

Children then go on a tour of the school and follow network cables that come out of computers, looking for the school switch and cable that leaves the school.

'Internet'

As explained, all information on the internet is stored on physical computers called servers, many of which are in huge buildings called data centres.

This is important for children to understand, as with phrases such as 'the cloud', information can seem like it is appearing out of thin air. 'The cloud' refers to the information and programs on these physical servers, which can be accessed through requests sent over the internet. The important thing about the cloud is that services are running on servers, not on your own computer.

Cloud computing, one of the major developments of the 21st century, is an extension of this, where computational power and storage takes place on computers elsewhere in the world.

The internet is the connection between devices all around the world, whether through wired or wireless connections. All connections are eventually connected via a wire, as wireless routers have wires going into them to connect them to the rest of the internet.

To connect all computers together across the world, huge cables are laid under oceans. This means that your computer can request and receive information from a computer on another continent within seconds. Modern cables are made of fibre optics, which allows signals to be sent via light meaning very fast transmission.

'World Wide Web'

The World Wide Web is a collection of websites that can be accessed over the internet. The internet is the network that data from these pages is sent across.

Webpages can contain text, images, or videos. When you request information from a webpage, data is sent to you by being broken down into packets and directed to your computer via junctions called routers.

'URL'

A URL (uniform resource locator), often known as a 'web address', is the address given to a webpage on the internet. By using a web browser (such as Chrome or Firefox), we can type in and specify which webpage we want to view on the internet by typing in the URL. What we are doing is specifying the IP Address that we want to receive information from, but it is a lot easier to remember a URL such as apple.com, than an IP address containing a string of numbers.

'PRIMM'

Sue Sentance, Chief Learning Officer at the Raspberry Pi Foundation, introduced the term 'PRIMM', which stands for **Predict, Run, Investigate, Modify, Make**. PRIMM is an effective way for children to learn about new code and create their own. It recognises the importance of reading code written by others, exploring, and discussing code, and then making code with varying degrees of scaffolding provided by the teacher.

Some coding lessons will not follow the PRIMM approach in its entirety. Lessons might instead focus on one element or a skill such as debugging. In Chapter 5, we will consider the place of PRIMM in teaching effective computing lessons.

PRIMM is an example of **metathinking**, teaching children **to think about what the thinking they are doing**, i.e., 'now we are in the predict phase'. Metathinking is an important concept to address in schools, teaching the children how to learn new concepts.

'Predict'

The first stage of the PRIMM process involves looking at code that others have written. There are two important aspects here:

1) Reading code – Just as children learn to write having read stories written by others, they learn to write code having learned from and been inspired by programs written by others. I often encourage children to read code as they would a story, reading it out loud and skipping over any parts that they do not understand, perhaps highlighting them for later.
2) Making predictions – Children should be posed questions that require them to have opinions about the outcome of code. This can involve what they think they will see happen, any bugs that might arise and any changes that they think could be made.

In computing lessons, the 'predict' phase will take part in different ways. It could be through whole class discussion, where the teacher puts code on the board for the class to discuss, before running it. Alternatively, the teacher could print out code for children to discuss in pairs or groups. Teachers could even share code via a virtual learning environment (VLE) such as Google Classroom. Teachers can either share screenshots of code for children to discuss, or share links to Scratch projects, other block-based code or typed code.

Another great way to get children talking about code is through **Parson's problems** – where the teacher gives children jumbled up code to put in order and discuss. This could be through cutting out blocks of code in Scratch, or Scratch Junior.

'Run'

This is the phase of the lesson or activity where children test their predictions and execute the code that they have been discussing. The quality of the discussions preceding this phase will affect the impact of this phase. Crucially, this approach allows children to run code that is slightly above the level of their current knowledge. In this way, they are working in Vygotsky's **zone of proximal development**, working at the level that will challenge and extend them.

'Investigate'

The investigate phase of PRIMM involves the children taking part in activities set by the teacher, to further explore the coding concepts that they are learning about. As mentioned above, Parsons problems can be used here too, where children physically move around blocks of the code to change its outcome. Children may write about the code or annotate it at this stage, or match sections of the code to particular outcomes. By the end of this stage, the children will be ready to start coding themselves and will have a good understanding of the concepts being taught in the lesson.

'Modify'

Children may have already modified the code in the 'Run' phase – this is often a natural extension of their running of the code for the first time. The 'modify' stage of PRIMM refers to children being scaffolded when they write programs.

'Make'

Now that the children are familiar with the code and the concepts being taught, they have a go at making their own. This is a really important phase, and it is important that the children have a go at coding without looking at examples by others. It is at this stage that children must draw upon their thinking and understanding. As mentioned above, children should have resources (scaffolding) to support them when they are stuck. For older children, this can include them learning to search online for examples of code that perform similar functions to theirs.

PRIMM in lessons

It can sometimes seem quite challenging to plan the PRIMM sequence into lessons. Children usually only have one computing lesson per week and are often eager to spend this time working at the computer, rather than doing writing on worksheets or other preparatory tasks. It can seem easier in a computing lesson to show children an example of the code that they are going to use, discuss it, and send them off to the computers to make something similar. Children (like adults) are eager to get started!

The key to employing the PRIMM approach properly is to be clear about the learning outcome desired. A teacher can give children Scratch Junior on iPads, Scratch on a computer,

Computing concepts 27

or a Lego Robotics set. With discussion and exemplification, children may make something exciting happen!

What the PRIMM approach is so good at doing is focussing the children's thinking and energy on the zone of development that the teacher has decided upon. In this way, children will not spend 20 minutes in Scratch either doing something that they can already do (such as designing a costume or constructing basic elements of code) and will instead be focused on the task provided to take their programming understanding to the next level.

One way to employ the PRIMM approach effectively is for the children to have a **computing exercise book**, in the same way that they have a book for other subjects. This makes it really clear to students when they are supposed to do some thinking around some code and acts as a record and a resource for them.

As stated above, not every lesson needs to follow all the stages of PRIMM. There should be some computer work in every computing lesson. Some lessons might be entirely based around running code written by others and changing the code to affect the outcome. This can be achieved via Scratch projects shared by the teacher or through activities selected from **Blockly games** or **code.org** (both covered in Chapter 5). Activities like these reduce cognitive load and allow children to focus on practising desired skills.

Some lesson might be entirely about debugging, teaching children the skills and process needed when code goes wrong. Children might do activities such as 'breaking' code written by someone else, for another to fix.

Some coding lessons should be focused all around the 'make' stage, where children draw upon their knowledge of coding to solve a problem.

Other coding lessons could be 'tinkering' lessons, where the teacher does not provide demonstration, but allows children to find out what they can through trying things out for themselves. These sessions, while being freer, will benefit from a thoughtful evaluation of what was found out and what is needed to learn, perhaps leading into one of the phases of the PRIMM sequence.

Cognitive load

Cognitive load theory refers to the 'processing power' of the brain. This is a limited resource. If a new concept, piece of software, or working environment is being introduced to children, this takes up a significant piece of that power.

As teachers of computing, we need to be aware of what children know, do not know, and what we want them to learn in that lesson. If children have not used the computers much and do not know how to log on quickly, the lesson might involve teaching them to log on and off until they can do this. If they do not know how to open and use the internet, the lesson might be about this, with activities for them to practise this. If we want inexperienced computer users to do some coding (as we might), we could set up the computers for them, already logged in with the software open on the screen. This way, their cognitive load is used on the programming task, not on logging onto the computer and opening the software.

Another element of managing cognitive load is breaking large tasks down into teachable elements. When teaching children to use Lego Spike Prime equipment for the first time, the whole lesson might be around making the motor turn one way or the other precisely. This can be through the children making a bridge that opens or closes, a ticking clock, or something else

28 *Computing concepts*

with a simple movement. If teaching the children to use the distance sensors, the whole lesson will be around this, with a simple outcome, such as making the brick 'bleep' when something gets too close. Teachers may even set up the code on the screen ready for children, with the brick connected to the computer. In this way, 100% of the children's cognitive power is used on the learning desired, not on 'how to plug in the brick', or how to put the code blocks in place.

This is not to say that children cannot do more than one thing at a time; as they develop their skills at using computers, they will be able to multitask using digital devices. But as computing teachers, it is important for us to recognise that many of the skills we require children to use in computing lessons are unique to that environment – these can include skills such as clicking the mouse, typing, and navigating the computer.

Paired programming

Paired programming is a method of two children working together to create a program. It involves one of the children being the 'driver' and the other child being the 'navigator'. The driver inputs the code and controls the computer. The navigator tells the driver what to do, thinking about solutions to the problem.

Paired programming is prevalent in activities on the website **code.org** which features an excellent video to show children, explaining how children should fulfil the roles of driver and navigator, and that they should swap over from time to time!

Using paired programming in the classroom

Paired programming can be an invaluable method for children working in computing lessons. It benefits several aspects of computing lessons, outlined below.

Sharing resources – computing teachers are often constrained by resources, whether it is laptops, sets of equipment, or other devices. It is perfectly fine for children to pair up to share resources. Using paired programming, children both have a clear role to play, enhancing the focus of both children.

Communication and collaboration – We often ask children to work together, but how often do we teach them *how* to work together? Paired programming sets out one method for children working together as an effective team. It emphasises communication and listening, as children in both roles need to explain what they are doing and rely upon the other person.

Verbalising and planning ideas – Similar to 'talk for writing', employed in English lessons, children's coding benefits from them talking about their programming before and as they do it. In the 'navigator' role, children must suggest solutions to the problem, using sequences of instructions and coding concepts such as loops and conditions. Children in both roles must ask questions of each other and talk about the code, helping to embed their understanding of the concepts being covered in the lesson.

The engineering process

The engineering process is a system that benefits any scenario where a problem is being solved. This way of working is often beneficial to computing lessons and children can be taught to follow its steps. Following the engineering process could be described as 'meta learning', that is, 'learning to learn', as we are teaching children to talk about the steps they go through to solve problems.

The engineering process is cyclical, so that the last step feeds back into the first. The engineering process is usually explained as follows:

- **Identify** the problem
- **Suggest** ideas
- **Choose** an idea
- Build a **prototype**
- **Test** and **observe** (repeat the process from step 1)

Teaching children to follow the engineering process is beneficial for their growth mindset. Growth mindset teaches children that hard work is what solves problems, rather than innate ability or talent. The engineering process reinforces this, as children see clear steps that they must go through to develop an idea, including the fact that there will be mistakes and problems to solve along the way!

The engineering process is a good approach to some of the problems children might tackle in computing lessons, as well as subjects across the curriculum. It will be referred to throughout this book.

E-safety

One of the most important facets of teaching children to use computers is teaching them to use computers safely and responsibly. Just as with any area of life, we can never prevent children from being exposed to every danger, but we can teach them to make good choices so that their exposure to danger is limited and so that when they come across danger, they know what to do, and not to do.

E-safety will be taught explicitly in lessons, including in computing and health and relationship education. As we will explore in Chapter 19, E-safety should also be an integral part of school life, talked about frequently and with a visible presence in school. This must be the case, as children are being exposed more and more to technology and the internet at home and at school.

Conclusion

As computing is still a relatively new subject, it uses terminology that is often unfamiliar. Schools need to ensure that the terms covered in this chapter become widely used and understood by all staff and children.

Schools can promote the vocabulary relating to computing through displays, events, assemblies, and staff training. The terms covered in this chapter may be unfamiliar in some cases, but they refer to simple and understandable aspects of technology use. The aim should therefore be that these terms become as familiar as terms used in maths, English, or other subjects. This empowers staff and children through enabling them to be precise about aspects of technology use.

30   *Computing concepts*

References

Code.org, https://code.org/
Computing Programs of Study: key stages 1 and 2, National Curriculum of England, Department for Education, 2013.Scratch, https://scratch.mit.edu/
Gearsbot, https://gears.aposteriori.com.sg/
VexcodeVR, https://vr.vex.com/
Apps for Good, https://www.appsforgood.org/

4 Computing schemes of work

The importance of a scheme of work

There are many computing schemes of work available for schools to select from, many available for free. One of the best pre-made computing schemes of work is the **Teach Computing curriculum**,[1] developed by the **National Centre for Computing Education** (NCCE), which is funded by the Department for Education (DfE). This scheme of work covers all areas of the computing curriculum, with well-designed and interesting units. It is a great starting point for schools to build on. Schools can rewrite and substitute units where they feel they have opportunities, strengths, and specialisms.

A computing scheme of work ensures lessons are strategic and working towards an established overall goal. It ensures that children have a good balance between different strands of computing, with appropriate time spent to explore topics and create outcomes. There will also be sufficient time to repeat concepts so that that knowledge is embedded. A priority for any computing lead will therefore be to examine the school's scheme of work and make improvements where necessary.

As discussed in Chapter 2, one approach to a scheme of work for computing is a 'spiral' approach, where skills and use of technology are repeated. A spiral curriculum repeats concepts within year groups, as well as between year groups. This approach means that children have a chance to develop their learning, embed their learning through repetition, and lessen the time that the teacher must spend introducing the basics of how to use a new piece of technology.

There is so much exciting technology that can be used in computing lessons and so many exciting projects that children can work on to meet the goals set out. When choosing, developing, or designing a scheme of work, schools must look at the resources that are available to them, the strengths of the school, and the interests and strengths of the staff. A school in the countryside may, for example, do projects relating to measuring data about animals and plant growth, planning, and purchasing technology accordingly. Schools in cities might develop schemes of work around transport, demographics, and local communities. Just as with any other subject, the ethos and identity of the school should be visible in the computing that is taught.

Having a scheme of work in place helps schools to make strategic decisions about purchasing new resources and technology. Once a scheme of work is established, schools can ask the question: "what technologies do we need to cover these objectives?", rather than

DOI: 10.4324/9781003502555-4

32 *Computing schemes of work*

"what technologies should we invest in?" Upon asking this question, schools may well decide that they can accomplish all of their computing objectives with free, online resources and a suite of computers or laptops.

Schools may decide that they want to improve their multimedia outcomes and purchase filming equipment. They may decide that data collection is an area of the curriculum that could improve and invest in sensors or data logging equipment. They may decide that physical equipment would allow for enhanced programming and design objectives and invest in this.

The important point is that having a well-developed and established scheme of work avoids the 'tail wagging the dog', in other words, decisions and purchases being made without educational needs and outcomes being established.

What makes a good computing scheme of work?

A skills-based approach

A good computing scheme begins by outlining the skills that are to be taught. In Chapter 18, there is an example progression of skills outline for computing, which could form the basis of a scheme of work. A scheme of work then outlines lessons and projects that will enable children to learn these skills, before finally, considering the technologies that are required.

Although the national curriculum for computing does not specify skills in detail, it is important to define and teach the whole range of computing skills that we need to teach children. This should include basic skills, such as using the mouse, keyboard, turning the computer on, navigating Windows and the internet and organising and saving work.

On top of these basic skills, we need to teach the full range of skills involved in the three strands of computing – computer science, information technology, and digital literacy. The skills in these strands are not laid out year-by-year in the national curriculum, so it is necessary for a scheme of work to provide this map, ensuring that children progress from reception to year 6.

Balance between skills-based lessons vs. project-based lessons

As with all subjects, in computing, there will be lessons with a focus on teaching and practising skills. These could be basic skills connected to computer operation, navigating Windows, the internet or other programs.

There will also be lessons where children apply their knowledge, creating their own work to express their ideas. This could be through building things physically and using programming to make them work, it could be creating documents, graphics, animations, or movies for an audience. Children love solving problems and the engagement that children demonstrate when working on a real problem is unmatched.

In any scheme of work, there needs to be a balance between children developing skills and freer application of these skills through tasks and problem-solving, including an element of creation of original work. Too much of a skills-based approach takes ownership of learning away from children, and it is difficult for the teacher to assess what children really know. Too many open tasks and exploration risks children not being pushed to practise and develop required skills.

One way to constantly reinforce the computing skills needed across the scheme of work is by setting short activities for children to do at the start of the lesson. These activities keep skills fresh for children. They can be connected to the lesson objective or separate from it. In Chapter 5, 'Teaching effective computing lessons', we explore examples of the types of activities that can be used here.

A modern and exciting curriculum

Things are changing so much in our world in terms of the technology available for children to learn about use. This includes free technologies, websites, simulations, as well as practical equipment, robotics, building sets, and mobile devices.

A good computing scheme of work should aim to deliver the learning according to the computing curriculum, while teaching children about some of the emerging technologies that will shape their world. This could include children learning to use a virtual learning environment (VLE), learning about artificial intelligence, the internet, robotics, filmmaking and animation, engineering, augmented reality, and other forms of digital media.

A spiral approach

With one computing lesson per week in most schools and a huge range of possibilities for topics and materials while teaching computing, it can be easy to design a scheme of work that constantly introduces new ideas, either within a year group or across year groups, with few opportunities for repetition.

This should be avoided, for the sake of teachers and children! Instead, there should be times when children re-use technologies within the year, otherwise they do not have the chance to build their skills in these areas. For the sake of teachers, always introducing new technologies means that teaching time is taken up explaining how things work, rather than developing children's computing skills with them using things they are familiar with.

It is possible to employ a scheme of work that has a spiral approach, both within the year and across years. Throughout the year, children have the opportunity to use and reuse technologies, such as Garageband, Google Docs, Scratch, and Spike Prime sets, becoming familiar with expression using these tools. In the same way, children use concepts such as conditions, variables, and E-safety frequently, achieving fluency and familiarity with these ideas.

Some schemes of work teach topics in half-term blocks of approximately six weeks. For some projects, this is a good amount of time to explore topics in depth. However, there is nothing wrong with shorter units, or even 'one off' lessons where children engage in activities like problem-solving, creating animation, or E-safety work.

PAUSE AND REFLECT...

A 'spiral' curriculum is one where concepts and skills are taught repeatedly, at ever-increasing levels of complexity. This can be over one year, or several years.

- What are the benefits of a spiral curriculum?
- How spiral is the curriculum you use in computing compared to other subjects?

34 *Computing schemes of work*

Appropriate level of challenge

Children are capable of amazing things when using technology to express their ideas. It is important that any scheme of work provides challenges and opportunities for children to reach their potential. This is especially true for children who are particularly able in an area covered in computing lessons, such as programming, graphic design, or animation. Many children will be engaged by computing and want to do more in their own time, either during school clubs or at home.

Any scheme of work should, as well as teaching basic computing skills, also offer sufficient opportunities to challenge children who are capable in any area of computing. This can be hard in computing, which is still a comparatively new subject. Many teachers lack confidence in teaching computing in ways that they do not, for example, in teaching subjects like maths, English, and science. It may well be the case that some of the children in the class are more confident than the teacher with aspects of computer use.

A good scheme of work for computing will ensure that all children meet the basic skills required, have the opportunity to explore these skills in depth and have the opportunity to access further challenges where appropriate. In Chapter 18, we will explore assessment and progression, looking at ways to extend children where appropriate.

Exciting and purposeful outcomes

Children love problem-solving. This is evidenced by how easily a lesson can go off track when a seemingly trivial problem arises! Children's imaginations are fired when real-world problems present themselves.

As with all subjects, in computing we can give children work to do with the goal of practising skills. We can also give them work to do that captures this love of solving real-world problems, while at the same time covering learning objectives.

In computing, there are so many opportunities for children to use computers to solve real problems and cover curriculum objectives at the same time. Any scheme of work should have at least some elements of real-world problem-solving alongside teaching computing objectives.

Of course, to solve problems, children need to have the skills in the first place, which is why a good scheme of work will offer a balance of skills teaching and practice, as well as application through problem-solving.

Linking a scheme of work to school strengths, celebrations, themes, and values

A well-designed computing scheme of work should reflect the strengths and values of the school. It is usually possible to adapt existing schemes of work to include piece of work that utilise strengths and resources within the school and fit in with the celebrations, topics, resources, and expertise within the school.

A school with links to another school abroad might teach parts of the computing curriculum through the children emailing children in another school. Schools with access to nature may teach the data handling parts of the curriculum by the children using technology to record animals or plant growth.

Computing schemes of work 35

Resources and staff expertise are also a consideration that should affect the overall computing scheme of work. Although ideally, resources would be chosen following the development of the scheme of work, the reality is that many schools have established technology available. Schools that have invested in mobile devices such as iPads may develop schemes of work that include creating digital content through filmmaking, animation, and photography. Schools with space and available resources may design schemes of work that utilise robotics systems such as **Sphero robots**, or **Lego Spike Prime** sets. Children might also develop their engineering skills through designing and building physical systems using technology like **Crumble kits** by **Redfern Electronics**, or **Arduino** sets.

There is also the question of how much ICT use will be incorporated into the teaching of other subjects. If, for example, as part of the children's English work, they are writing and producing an animated film, it would be advisable to teach some of these skills in computing lessons prior to this kind of project. The same would be true if the children were planning to use robotics in maths lessons, or data loggers in science. It therefore depends upon where the school is on its journey of incorporating technology into the overall curriculum, as to which topics will be taught in computing and when they will be taught.

A logical approach is to start with a purchased scheme of work and gradually adapt it by replacing units as time goes on. Most units under computing schemes of work can be shortened, if, for example, the school wants the children to create animations on a particular topic in computing lessons.

Assessment opportunities

Assessment is a vital part of teaching. For teachers, assessment enables teachers to give learners the correct instruction and activities to progress their learning. For children, assessment and feedback give them a measure of how successful they have been, both with their last activity and in terms of their overall learning.

Any scheme of work should therefore include a system for measuring children's progress and opportunities to share this as feedback to the children.

Chapter 18 deals with assessment in computing in more detail, examining ways in which teachers and students can assess learning in computing.

Early years progression of skills and planning is covered in detail in Chapter 9.

Conclusion

It can be highly rewarding to develop a scheme of work for a subject. By mapping out the skills that should be taught across year groups, it is possible to ensure that every lesson that children receive is purposeful and progresses their understanding of computing.

Developing a scheme of work for a subject is also a large task. However, by starting with a progression of skills, a school can ensure that the activities that they use in lessons are focused and purposeful. Chapter 18 of this book features an example progression of skills, based on an interpretation of the requirements of the national curriculum.

In any school, the computing coordinator will assess the current computing scheme of work and evaluate what is taught in each year, as well as progression between years. The

36 *Computing schemes of work*

computing coordinator will then suggest ways that the scheme of work could be improved to school management and teachers. Having a strategic approach that focuses on the skills that children learn leads to clear and focused conversations around suggestions for developing whole-school computing.

Note

1   https://teachcomputing.org/curriculum.

References

Computing Programs of Study: Key stages 1 and 2, National Curriculum of England, Department for Education, 2013.
Teach Computing curriculum, https://teachcomputing.org/curriculum

5 Teaching effective computing lessons

Introduction to teaching computing

This chapter discusses how to teach effective computing lessons. There are aspects specific to computing that can make lessons effective, as well as general good teaching practice that applies to computing lessons.

Lesson structure and routines

Having a clearly established routines and procedures is important in computing lessons. Routines and procedures in computing help develop children's independence, responsibility, and resilience, minimise teacher time spent on technical support and reduce cognitive load on children.

Many subjects have a period of setting up, response to teacher feedback and starter activities at the start of the lesson and computing lessons can also start in this way. Giving children time to set up their equipment, respond to any teacher feedback, and work on a short independent task is a good way of using the opening five-ten minutes of the lesson and helps to start the lesson in a calm and structured way.

As in any lesson, the teacher should share the learning objective, or learning outcome with the children at the start of the lesson. This is sometimes referred to as WALT ('We are learning to'). The teacher will also share success criteria at the start of the lesson, sometimes referred to as WILF ('What I'm looking for'). At this stage of the lesson, it can be beneficial to give children an idea of how their learning fits into an overall picture. They may recap what they learned previously or consider why they are learning this lesson's skills. In some cases, children may also help agree the success criteria for the lesson.

Carefully chosen success criteria are especially important in computing lessons, particularly on tasks that are open in their nature. On more open tasks such as programming, problem-solving, and engineering, children will naturally want to be creative and try out ideas which are perhaps different to those talked about earlier in the lesson. Success criteria tell them that it is okay to do this, as long as certain skills are demonstrated.

Basic skills

It is important to recognise that children need to be trained in many of the routines necessary for using computers. Turning on a computer and logging into Windows presupposes certain

DOI: 10.4324/9781003502555-5

38 *Teaching effective computing lessons*

knowledge – knowing where the 'on' button is, knowing about 'caps lock' affecting usernames, knowing that 'tab' takes you into the next field, knowing that 'enter' can be pressed to enter the username/password, etc. Once the operating systems has loaded, the same can be said of opening software or internet pages.

It is beneficial to train children to do these things, spending the time to practise them. There may be lessons where the class practises logging onto the computer and opening a website or a program, before logging off again – perhaps the whole class could be timed to see how long it takes them to do this! While we are all eager to get to the exciting parts of teaching computing, practising skills and routines like this will pay dividends later in the year.

It is important not to assume that children have skills relating to computer use. Just as in PE lessons, where children practise bouncing a ball and kick ups, in computing, we need to give children time to practise basic computer skills. This could include double clicking, using keyboard shortcuts, typing properly, highlighting text, clicking in the right place on the screen, navigating folders and internet pages, etc. Children may groan a bit being asked to practise such basic skills, but the alternative can often mean lessons delayed because teachers have assumed that children have skill that they do not.

One way to address the need to address the need for basic skills is through a **computer licence**. This can involve children demonstrating a checklist of skills which they keep track of. When children have ticked off a skill a number of times, they can qualify for different levels of licence, i.e., 'gold', 'silver', etc. Licences can be for years groups or key stages. This system has the added benefit of allowing the teacher to assess and identify children who need extra support or children who are confident and can help others.

Start of lessons

The opening five-ten minutes of a lesson can be a great time to settle children, allow them to practise skills independently, respond to teacher feedback, and start priming themselves for learning.

Children from year 3 upwards should be able to log onto a virtual learning environment (VLE), i.e., **Microsoft Class Teams** or **Google Classroom**. This is then ready for them to use in the lesson. Another benefit of children logging into an account is that their bookmarks are usually then visible at the top of the screen, saving them having to type the address of webpages.

Once children have logged in a VLE, they respond to any teacher feedback and then work on an independent starter task. The teacher can specify instructions for the starter task in the VLE. This could be a question that the children should answer, or a problem that they should try to solve. This is a routine that serves them well throughout key stages 1 and 2, although children in years 1 and 2 may require support logging into the VLE or may use a simpler VLE, such as **Seesaw**.

For children in years 1 and 2, having them log onto the computer and open their last piece of work is also an effective initial starter activity. Children enjoy looking at what they did in the previous lesson and having the opportunity to make changes or improvements in the starter part of the lesson.

Teaching effective computing lessons 39

Of course, there will be situations when these routines are not followed. For younger children, the starter task might be a case of setting up their equipment according to a photo shown on the screen or finding and opening an iPad app, before coming to sit down on the carpet.

Whichever format of starter task is chosen, it is important to recognise that it will take time to embed this and the first two or three lessons of the year could be spent navigating to a VLE and completing simple tasks. The first lesson delivered to all year groups should demonstrate navigating to the VLE and explain lesson procedure.

Independent starter activities

Independent activities at the start of computing lessons allows for the differences in speed in which some children will be ready for the lesson. It also reinforces children's independence and is a good way for them to develop the skill of reading instructions from the screen.

The start of the lesson is also a good time to reinforce children's basic skills. With computing lessons often taking place once per week in schools, it can be a long time between units of work. The start of the lesson can be a good opportunity for children to revise basic computing skills and concepts.

Independent starter activities can include:

- Problem-solving
- Typing practice
- Responding to teacher feedback and improving work
- Starter activities to get children thinking about lesson concepts
- Mini-assessments, such as in forms sent via **Google Forms** or **Microsoft Forms**, or using participation software such as **Mentimeter**, **Kahoot**, or **Quizziz**

Independent problem-solving

Code.org is a website with work that covers all eras of the computing curriculum. Teachers can set up classrooms there, and set and monitor children's work. It has some tasks that are ideal for the start of the lesson, and which could link well to the topic being taught in the lesson. One of the good things about the tasks in code.org is that on each course of about ten lessons, the tasks gradually get harder. The teacher could, therefore, give a link to the task one of these levels as the starter task.

Blockly games[1] is a website that features well-designed activities to develop children's problem-solving. The puzzles gradually increase in difficulty, meaning that children can usually work on them independently as their skills develop.

Lightbot is now only available as a mobile app, on both iPads and Android devices. It involves children controlling a little robot that moves around and lights up tiles. The problems start off as quite simple, using movement and 'light up' commands, but quickly get quite hard, requiring understanding of loops and functions. It is a fun and accessible app though, and children could be challenged to complete one level at the start of the lesson.

Cargobot is available for free on the Windows store and as a mobile app. It requires children to create programs to move a crane around to place coloured boxes in specific places,

40 *Teaching effective computing lessons*

according to a picture. The 'tutorial' levels start simply but get quite challenging! The 'easy' and 'medium' levels are really challenging. Cargobot teaches children to problem solve, break problems down, and use loops and functions. In a similar way to Lightbot, children could be asked to complete one level at the start of the lesson.

GearsBot[2] and **Vexcode VR**[3] are both tools that simulate robots and robotic challenges. Children can program robots to complete tasks such as line following, tower demolition, and obstacle avoidance – all classic robotics challenges. For a starter activity, the teacher could share some code for the children to test and improve, debug, or otherwise modify.

Independent typing practice

Developing children's typing skills is a good activity for the opening five-ten minutes of any computing lesson. Children are, more and more, expressing their ideas using a keyboard and being able to type quickly and accurately is becoming an important skill. Another benefit of practising typing skills is that this is a measurable skill – children can receive a word per minute (WPM) score and an accuracy score, usually a percentage.

Two of the best websites for practising typing at the start of the lesson are **Typing Club**[4] and **Monkeytype.com**.[5]

Typing Club has both free and paid levels. The free level is restricted to the number of classes and teachers that can be set up, but still offers an excellent environment for children to practise their typing. I really like the way that in Typing Club, the children are gradually introduced to new keys on the keyboard and gradually build up their ability to type words and sentences using these keys. Children should be reminded that they can (and should) go back and practise letters they have learned to type previously, as the course keeps on introducing new keys as it goes on. There are hundreds of lessons and games on this platform, not just for typing practise but for other computing concepts such as E-safety.

Monkeytype can be used with or without logging in, but it is a way for children to quickly practise typing in full sentences. They type as much as they can for a minute and then receive an accuracy and WPM score.

A golden tip for developing children's touch typing is to cover their hands with a piece of cloth! This makes it clear to them which keys their fingers know the location of and which they still need to learn, making it much more likely that they will go back and redo previous lessons. Generally, the teacher should try to emphasise accuracy and correct finger usage in typing over speed. Teachers can use the analogy of learning to play a musical instrument, where musicians start off slowly and then gradually speed up when their fingers learn where the notes are.

Lesson preparation starter activities

Jamboard/Microsoft Whiteboard are digital whiteboards that multiple people can join and collaborate to. The website, **whiteboard.fi**[6] allows children to project their devices to the screen.

A good starter activity could be for the teacher to ask a question and for the children to respond using digital devices. This could then form the basis for the opening discussion in the main part of the lesson. This could be done for any topic, including asking a question about E-safety, or asking children where the bug is in some code.

Children could all contribute to the same Jamboard/Whiteboard although it can be more manageable for children to work in smaller groups. On Jamboard, different pages can be created within the same Jamboard, so that each group could work on one page. It can be useful to provide the children with pre-made templates on which to structure their answers. This could be that the teacher shares pages with blank notes for the children to fill in, or a 'pros and cons' table for the children to populate.

Kahoot[7] and **Poll Everywhere**[8] are websites that allow teachers to set up quizzes for children. Kahoot features real-time quizzes and assignment quizzes. Assignment quizzes can be done quietly by children as part of a starter activity. The children's answers are marked by Kahoot, and the assessment data is viewable. The basic version of Kahoot is free, with some limitation on question types. Kahoot can be an effective tool as a starter activity when used in this way, as it primes the children by making them think about either learned topics or upcoming topics and generates useful assessment data.

Poll Everywhere is a similar concept to Kahoot, where teachers can ask questions to children and have them respond on devices. Poll Everywhere is beneficial owing to the amount of different displays of answers it includes, even in the free version. These include graphs and wordwalls, where the more common the answer, the bigger the word appears on the wordwall. Answer types that require the children to click on an area of a picture are also included in the free version.

Using a VLE

Using a virtual learning environment (VLE) is essential in computing lessons. Examples of VLE's include **Google Classroom**, **Microsoft Class Teams**, and **Seesaw**. These three platforms can be set up as tools for communicating in a classroom environment, sharing resources, handing in work, and giving feedback.

Training children to log into a VLE as the first thing they do in a computing lesson is highly beneficial. Most of the work that children do in computing lessons will be digital and submitted digitally, as screenshots, files, or weblinks. By logging into a VLE, children can view digital feedback that the teacher has given them on their digital work. This gets around the problem of amazing work being done by children in computing lessons but remaining unseen on computer hard drives.

Sharing work and materials digitally is enormously beneficial in computing lessons. Teachers will wish to direct children to use websites and posting a clickable link to websites on a VLE saves the children time. (Children should also be trained to add bookmarks to useful websites, as well as navigate to websites.) One particularly useful use of a VLE is providing links to specific projects via a VLE. In this way, the teacher can create a piece of work using Scratch, copy the link to the project and then paste this in the VLE for the children to remix. This remixed work could then be done as a task, for example, fixing broken or incomplete code, or could form the basis of the children's own work, in a similar way that they might be given a writing frame in an English lesson.

It can be beneficial for children to have **computing exercise books**. This is because handwriting is still the principal method of working, especially when planning things out. If children

42 *Teaching effective computing lessons*

are being asked to plan an algorithm as a flow chart, for example, this might be best done on paper, even though it is also possible to make flowcharts using digital devices.

Some VLE's feature assessment tools, meaning that children can view and respond to feedback. Google Classroom now allows teachers to respond to digital work using teacher-created **rubrics**, meaning that the teacher and children can see the level at which they have met pre-determined skills.

Google Classroom also allows teachers to set quizzes and keep a record of the correct answers that children give.

Using Google Classroom, children can be awarded marks from 1 to 3 for work that they have handed in, 1 being 'working towards expectations', 2 being 'working at', and 3 being 'working beyond', or a similar scale. This then generates a spreadsheet giving an overall picture of children's success.

Finally, A VLE can be an exciting and supportive environment for the teacher and children to share work, links, materials, and ideas. A VLE is a good environment for children to practise posting appropriate comments and content and highlight some of the work that they have been doing outside lessons.

PAUSE AND REFLECT...

The start of the lesson can set the tone for the rest of the lesson. It can be exciting, calm, or focused. It can also be a valuable opportunity for children to complete activities to prepare them for the rest of the lesson.

- Should all lessons start in the same way?
- How would *you* like to start a lesson, if you were one of the children you teach?

Independence and problem-solving

According to the national curriculum, it is important that children develop and demonstrate logical thinking in computing lessons. The opening lines of the national curriculum for computing state:

A high-quality Computing education equips pupils to use computational thinking and creativity to understand and change the world.

One of the requirements for key stage 1 computing is that:

Children use logical reasoning to predict the behaviour of simple algorithms.

At key stage 2, the national curriculum requires children to:

"Solve problems by decomposing them into smaller parts" and "use logical reasoning to explain how simple algorithms work."

In computing lessons, teachers will need to decide what kind of lesson they are teaching. Is the lesson a knowledge-building lesson, where a concept is introduced and explored with children? Is the lesson an exploration lesson, where children try out new equipment and realise

Teaching effective computing lessons 43

what they can do and can't yet do? Or is the lesson a problem-solving lesson, where the children will approach a problem in the way that a programmer would, breaking it down before writing code for each section?

To be taught effectively, computing must be a combination of all three kinds of activities. Children who are given too much problem-solving will gradually learn but will not have the knowledge to solve problems effectively. Conversely, too much practice of concepts will develop knowledge, but children will not have had the opportunity to use this knowledge to solve problems by themselves.

> ## PAUSE AND REFLECT...
>
> Computing lessons can involve problem-solving, acquisition of knowledge, and exploration.
>
> - What balance should be given to the above aspects of lessons?
> - Should lesson be a mix of the above aspects, or focused on one at a time?

Strategies for ensuring good problem-solving in computing lessons

Use of computational thinking

For effective problem-solving lessons, children should have been taught how to use computational thinking beforehand. They should have had the experience of breaking a problem down and planning solutions for each stage, and they should demonstrate pattern spotting and awareness of abstraction at a level which is appropriate to their age. This kind of lesson would also usually follow lessons where they have learned how to use the technology in question.

Materials to support problem-solving

Children should have access to appropriate materials to support the problem-solving process. The best material for planning an approach to a problem can be a pencil and paper and computing exercise books can be beneficial for this reason.

The classroom can also be set up in a way that allows for effective problem-solving to take place. This can include quiet areas for thinking, materials for planning, seating set up for discussion and displays of thinking processes, including design thinking or computational thinking.

Raising the profile of thinking

Problem-solving and computational thinking should be high profile and celebrated in the class. Many schools are doing this already by promoting growth mindset, which includes the importance at working at a problem and making mistakes, before finally solving it. The more the teacher models and uses the language of computational thinking, the more second nature it will become to children. Once children have developed this way of approaching problems, it is a skill that will remain with them for life.

44 *Teaching effective computing lessons*

Many children will, in fact, already have computational thinking skills. Children who build models, build Lego, or do anything else creative will already possess much of the resilience and ability to break problems down that we call computational thinking.

PRIMM

As discussed in Chapter 3, PRIMM stands for **Predict, Run, Investigate, Modify, Make**. The term was introduced by **Sue Sentance**, Head of the Raspberry Pi Foundation.

The PRIMM approach is useful because it highlights each stage of the process of learning about coding. In the same way that children read books before writing their own stories, children should learn to read code before writing their own. This reading of code will be guided by a teacher, who will challenge the children with questions, encourage them to make predictions, and model reading code using the structures within which it is written.

When teaching programming, teachers can combine the **predict** and **run** phases into one lesson. This allows for plenty of time to teach children to read code. They need to learn to ready code line-by-line, skipping over parts they do not understand and looking for structures like loops, broadcasts, conditions, and functions. Teaching children to read code in this way is not something that can be done quickly at the start of the lesson, and it is far better to spend time doing this properly. Children can answer comprehension questions about the code, before running it and seeing if their predictions are correct. Code can be shared with children using a VLE, so that they can click on a link to a project that the teacher has created using Scratch, or another platform.

Investigating code can form a part of many lessons. Class or group discussions about code are valuable for many stages of the lesson, including the starter, main activities, or plenary.

Modifying code can be done as part of a lesson. It could be done following children running code that they have made predictions about (almost all children will modify the code as a natural progression of running it!). Other 'modify' activities include giving children code that is broken and asking them to debug it, or asking them to 'break' someone else's code by changing one or two things and asking the creator to fix it again.

Making code refers to children solving problems using their understanding of code, making their own programs to control on-screen programs or devices.

The PRIMM process is useful both as having clearly defined phases, but also as a more organic process. There might be some lesson that have all the aspects, or some that only have one or two aspects. The aspects of PRIMM do not have to take place in order. Mini plenaries in the lesson might, for example, challenge children to make a quick prediction about a new piece of code. What has been particularly beneficial to me and my teaching (and hopefully the children's learning) about the PRIMM process has been the increased emphasis and time spend on reading code, with the impactful activities and discussion that follow this.

Paired programming

Paired programming is where children take on specific roles while programming and sharing technology – one the 'navigator' and the other the 'driver'. On the website, **code.org**,[9] there is an excellent video explaining the two roles.

Teaching effective computing lessons 45

Paired programming may be a part of effective programming lessons for several reasons. For one thing, it allows children to share technology when devices are limited. This may be the case especially where the school has purchased robots or robotic sets, such as Spheros, Lego Spike Prime, or OhBot robotic heads. Children can also use paired programming for on-screen programming. This works well when children are using a laptop to program a physical device such as a robot or a crumble set.

Assigning each child a role encourages each child to perform their role to the best of their ability, since the other person in their partnership is depending on them. The **navigator** should do all of the thinking and problem-solving, with the **driver** pressing all of the buttons and constructing the code. The children will swap roles frequently, either when the teacher directs them to or when they choose to.

Paired programming also develops children's communication skills, chiefly their ability to express their ideas and to listen to the ideas of another.

Children usually enjoy this way of working but need time to practise and adapt to it. Although paired programming can see a little strange at first, assigning roles for other tasks is perfectly legitimate, such as when the children do animation, and children take on the roles of animator and photographer. Paired programming works well when robotics are involved, whether this is with younger children with Beebots, or older children and more advanced robots.

A natural development of paired programming is assigning roles when children work on larger tasks or engineering tasks. Children who have engaged in paired programming are more likely to have the discipline and communication skills to carry out roles effectively.

Extending learners

One characteristic of effective lessons is that all children's needs are met, allowing children to progress with their understanding and ability at all levels.

Just as in any subject, there should be provision in place to support children who need it during the lesson. There should also be ways to further challenge children who either quickly grasp the learning, or who come to the lesson and already have the knowledge being taught. Since the inception of the national curriculum in 2014, there is now more focus on children exploring topics in **greater depth** once they have grasped the material being taught in the lesson. Accordingly, there is less focus on pushing children to learn more and more and perhaps moving into the objectives of the next academic year up. Having said this, the children who are ready to start exploring content that is above their age-related expectations should have the opportunity to do so, as long as it does not mean that they are covering any objectives at any stage in a superficial way.

This approach of 'greater depth' works well in computing. The objectives in the national curriculum require teachers to teach them in greater levels of depth, since objectives are grouped by key stage, not by year group. Even when skills are broken down by year group, they can be explored and taught at different levels of depth.

We will now look at several examples of lessons where learners who have grasped the topic well might be encouraged to work at greater depth, or to extend their learning beyond what is being taught to the rest of the class.

46 *Teaching effective computing lessons*

Example 1 - year 1 lesson

Learning objective: *To choose movement commands and put them in the correct sequence*
   Lesson overview: The children program Beebots to reach designations on a treasure map. Children are provided with direction cards which they use to help plan the instructions they give to the Beebots.

Table 5.1 Example outcomes from a year 1 lesson

Meeting the learning outcome		Exceeding
Expected outcome	**Greater depth**	**Working beyond**
Children discuss the movement of the Beebot with a partner, before placing the movement cards in the correct order. They then press the buttons on the Beebot according to these movement cards.	Children are given obstacles to place on the maps. They explore how placing these obstacles on the maps changes their algorithms and makes them longer.	Children use loops in their algorithms, being able to use the same movement card but indicate that it is repeated several times. Most able children could loop patterns of more than one command, i.e., (forward, right) × 3

Example 2 - year 4 lesson

Learning objective: *To understand how variables are used in programs to keep track of values*
   Lesson overview: Children, having already looked at Examples of code that use variables, are tasked with adding a variable to a game that either they or the teacher has made.

Table 5.2 Example outcomes from a year 4 lesson

Meeting the learning outcome		Exceeding
Expected outcome and learning	**Greater depth**	**Working beyond**
Children create algorithms, written in pseudocode, for when the amount stored in the variable should change, i.e., 'when touching the apple, change the score by 10'. Children program a sprite to change this variable amount in a game, using a 'forever if' conditional structure.	Children explore other ways that the score variable could change, writing algorithms and creating code for this. For example, 'when touching the blue apple, change the score by 20'. 'Every 1 second, change the score by minus 1'. 'When the score = 100, say "You have won!"'.	Children combine manipulation of variables with a 'repeat until' logic. They create pseudocode and programs using this, i.e., 'if the timer variable is greater than 0, decrease the timer by 1 every second'.

These examples should show the difference between children exploring the lesson content at greater depth (hopefully a good proportion of the class) and children who are working at a level above the lesson objective (maybe one or two children). For this second category of

Teaching effective computing lessons 47

children, the teacher will need to know the children well and ideally, have had conversations with them about what they need to develop their learning in computing lessons.

Supporting learners

Just as it is important to provide for learners who quickly grasp the learning objective, it is important to put into place support for those children who need it in order to meet the learning objective. This is most often done through providing extra layers of **scaffolding** for children who need it. The scaffolding is gradually withdrawn from children as they become more confident and can be put back if children need it.

In the example of the year 1 Beebot lesson, the learning objective is that children choose movement commands for the Beebot to reach a position on a map. One way that the teacher could scaffold this would be to provide children with a choice of two or three sequences of movements commands, instead of children making their own sequences of movement commands. The children would need to read the sequences provided, look at the map and then make a choice about which one to use. These sequences could start off as being made of only a few movement commands.

In the example year 4 lesson, where the children were learning to modify a game and add a score variable, the teacher could share an example of the game where the score variable has been created and perhaps the commands are present, but in the wrong order. Children are therefore provided with an extra layer of scaffolding to support them in modifying the game to add in a variable. These children are still free to explore the concept of variables in greater depth, as they could make certain colour apples affect the score by different amounts, for example.

Of course, there are many reasons why children may need support in computing lessons, some connected to needs that the children may have. This is explored further in Chapter 14, which discusses inclusion in computing.

PAUSE AND REFLECT...

Effective computing lessons extend all children's learning, either through allowing them to explore concepts more deeply, or by teaching them new knowledge.

- How do you provide opportunities for children to achieve the learning objective at different levels of depth?
- Do you provide opportunities for children to learn beyond the learning objective?

Managing cognitive load

Cognitive load theory describes the amount of working memory that the brain is drawing on at any given time. Teachers need to be aware that every time the children must consider a new or unfamiliar task, this adds to cognitive load. Cognitive overload occurs when children have too many new concepts to process and this negatively affects how much they can learn.

48 *Teaching effective computing lessons*

Consideration of cognitive load is important in computing lessons. There are potentially several challenging activities that the children must go through before they can start to engage with the topic of learning. For example, if we wanted children in year 4 to learn about how conditions work in Scratch, they first need to turn on the computer, log in, then load up Scratch, possibly open a project of teacher example before they are even in the Scratch environment. Even within Scratch, to use conditions, they must select the conditional block, drag it into place, place an operator block in the correct place, and make sure their program is joined up in the correct sequence.

Year 4 children may well be able to cope with these steps, but it is important to recognise the steps, nonetheless. If the teacher is asking children to produce some advanced thinking and work around conditionals, the teacher should be aware of how much cognitive load the children are already under before even starting the task.

There are two approaches that teachers can use to reduce the cognitive load upon children in computing lessons. The first is to gradually train children up with the skills that they need, so that when they come to do a complex task, they can use their cognitive abilities to address the task, without having to think too much about how to set up the technology. The second approach is for the teacher to set up the technology prior to the lesson, so that the children sit down at a computer or equipment that is ready to go. In this second approach, the children can straight away use their full cognitive abilities on the task at hand. The second approach might be used with younger children, or in cases where lesson time is at a premium, but both approaches will effectively reduce cognitive load on children.

When using a piece of technology for the first time, they should not be tasked with producing a high level of outcome. Instead, children should be given the chance to explore the new technology. This helps to reduce the cognitive load, recognising that when children first encounter a piece of technology much of their cognitive load will be used familiarising with the device or technology. In these first lessons, the teacher can give the children time to explore the device for themselves, pose their own questions and think of their own ideas, without the pressure of a task set by the teacher.

Whatever approach teacher in computing lesson choose to employ to manage cognitive load, the most important thing is that teachers are aware that there may be several taxing tasks that children must do before they start the learning that the teacher has planned. Teachers must plan lessons so that children have sufficient cognitive power to tackle the main learning activity. Whether this means training children in technology use or setting up the lesson so that children can get straight on with the activity, the best computing lessons are the ones where the teacher is clear about exactly what skill the children are to develop and has set up the lesson so that children are able to devote themselves to this.

PAUSE AND REFLECT...

Cognitive load refers to the finite processing capacity of the brain.

- What are the contributors to cognitive load in your computing lessons? Are they planned for?
- What strategies do you use to manage cognitive load in your lessons?

Blended learning

Children can receive instruction in lesson directly from the teacher. With modern technology, they can also receive online instruction that the teacher has shared via a virtual learning environment (VLE). This online instruction could be materials or videos that the teacher has created themselves, or materials created by other people. The term **blended learning** refers to using a combination of direct, classroom teacher instruction and online instruction.

Nothing will ever replace the direct interaction that children have with a teacher in the classroom. Children benefit from teacher explanations, being able to ask questions, view teacher modelling, not to mention the encouragement, and support that teacher give children in every lesson. But some teachers may wish to combine this direct instruction with video tuition to support learners. With VLEs, we now have a platform for teachers to easily share instructional materials and videos with children. Most adult learners, when they want to learn something, will watch, pause, and rewatch online videos to help them to learn it. Some teachers may well with to try creating videos of them explaining or demonstrating computing concepts for the children to watch at their own pace.

The intangible 'buzz'

One of the defining features of an outstanding lesson is the intangible 'buzz' in the classroom. This involves all children being excited, focused, and challenged. Any teacher will know that creating this 'buzz' involves a lot of hard work – planning the lesson, knowing the children in order to challenge them appropriately, and delivering the lesson.

One surefire way to achieve this 'buzz' is through all children being successful in the lesson. This success depends on well-planned activities, children being able to access support independently and children being motivated by the task set.

Conclusion

Children's needs in lessons resemble many of the needs we have as adults. They need lessons that are well-structured, building on previous knowledge and challenging them to apply and extend this. They need to be able to focus on achievable goals and to recognise where they experience success and reasons for when do not.

Effective computing lessons require some elements of particular consideration, which we have explored in this chapter. Teachers may also find that the elements of effective computing lessons have benefits in other subjects across the curriculum.

Notes

1 https://blockly.games/.
2 https://gears.aposteriori.com.sg/.
3 https://vr.vex.com/.
4 https://www.typingclub.com/.
5 https://monkeytype.com/.
6 https://whiteboard.fi/.
7 https://kahoot.com/.
8 https://www.polleverywhere.com/.
9 https://code.org/.

References

Blockly Games, https://blockly.games/
Code.org, https://code.org/
Computing Programs of Study: key stages 1 and 2, National Curriculum of England, Department for Education, 2013.
Gearsbot, https://gears.aposteriori.com.sg/
Kahoot, https://kahoot.com/
Monkeytype, https://monkeytype.com/
Poll Everywhere, https://www.polleverywhere.com/
Typing Club, https://www.typingclub.com/
Whiteboard.fi – a Kahoot company, https://whiteboard.fi/
Vexcode VR, https://vr.vex.com/

6 Teaching computer science

What is computer science?

Computer science is one of the three strands of computing. The national curriculum states,

> The core of Computing is computer science, in which pupils are taught the principles of information and computing, how digital systems work and how to put this knowledge to use using programming.

This can be read in conjunction with the opening line of the national curriculum for computing, which states,

> A high-quality Computing education equips pupils to use computational thinking and creativity to understand and change the world.

Computers work by running programs which control the actions of a machine (the output), depending on information that goes into a computer (the input). Much of what children will learn about through the computer science strand is understanding how programs work, including creating their own programs.

At **key stage 1**, computer science includes the following objectives relating to programming:

- Understand what algorithms are; how they are implemented on digital devices; and that programs execute by following precise and unambiguous instructions
- Create and debug simple programs
- Use logical reasoning to predict the behaviour of programs

At **key stage 2**, computer science includes the following programming objectives:

- Design and create a range of programs, systems and content that accomplish specific goals, including controlling or simulating physical systems; solve problems by decomposing them into smaller parts
- Use sequence, selection and repetition on programs; work with variables and various forms of input and output
- Use logical reasoning to predict how some simple algorithms work and detect and correct errors in algorithms and programs

DOI: 10.4324/9781003502555-6

52　Teaching computer science

In addition, as we saw in Chapter 2, at key stage 2, computer science also covers the following objective:

- Understand computer networks including the internet; how they can provide multiple services, such as the world wide web; and the opportunities they offer for communication and collaboration.

In this chapter, we will explore ways in which children can be taught to develop ideas into algorithms and how these can be used to create programs to control devices. We will also explore activities that can be used to teach children about networks and how these operate.

Algorithms

The word 'algorithm' is challenging for young children to say, but the concept of an algorithm is easy to understand. An algorithm is any set of instructions to complete a task. Children will be able to give many examples of instructions for tasks that they complete in their day, from brushing their teeth in the morning, to entering school, to taking a penalty in football.

Discussing algorithms also has good links to a lot of the English work that the children do such as writing instructions, using time connectives, using adverbs, etc. There are, therefore, plenty of opportunities to discuss algorithms in class. In maths, children can follow and create algorithms for calculating, and in PE, they can create and follow algorithms for physical activity.

Children can even create algorithms for lining up for lunch, what to do if someone is upset, how to end the lesson properly, etc. In this way, the word 'algorithm' can become part of the children's everyday vocabulary.

Some of the key features of algorithms are that they:

- Are in the correct sequence. The same instructions in different sequences have the wrong results! *(See discussion of sequence in 6.3).*
- Have a starting event and an outcome. The starting event for an outcome being 'when something happens'. Helping children to think like this helps them structure their programs later, using inputs and outputs.
- Use succinct language. Children usually don't need to compose algorithms in full sentences and using more succinct language with key words prepares them to plan their programs using pseudocode.
- Use the logic of computing. Simple algorithms with an event and an outcome easily translate into computer programs and help children with their programming. As children get progress with their thinking, they can be encouraged to use more sophisticated logic in their algorithms. They could use questions and 'if/else' structures. They could use repetition for repeated instructions. They could start to incorporate variables into their programs, i.e., 'if noise level > 50%, turn on light'. Children could even incorporate sets of predetermined instructions, called functions, into the algorithms they devise. The website code.org has a brilliant video about functions, explaining them as being like predetermined 'plays' in sport.

Teaching computer science 53

For younger children, they should start to use the word 'algorithm', as the national curriculum for computing at key stage 1 states:

Children should be taught what algorithms are, how they are implemented as programs on digital devices and that programs execute by following precise and unambiguous instructions.

For younger children in early years or year 1, giving them a scaffold for their instructions helps ensure that their algorithms have a starting event and commands that are clear and precise.

Tools for teaching children to use algorithms

Although it is possible to teach children to use algorithms for non-computer related activities, objects that can be programmed are an ideal way for children to test the effectiveness of their algorithms. In this section, we will consider some of the most effective tools for teaching children to develop algorithms and program. Schools do not need to invest in all of these but should look at their curriculum and select the one(s) that meet the needs. The excellent **Apps for Good**[1] projects, for example, uses the **App Lab** in **code.org**, and it would be possible to teach all computing at key stage 2 using this.

Some of the best tools for teaching children to construct algorithms are summarised in Table 6.1.

Table 6.1 Physical and digital tools for teaching computer science

Age group	Physical tools	Digital tools
Early years	Beebots Bluebots Duplo Coding Express Dash and Dot	Scratch Junior (iPad)
Key stage 1	Beebots Bluebots Duplo Coding Express Dash and Dot Lego Spike Prime (picture blocks)	Scratch Junior (iPad) A.L.E.X. app (iPad) Code.org
Key stage 2	Bluebots Lego Spike Prime (word blocks) Redfern 'Crumble' sets Sphero robots OhBots Microbit Arduino (advanced)	Scratch 'App Lab' (part of code.org) Flowol 4 CoSpaces Tinkercad Cargobot (iPad or PC) Lightbot (iPad app) Code.org activities Beetleblocks VexcodeVR Gearsbot Makecode Minecraft Kodu

54 *Teaching computer science*

Duplo Coding Express

Duplo Coding Express sets are excellent tools to use with children in nursery and reception. These sets feature blocks of different colours that are placed on the train track and which make the train respond in different ways *(stop, blow the horn, turn on the lights, change direction, drink fuel)*. Children can be provided with picture cards relating to these actions and picture cards relating to the colour. They can then stick these cards onto an algorithm skeleton provided and be encouraged to talk about their algorithms prior to setting up their scenarios. Children can be extended by having more than one outcome in their algorithm. For example, when it gets to the station, the train could stop and blow its horn.

Duplo Coding Express sets are expensive, retailing at approximately £200 per set. They are, however, a versatile resource, including blocks that can be used for maths, roleplay, and other activities.

Beebots/Bluebots

Many schools have purchased Beebots to use for teaching children in key stage 1 about algorithms and programming. The newest version of Beebots, Bluebots are chargeable and controllable via Bluetooth. They can also be programmed using a simple block-based programming environment in the Bluebot app on mobile devices. This app enables the Bluebots to be programmed to drive specific distances and turn amounts measured in angles, extending their usability in terms of maths teaching.

Beebots and Bluebots are versatile and robust tools for teaching children to program. They are expensive when bought new, with a set of 12 Bluebots retailing at over £1000. Below, we will also consider some alternatives to Beebots for programming at key stage 1.

Just as with teaching children in early years to construct algorithms using Duplo Coding Express sets, it is useful to provide scaffolding when teaching children to construct algorithms for Beebots. Children should be able to use their cognitive power on the instructions and logic for the robots. Providing instructional cards for them to arrange and a scaffold to place their instructions on lessens cognitive load in other areas. Drawing directional arrows is a challenging task for some children! Of course, teachers may use this activity as a chance for children to practise drawing symbols like arrows, but this decision should be thought through and taken prior to the lesson.

When setting up tasks for children to do using Beebots, or similar robots, the tasks can fall into one of several general categories. These are:

Stopping at a destination - this is the simplest and most common type of task that children will do using Beebots. It involves children thinking of algorithms to make the Beebot stop on a specified point. There are several types of Beebot mats available to buy. Teachers could also produce their own mats by drawing grids using the measurement of the Beebot for one square.

To prepare children to construct their algorithms for the Beebots, it is a good idea to first ask children to give each other instructions to move around the room. Children can write simple sequences of instructions on whiteboards and give it to their partner, starting with one or two instructions at a time and gradually building up longer algorithms. This helps

Teaching computer science 55

children to conquer two misconceptions. The first misconception that children often have with Beebots is that the 'left' or 'right' arrows mean go left or right, not turn left or right. Children also have to realise that 'left' and 'right' are from the point of view of the Beebot. Doing some class work on this is beneficial. The teacher can instruct one child at the front of the room and model the importance of turning from the point of view of the robot. The second misconception that children must get over with Beebots relates to running the program. Children must understand that they write the whole program, then press 'go' on the Beebot. A lot of children think that as soon as they give one single instruction, the Beebot follow this, or should follow it. Writing a set of instructions on a whiteboard for a partner and physically giving the instructions to them helps them to get over the misconception that the instructions are executed individually.

There is so much scope for using Beebots in early years and key stage 1, and even into key stage 2 with the new Bluebots, which are programmable using centimetres and degrees. Depending on the mats used, children can give instructions for the Beebots to visit islands, farm animals, stop on letters to spell words, or stop on numbers. It is worth remembering the idea of cognitive load here; programming the Beebots to get to the correct destination can be challenging. Asking the children to spell out words or do maths at the same time adds to this challenge significantly!

To extend children who are creating algorithms for Beebots, a good way to challenge them is to ask them to include instructions for the return journey. This activity has the benefit of helping children to start seeing patterns as the return instructions will mirror the outward ones.

Another good extension activity for creating Beebot algorithms is to place obstacles onto the grid. Children can compare the algorithm for the straight-line journey against the algorithm when obstacles are laced in the Beebot's path. Thematic obstacles could be used, i.e., the wolf on Red Riding's Hood's journey.

Navigating a path - This is a similar task to programming the Beebot to reach a destination, but it extends the children by having to make the Beebot reach many destinations along a path. It is possible to either buy or make mazes for the Beebots to navigate. To program the Beebot to navigate a maze, children will usually have to decompose this problem - break it down and tackle it step by step. They can also experiment with trying to write an algorithm to solve a whole maze and talk about which approach is better - a good opportunity for some metathinking.

Creative tasks - It is possible to attach pens to the Beebots and program them to draw shapes and patterns. It is possible to either purchase special Beebot pen holders, or to attach pens in other ways. Children can begin by attaching the pens and experimenting with shapes that the Beebots draw. The teacher should then challenge the children to draw agreed shapes by constructing algorithms for the Beebots prior to programming them. The shapes could include squares or rectangles, as well as zig-zag lines or stars. Programming the Beebots manually, children are restricted to 90 degree turns. Using the iPad app and the Bluebots, children can draw shapes with any angle.

Scratch Junior

Scratch Junior is a free, mobile app available on iPads and Android devices. It is one of the best ways to teach children about creating algorithms for computers to follow as programs.

56 *Teaching computer science*

Most children from the reception age can create simple algorithms to make the sprites move around the screen. The teacher must emphasise that each program either starts with the 'green flag' or another event block. Children are then quick to discover how they can make sprites move around, speak, grow, shrink, and make sounds. As with introducing any new technology, the first lessons where Scratch Junior can give them time for exploration without a required outcome. When children start aiming for specific outcomes, they will benefit from planning their instructions as algorithms, either written out with words and symbols or using command cards that the teacher has cut out for them. The more that the teacher models this process of planning, fixing errors, and thinking about algorithms, the more success the children will have when creating their programs.

There are many creative and thematic possibilities for using Scratch Junior in class. The teacher or the children can take a photograph to use as a background, meaning that any printed image can be used as the background. In this way, children could create an animated scene from a book they are reading, a historical scene or a factual scene about a topic they are studying. By considering the algorithms for the sprites in their scene beforehand, children will experience greater success when they turn their planned algorithms into programs.

Scratch Junior also has mathematical application, as the children can be challenged to create algorithms to make sprites reach specific destinations on the togglable grid, superimposed over an image. Children can be tasked to make the sprites move to specific destination or visit multiple destinations. I have used this with young children who were learning about programming self-driving cars, and we programmed the cars to move around a city.

A.L.E.X.

There are many programming apps available for iPads, including **Daisy the Dinosaur**, **Hopscotch**, and **Kodable**. **A.L.E.X.**, is a simple app, which features free and paid versions. The free version has enough features for most classroom use.

A.L.E.X. features a distraction-free environment and puzzles which emphasise directional movement at a level that progresses nicely from using Beebots. One of the best features of A.L.E.X. is that the algorithm is displayed as the program is running, helping children to debug mistakes. As with using Beebots, children will benefit from planning their programs out as algorithms, either by writing or drawing commands or by using directional cards that the teacher has provided.

Code.org

Code.org is an educational website that is free to use. It features courses of coding challenges for all abilities and has excellent tracking and assessment tools when set up for classroom use. Teachers using code.org need to set up a class and add children's names. Children then sign in by slicking on a link shared with them via the VLE and entering a passcode. The teacher can then assign courses to children and view their progresses on these courses, as well as their own projects.

In Chapter 16, 'Green opportunities', we consider computing projects that the children can engage in to improve their world. The website code.org features the excellent **app lab**, as well as the **Introduction to app lab** course. Children can use these tools to enter the **Apps for Good** competition. This is an incredible engaging and meaningful way to structure computing at key stage 2.

For children who have learned to use the mouse and keyboard, the tasks on code.org are a good way for them to practise creating algorithms for computer programs. They will be able to solve many of the problems by working on screen but will benefit from having materials available to write on and plan out their algorithms before creating programs.

Code.org also features opportunities for children to engage in creative projects, as well as complete problem-solving tasks. This is important, as while problem-solving tasks are great for practising algorithm design and problem-solving, the creative element is necessary, from both the point of view of the national curriculum and for children's own satisfaction.

Lightbot

Lightbot is another onscreen, problem-solving task that children can access on mobile devices through the Lightbot app. Lightbot is a free app. Unfortunately, as Lightbot uses Flash Player to run, it does not run on many modern computers, as Flash is no longer supported. Lightbot is deceptively simple; the first few puzzles involve directional movement and could be attempted by children in years 1-3. However, the puzzles quickly become harder, requiring use of loops and prewritten commands called procedures (procedures are sometimes referred to as functions).

Nevertheless, in a similar way to the puzzles in A.L.E.X., or in code.org, children enjoy solving the problems in Lightbot and they are great for reinforcing solving problems using decomposition, resilience, and computing concepts such as sequence, loops, and functions.

Lego Spike

Lego Spike is one of the current Lego Education systems, designed to allow children to build and program physical systems. There are different versions of Lego Spike: **Spike Prime** and **Spike Essentials**. Spike Essentials is a simplified version of the Spike Prime set, featuring a programmable 'brick' with fewer input/output slots. However, even the more advanced Spike Prime set is suitable for key stage 1 children, being programmable using picture blocks which resemble blocks in Scratch Junior, word blocks which resemble blocks in Scratch and Python.

Lego Spike Prime is an expensive investment for schools, priced at over £300 per set. However, the results that children can achieve using SPIKE Prime are excellent and, along with the fantastic range of educational lesson plans and resources that Lego provide, schools who can afford the investment may well choose to buy 10-15 Spike Prime sets for paired classroom usage. Another benefit of Lego sets is the speed at which they can be assembled and disassembled, meaning they can be used for quicker, problem-solving activities. There is also a large community dedicated to Lego Education, including the **First Lego League** events, offering children opportunities for competitive robotics.

From the point of view of algorithm design, an effective way to use the Spike Prime sets is to give the children one or two new components at a time. Children should be encouraged

58　*Teaching computer science*

to develop algorithms that control components precisely, before requesting additional components.

Good projects for children to begin constructing precise algorithms include a ticking clock, a bridge that opens and closes, a motion detector alarm, and a colour sorter. All of these projects can be built with less than ten parts. I would introduce one part per lesson and have the children master it, for example, in lesson one, the children might work on the 'ticking clock' project, making the hand turn around when the program starts.

While thinking about their algorithms for this ticking clock project, the children will be required to decompose the task. How fast should the hand turn? Should it pause after every 'tick' and if so, for how long? What should happen when it has gone around once? Should anything be shown on the screen of the Lego 'brick'? Giving children a worksheet with these kinds of questions on will help them to decompose the problem like this and construct an algorithm, prior to programming.

Once the children have mastered controlling a Lego motor precisely, the next step might be for them to be introduced to a sensor. They could, for example, work on a 'motion detector', which triggers an output when someone gets too close. (*This is a great example for the teacher to build such a device and challenge the class to take something from it!*) Children should now be challenged to decompose the task and answer questions including 'How close should someone get before the alarm is triggered?' and 'What should the motor do when the alarm is triggered?'

Projects like the two detailed above are limited, but I have found them extremely effective ways of getting children to construct algorithms and program precisely during a lesson. It is far more effective to give children manageable challenges like the above that really make them think about how they want motors to move. Developing the ability to program motors precisely like this paves the way for them to build more advanced robotics systems.

By the time children have been using Spike Prime sets for a while, perhaps by year 5 or 6, they should be ready to undertake engineering tasks, combining motors, sensors, and Lego construction. When working on more complex engineering tasks, children may well benefit from and have been taught to use, the engineering process (define the problem, imagine solutions, decide on a solution, build, test, improve). Here, the algorithm design will fall into the 'imagine solutions/decide on a solution' phase.

Scratch

Scratch is a block-based coding environment, developed by Massachusetts Institute of Technology (MIT). Scratch is available for free to use and has for many years, been the mainstay of teaching children to program in education. It remains as powerful and as versatile as ever.

Children can navigate to the Scratch website and create without making an account. They can also sign into an account, although this opens up the possibility of sharing and communicating online.

Scratch can be compared to a set of paints and sheet of paper. This is because children using Scratch could produce a masterpiece. Equally, they could find it difficult to know where to start, especially if they are new to the environment or to coding.

Fortunately, there are ways to help children to structure their programming in Scratch and allow them to be successful.

Principles of using Scratch

An important principle of using Scratch is that children do not always have to start from a new project. The teacher can share projects with the class via a VLE, which the children can 'remix'. This ensures that children can focus on the programming skill taught. It also enables the teacher to support children by giving them code to adapt, or blocks of code to use.

Pre-planning work before starting in Scratch is important. Prior to sitting down at the computer and constructing a program, children should have had time through class discussion and planning time on paper to consider the task, decompose it into the different things that need to happen and make sure they understand the coding logic that will be needed for each aspect. There are lots of things that the teacher can do to facilitate this planning stage of the lesson, from providing children with worksheets to structure their thoughts and algorithms, using Parson's puzzles to provide children with mixed up code for them to rearrange.

The key thing for children to remember when developing their algorithms is that computers work in terms of an input and an output. In Scratch, the inputs are represented as any of the following: brown 'event' blocks, orange 'when broadcast received' blocks, light blue 'sensing' blocks (embedded within an 'if' block). Children should be asked to think about when they want something to happen in their program and which of the above inputs is going to be the cause of a section of their program. If children write their algorithms with this clear event (input) → outcome (output) structure, they will find it much easier to program in Scratch.

Some great discussions can be had with children about input and output and the algorithms that cause everyday devices to function. Automatic doors are a great device to get children thinking and planning algorithms. How close do you have to be to trigger them? How fast do the doors open? What does 'open mean?' (turn the motor one way!) What happens if someone is standing in the way when they start to close? The more that children can be given the chance to plan algorithms for devices like this, the easier they will find it to decompose tasks in environments such as Scratch into precise and programmable commands.

Game design using Scratch

One of the most common projects that children undertake using Scratch is designing computer games. Computer games are good projects for children to work on because they involve so many aspects: sprites moving around on the screen, sprites having to sense other sprites, scores, and other variables that need to change and graphic design. Children love the idea of working on a game, but quickly realise just how much work is needed to make even simple things happen in their game!

With any game creation, planning and algorithm design is key to success. Children should be given opportunities to draw their game, label parts of it, and consider how each part will work. Once they have done this, they should be guided in decomposing the elements of their game as much as possible, before constructing algorithms to tell each part what to do. Common ideas for games can be decomposed in Table 6.2.

What children will discover when they start planning their games like this is that the game can be decomposed into its elements. These elements can then be decomposed and

60   *Teaching computer science*

Table 6.2 Game ideas decomposed with pseudocode

Idea for game	Decomposed element	Pseudocode (further decomposition)
Enemy chases you	Enemy sprite moves towards your sprite	If distance between sprite <= 10 pixels, enemy sprite moves towards you.
Pressing 'space' make your jump	When you press 'space', you go up and then come back down again	When you press 'space', the position of your sprite changes the 'y' value by 20. The 'y' value then decreases by 20.
When you pick up a cherry, your score increases	When your sprite touches a cherry sprite, your score increases	When the player sprite is touching the colour 'red', change 'score' by 10.

then decomposed even further, until you end up with statements that closely resemble code (pseudocode). This is how we move from concepts to algorithms to code.

As stated above, it is useful to give children pre-started projects on which to work. This allows the teacher to focus their attention and work upon a specific part of the desired. It allows the teacher to differentiate work by setting differently completed versions of the task, or to allow children to self-differentiate by choosing the version that they think they can do. Furthermore, this approach lets children all have a much greater chance of succeeding in creating a working project within the time constraints of a lesson.

For example, if a teacher wanted to develop children's understanding of how sensing logic is used, they might create a version of a game where the maze was drawn and the sprites moving around, but without any sensing logic in place. This allows the teacher and the children to spend the whole lesson considering ways that the sprite can bump into walls and move towards or away from each other. It is possible to create work for the children to do like this by the teacher creating a Scratch account and then sharing a link for the children to remix the project on their VLE. Children do not need to sign into Scratch to work in this way.

Scratch art and patterns

Another way to use Scratch and to develop children's algorithm design is to task them with drawing shapes and patterns in Scratch. This can be accomplished by using the 'pen' commands (click on 'extensions' and select the 'pen' extension).

Drawing shapes is a great context in which children can develop algorithms. There are great links with maths here, so that this kind of task could be done in a maths lesson.

Prior to attempting to code, the teacher would ask the children to plan out how their sprite is going to move, using a physical object to represent the sprite on the table. Once children have written an algorithm to move their sprite, they can give this algorithm to a friend and see if their friend can follow the algorithm to get the same shape.

When drawing shapes like this, the children are required to tell the object to turn according to the **exterior angle** of the shape, not the interior angle. (The exterior angle is the difference between the interior angle and 180 degrees, as if the side had been carried on.) This will only become apparent to children when they try to construct shapes other than squares and rectangles, as with squares and rectangles the interior and exterior angles are the same.

If planned around children's maths learning, they could receive a maths lesson on interior and exterior angles before attempting to draw shapes in Scratch. This is much easier than trying to teach them the maths in a computing lesson. When constructing their algorithms, children should spot a pattern where the movement and turns are the same. This will allow them to create more efficient algorithms and programs.

The next step on from drawing shapes is to draw patterns. The teacher could start this kind of activity by showing children examples of patterns created with coding and talk about the algorithms that make them. This is the important part of this lesson, as it is this thinking and planning that will later allow children to construct other patterns.

The basic premise of drawing a pattern is to draw a shape and then either move or rotate, before drawing a shape again. The teacher would point this out to the children and ensure that they are all familiar with this basic algorithm. Once children understand this, they can use the same code that they drew shapes with and put this into a repeat loop, with a movement block at the end of the loop. If they used a loop to draw their original shape and they put this loop inside another loop, they have created a **nested loop**. Nested loops are used a lot in programming and discussion of them might challenge the most able coders in key stage 2.

As an extension from this work so far, the children could try using a variable to change the length of the line each time it is drawn.

Drawing shapes is a good opportunity to introduce functions to children. Once they have created a piece of code to draw a shape, they can 'create a block' in Scratch and name it, for example, 'triangle' with their original code. They can then reuse this block as many times as they wish. This is called defining and calling a function, sometimes called a procedure. Under the national curriculum, this is not required until key stage 3, although some children are ready for this kind of structure in key stage 2.

User interfaces in Scratch

As well as creating games and drawing patterns in Scratch, children can create projects where the computer responds to input that a user provides, creating a type of user interface. Quizzes are some of the most popular projects that children can create way. Children can create quizzes for any subject, applying their knowledge of algorithm design and program design outside of computing lessons.

The algorithm that children would create when planning a quiz would follow a branching 'if/else' structure, as shown. Children could extend their algorithms by allowing for more than one possible answer, by using 'not' logic, or by including a score. Children can also add animations and graphical effects to their quizzes.

As with using Scratch to create games, these types of projects can benefit from the teacher creating a template for the children to work with. The teacher can set up their own Scratch account, create a project that is unfinished, and share this with the children as a link to remix. This gives all children a starting point, allows them to experience success, and allows them to concentrate their thinking on the learning point at hand.

62 *Teaching computer science*

Creating simulations using Scratch

One of the most exciting uses for modern computers is their ability to simulate complex systems. This can include simulating environmental systems, mechanical systems including robotics and abstract systems such as voting trends and evolution.

The national curriculum for key stage 2 states that children should:

> Design, write and debug programs that accomplish specific goals, including controlling or simulating physical systems.

Creating a simulation of a physical system is a great way for children to consolidate and demonstrate their knowledge about it. Scientific systems such as the solar system, water cycle, evolution, growth of plants, states of matter, and electrical flow can all be simulated by children using Scratch.

Creating any simulation of a physical system requires children to decompose the problem into programmable steps. Children should be encouraged to do this gradually, starting off with the scientific concept, decomposing it and then decomposing it further, using pseudocode to explain what is happening using language relating to programming. This is demonstrated in Table 6.3.

Example 1 - The water cycle

Table 6.3 Ideas for programming the water cycle decomposed with pseudocode

Scientific concept	Decomposed	Decomposed further and pseudocode
Water evaporates from the ocean when the Sun shines	Water droplets go up when the Sun appears	When Sun clicked, broadcast 'evaporate'. When droplets received 'evaporate', change y by 20.
Clouds get heavier as water evaporates	Increase the size of the cloud sprite	When water rises, broadcast 'cloud heavy'. When cloud receives 'cloud heavy', change costume to grey and change size by 50.
Heavy clouds drift over mountains	Move the cloud left on the screen	When cloud receives 'heavy', wait 5 seconds and change x by −100.

Example 2 - The Solar System

Table 6.4 Ideas for programming the solar system decomposed with pseudocode

Scientific concept	Decomposed	Decomposed further and pseudocode
The Earth orbits the Sun	The Earth sprite moves in a loop around the Sun sprite and draws a trail	Pen down. Earth moves forward 1, turns 3 degrees, repeat forever.
Mars orbits the Sun	Mars sprite moves in a loop around the Sun sprite and draws a trail, a bit further away than the Earth	Pen down. Earth moves forward 1, turns 2 degrees, repeat forever.

Teaching computer science 63

The example of the solar system in Table 6.4 is a great puzzle, that children really enjoy doing, with some thinking beforehand! (The values in the tables above are not correct!)

Both examples are simulations that will benefit from careful and thoughtful algorithm design prior to coding and will produce excellent outcomes demonstrating children's scientific understanding.

Flowol 4

In 2013, when the subject of computing was still in its early stages, Flowol 4 was the one of first pieces of software used in schools for teaching algorithm design. The software is so good that it is still being used ten years later and it is a great way to practise algorithm design and simulate physical systems. Flowol 4 allows children to program simulations of everyday scenarios called 'mimics'.

The mimics are all situations that the children will be familiar with, such as crossing lights, traffic lights, level crossings, and Christmas trees. The class discussion that can be had prior to creating algorithms and programming these mimics is fantastic. Teachers can have great discussions with children about the sequence of traffic lights, when the green man should come on, how long it should be one for, etc. Children can watch videos of devices such as level crossings working and talk about how level crossings keep people safe.

Once children have had time to discuss how the mimics could work, they can plan their algorithms, decomposing the problem into its elements. The more carefully children think about their algorithms, the easier it is going to be for them to program the devices in Flowol.

Programming in Flowol is done as a flow chart, with a round starting event, parallelogram-shaped outputs, rectangular delay commands and diamond shapes decisions. These decisions are the inputs; the computer asks the question as to whether it has received an input from a button or sensor. Depending on whether the answer is 'yes', or 'no', the computer takes the next path on the flowchart.

Vexcode VR/Gearsbot

As mentioned in Chapter 3, **Gearsbot** and **Vexcode VR** (vr.vex.com) are both websites that are free to use and offer excellent simulations of robotics challenges. These websites therefore allow children to solve simulations of robotics problems, preparing them for when they encounter physical robots that they can program.

Robots in Vexcode VR feature motors, front facing touch sensors, front and down facing colour sensors, front facing distance sensors, and down facing magnets. In the free version, the children can choose 1 of 15 'playgrounds' that simulate common robotics problems, such as navigating a maze or picking up and returning obstacles.

As with any programming problem, thinking about the problem, planning algorithms, and decomposing the problem are key to success. During this process, children may well sport patterns too to help them. They might realise, for example, that in the block collection exercise, the same code is used three times with the robot just needing to change its starting point. Teachers can experience success using Vexcode VR with children in year 5 and later,

64 *Teaching computer science*

when they have encountered physical robotics problems, they have been able to apply some of the thinking they did using VexcodeVr (this is called 'generalisation').

Gearsbot (https://gears.aposteriori.com.sg/) also allows children to simulate robotics challenges with a slightly different range to those in Vexcode VR. Programming in Gearsbot is slightly harder than in Vexcoede VR due to the language used relating to movement. One of the most useful challenges for children to work on is the 'line following' task, which is a task commonly used in robotics. This task is brilliant for children to decompose and create algorithms to solve. There is no singular way to make the robot follow the line, and children should be encouraged to approach the task in a way that makes sense to them.

Sphero

Sphero robots are small, spherical robots designed to teach children about block-based programming, problem-solving, and data collection. Spheros are great to use because they are easy to connect to mobile devices via Bluetooth and start programming, they are robust, and they feature a simple, block-based programming interface that emphasises movement using bearings (measured in degrees).

When using Sphero robots with children, teachers should set them simple challenges to start with until they are satisfied that children can control their robots precisely. It is important that the children 'aim' their robots before they start using them, so that the blue light is at the back of the robot. It is also important that the children mark their starting point so that their program runs identically each time.

Even simple challenges such as getting the robot to drove forward and stop on a point can generate good algorithmic thinking for children. Children are required to decompose their movement commands, telling the robot at what power level to move forward, at what bearing and for how many seconds. These simple tasks can be extended by the children programming their robots to return to the starting point. This can then be extended further by children programming the robots to move in squares, rectangles, etc.

Once children have mastered making the robot move reliably, they can begin to decompose and plan algorithms for more complex tasks. These can include the robots navigating obstacles, navigating mazes, displaying messages on the LED screen, and even communicating with other robots.

Ohbot

Ohbot robotic heads can be bought as wither constructable sets, or prebuilt sets. Buying the pre-built sets may be a good option, as the constructable sets are very challenging to build.

Ohbot heads let children experience devise algorithms for and program anthropomorphic (human like) robotic devices. This leads to some interesting discussion about how robots are controlled. We take certain commands such as 'walk' or 'smile' for granted, knowing all the movements that are contained in each of these actions. In a sense, 'walk' and 'smile' are like functions, commands that contain many smaller commands.

A good first activity to do with the Ohbots is to ask children to make their eyes change colour when a button is pressed. This is a good lesson when the children are still getting used to the

Teaching computer science 65

OhBot interface and how to connect/disconnect the robots, so a simple outcome is preferred. However, even with this simple task, it is worth children planning out the algorithms they will use to make the robot's eyes change colour. Children can draw their algorithm out as a flow chart, being asked to consider the input (which button is pressed) and the output (the eyes changing colour). Children must think about how long they want the eyes to be that colour and whether they should change back again. Children can also consider changing to more than one colour.

A natural progression from this introductory lesson is to consider facial expressions that the robot could show. Children can be asked to smile and frown at each other and decompose the words 'smile' and 'frown'. What happens when we smile? Most people will say that the corners of their mouth go up and their eyes wide, with the opposite happening for a frown!

Moving on to examine the parts that the robot has, children can then think about algorithms to control the motors attached to the robot's eyelids, top lip, bottom lip, and even eye colour. Children can be asked to write precise algorithms for each part and model what is meant by a precise algorithm. 'Top lip moves down' is not precise, but 'top lip moves down 45 degrees for 3 seconds, then move back' is more precise. Having done this, children can use their algorithms to program the robots.

From here, children could go onto explore more robotic anthropomorphic behaviour, such as blinking, turning the head to track people (using a webcam with the robot), making the lips sync with speech and asking/answering questions. Fun projects could be to make the robots tell jokes, give advice, sing together, or answer questions. There are some good materials available on the OhBot website to help teachers and children think of ideas and solutions for the robots.

Kodu

Kodu is an old piece of software that is still available to download for free. Kodu is a 3D programming environment which can be used for making games and 3D environments.

In Kodu, the coding commands closely resemble standard English, far more so than in other block-based coding languages. For example, to program the sprite to move, only two blocks are needed: 'when buttons pressed' and 'move'. This makes Kodu very accessible to children, although it is also powerful enough to create some complex programs.

The fact that Kodu is a 3D environment is also exciting for children. They are able to quickly create a character that moves around in a 3D world, create character that reacts to the player sprite. Children also love drawing mountains, trees, and rivers for their world. One of the most significant features of Kodu is that the sprites can be programmed to follow paths. Again, this makes it very easy for children to program sprites to move along paths for a game, with an algorithm consisting of the commands: 'always', 'move', and 'on red path'. With nearly all the commands in Kodu, more detail can be added to a command, such as 'move', 'on red path' + 'quickly'. Once children start thinking in this way, they can usually create programs with a high degree of independence.

Algorithms 'unplugged'

While there are some exciting technologies available to teach children how to construct algorithms and programs, so much good quality thinking about algorithms can be done without

66 *Teaching computer science*

using any technology at all. Learning about concepts in computing without using digital technology is referred to as 'unplugged' computing. This is explored in detail in Chapter 12.

Any activity or game that the children take part in has procedures or rules and as such can be decomposed into algorithms. Nursery rhymes or simple songs that repeat phrases can be written as algorithms. Writing algorithms for dance routines is a very popular activity – the test is whether someone else performs the same dance as you! Children could write algorithms for sports moves such as taking a penalty, shooting a basketball, navigating an obstacle course, or doing a gymnastics routine. They could then ask someone to test their algorithm by following it precisely while doing the physical activity.

Popular ways to introduce algorithms are by the children coming up with an algorithm for a potentially messy activity, such as making a sandwich or brushing teeth. Phill Bagge, teacher, author, and computing inspector, made famous the 'jam sandwich' demonstration, which resulted in both hilarity and great discussion about the need to be precise with algorithms!

Children can make up their own games, either board games or physical games and devise algorithms for these, so that players can play their games. When doing this, children should be encouraged to use computational language such as 'if' and 'until'. Children could then make versions of these games using Scratch, or another coding environment.

Music is another area that follows very specific instructions, and musical scores are an example of algorithms. Children can use musical instruments and compose their own pieces, writing algorithms for others to play their pieces. The children could make use of loops for repetition of notes and even nested loops (loops within loops) to repeat whole sections of their music. Functions could also be introduced there, saying 'chorus' is telling the player to carry out a pre-determined sequence of instructions and is therefore an example of a function!

PAUSE AND REFLECT...

Algorithms are step-by-step instructions for accomplishing a task.

- How can you make algorithms part of children's everyday lives and vocabulary?
- What tool(s) would you choose for teaching children to create their own algorithms through programming?

Teaching children to use sequence

The national curriculum for key stage 2 states,

> Children should use sequence, selection and repetition within programs; work with variables and various forms of input and output.

Putting instructions in the correct sequence is closely related to correct algorithm design. The importance of the correct sequence of instructions is something children sometimes forget, causing errors when they run their programs.

It is important to remember about computers do exactly what we tell them to, in the exact order. This can sometimes be different to the order that we have in mind!

Teaching computer science 67

Children very often forget to put 'wait' commands into programs. Computers run commands in a program immediately after the previous command has finished. If we tell a computer to turn on a light, then turn it off, we will only see the light off. The computer will turn on the light, but only for a fraction of a second, before running the next command.

In **Scratch**, children can choose between 'play sound' and 'play sound until done' when they are adding sounds to their programs. The difference is, with play sound, the next command in the program will execute as soon as the sound starts playing. This can be useful, or can cause problems, particularly if the next command is a different sound!

Controlling or simulating physical devices is another good way to demonstrate the importance of sequence. Using **Flowol 4**, one of the first challenges is to program the crossing light to flash one and off. 'Easy!' exclaim the class! 'The algorithm is 'light on, light off, repeat!'' (If they don't suggest this, the teacher can model this incorrect solution on the board!) Of course, the correct solution requires a delay after each command. As this is an introductory lesson, the teacher can let the children figure out the correct delay themselves. After this activity, they are usually much better at remembering 'delay', or 'wait' commands in their algorithms and programs.

A great way to explore the effect of sequence is by using **Parson's puzzles** with the children. These are when the teacher provides children with all the correct code but jumbled up. Children must either individually, or in pairs, place the commands in the correct sequence. In doing so, a good amount of discussion about the right order of the code is created.

Teaching children to use selection

Selection occurs when a computer checks a situation against a condition and makes a choice of what to do next. This is most commonly represented using the language 'if' and 'else', such as 'if the robot detects green, start moving, else stop'. Selection is sometimes shown on flowcharts using questions, such as in Flowol 4. As children develop their understanding of selection, they will consider algorithms where there are more than two possible outcomes. Computers use 'else if' logic to ask a second question after the first answer is false. For example, 'if the robot is detecting green, then go, else if the robot is detecting yellow, then bleep, else turn off'. This branching question structure can continue indefinitely, with as many questions being asked as necessary.

Selection is not required until key stage 2. The national curriculum for key stage 2 simply states,

> Children should use sequence, selection and repetition within programs; work with various forms of input and output.

By years 5 and 6, children should be starting to think about selection with more than two possible answers.

Children will probably also want to start using 'or' and 'not' operators in their selection. There is, therefore, a natural progression from children starting to use conditions with a simple 'if/else' structure, to more sophisticated forms of selection. There is also a really good opportunity to combine teaching about selection with using inputs and outputs, since most inputs involve an element of selection logic. For example, a distance sensor will ask the

68   *Teaching computer science*

Figure 6.1 A screenshot of a branching conditional structure in Scratch. Screenshot taken by the author. Taken from Scratch, owned by the Scratch Foundation, screenshots are used under CC BY NC 2.0 DEED.

question, 'is the distance less than 100cm?', or a switch will ask the question, 'is the switch pressed?'

The first aspect of teaching children to use selection in their programs is to challenge them to think about how digital devices and programs work. A device like an automatic door is a perfect opportunity to explore this and something that all children should have experience of. Challenge children to write instructions (an algorithm) for how the doors work, and tell them that the program needs to involve a question. This question will be along the lines of 'is someone close to the doors?' Now challenge children to plot a sequence of events for the answer 'yes' and the answer 'no'. The answer 'yes' will involve a whole range of actions, such as the doors opening, (hopefully waiting) and then closing again. The children will realise themselves that when the answer is 'no', the question must be re-asked! The children can be further challenged by asking them to be precise with their algorithm – how close does someone need to be? How big does an object need to be to trigger the doors?

While it is unlikely that children will construct automatic doors, the above activity is a useful one for making children think about selection within a process of instructions. It also gives children practice at writing out an algorithm for a device – something that will benefit them in other projects. If the school has access to software like Flowol 4, the children could attempt

Teaching computer science 69

to construct flowchart-style algorithms for simulations of physical devices, also fulfilling the national curriculum objective for key stage 2: 'design, write and debug programs that accomplish specific goals, including controlling or simulating physical systems'.

It is also important that children recognise how selection is used to control results displayed on a computer screen. Again, the first stage of this is encouraging children to analyse how computer software that they use works. Computer games are a good example of this as they feature decisions and behaviour that can be analysed. Children could write algorithms for a popular game, writing questions to control the behaviour of elements in the program. For example, 'is the sprite touching the fruit?' If 'yes', fruit disappears and the sprite scores points, otherwise ask the question again. Once children are familiar with this type of logic, they should be able to use it to represent ideas in their own games.

Teachers should not underestimate how difficult some children find it to break behaviours down into conditional statements. Many games that children create will feature the character 'bumping' into objects. Children will find it hard initially to break this down into a question, such as 'is the character touching the wall, if yes, go backwards a bit'. However, with practice, they will start to think in this way when creating their own computer programs.

A good way to practise using selection is for children to create a 'quiz' game, or 'object identifying' program. This can also have links to other subjects, including maths, science, or history, as the children can create decision trees using their knowledge from within the subject.

As an example, a great way to teach children to think about the properties of 2D shapes is to encourage them to create a decision tree to sort 6-10 shapes. They need to think of questions that separate shapes at each stage, such as 'is it a quadrilateral?' Better questions will result in an even number of shapes being left on each side of the decision (i.e. not 'is it a square?', followed by 'is it an equilateral triangle?') Children could create science quizzes to identify plants or animal, create quizzes about people in history, etc.

Once children have created their decision trees, it is fairly easy to use these to create a program, although some children will find the process of creating a branching structure in a block-based program hard. One way to help them is to remind them that after every question, an 'if/else' block should be used.

Other types of programs that can use this idea are 'right/wrong' quizzes, where children use their knowledge to create quizzes about concepts in any subject. This is also a good opportunity to extend children by them using the 'or' operator, to consider that there may be more than one way of expressing the correct answer, such as '6' or 'six' as the answer to 'What is 2×3?'

As we have seen so far, what is important when teaching selection, is that children have the answer to think about how things around them work and to replicate this by asking questions in decision trees. They should also have the opportunity to construct their own decision trees to control imaginary and real devices and software.

Once children are familiar with this process of using decision trees, there are many opportunities for them to practise using selection in programs. Code.org has some excellent puzzles that children could work in in lessons which encourage children to think about selection in a range of contexts. Kodu lets children create 3D games and environments. The language

70 *Teaching computer science*

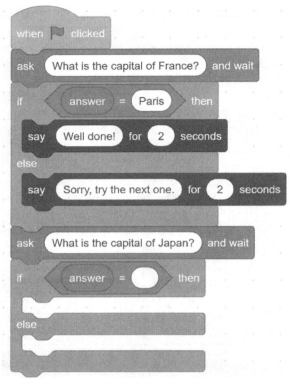

Figure 6.2 A screenshot of some code from Scratch showing a quiz game. Screenshot taken by the author. Taken from Scratch, owned by the Scratch Foundation, screenshots are used under CC BY NC 2.0 DEED.

in Kodu is different to most other block-based environments, but children will still benefit from planning out their ideas using decision trees.

Robotics is another excellent field for children to practise using selection. Children can create simulations of robots using Scratch and program them to respond to user inputs. Children in schools that buy OhBot robotic heads can program these to react in different ways using selection. Children can also use selection to program robots in the excellent on-screen robotics environments, Vexcode VR and Gearsbot. Both of these simulate common robotics challenges, such as programming a robot to navigate a maze and follow a line. These situations both use selection which can be explored with the children and mapped out using a decision tree. The first stage of programming a robot to follow a line might be, 'is the colour sensor detecting black?' The children could be challenged to complete the instructions for 'yes' and 'no' being the answer to this question. To navigate a maze, the robot might ask the similar question, 'is the distance to the wall less than 20cm?'

For schools that decide to invest in it, Lego Spike Prime sets offer an excellent medium for teaching children to use selection. This is because the sets feature a range of inputs, including touch, colour, and distance sensors. Children can create simple devices that use these sensors and conditional logic. A favourite of children is the 'alarm system', where the device

Figure 6.3 A screenshot of some code from Scratch showing maths quiz about shapes. Screenshot taken by the author. Taken from Scratch, owned by the Scratch Foundation, screenshots are used under CC BY NC 2.0 DEED.

bleeps if someone tries to steal a pencil (by their hand getting close to the distance sensor). Of course, more complex systems can be built using these Lego sets, including robots that drive around and grappling devices. Good advice to any teachers starting out using Lego, or any other physical system would be to set challenges that use one or two components to accomplish a simple task. This encourages children to really think about the movements and measurements in their device and is a much better approach than providing a whole Lego set and expecting thoughtful work within the lesson.

Of course, as all digital devices operate using selection logic within their programs, once children understand selection, they can use it to build devices that feature any kind of user input. In Chapters 10 and 11, we will explore robotics and physical computing in more depth.

Teaching children to use repetition

The computing national curriculum for key stage 2 states,

> Children should use sequence, selection and repetition within programs; work with variables and various forms of input and output.

72   *Teaching computer science*

Teaching children to use repetition in programs is the second of three programming elements that children should be taught at key stage 2. Repetition is not required to be taught at key stage 1, although it is something that will inevitably arise, and it could distinguish more efficient year 2 algorithms from algorithms written in year 1.

Repetition means telling a computer to use the same instruction, or sequence of instructions, more than once. This is why it will inevitably arise as soon as children start giving instructions to devices, or each other! It is far more efficient to say 'go forwards three times', than 'go forwards, go forwards, go forwards'. Why this is better should be explored with children as soon as they start writing instructions, for Beebots, everyday tasks, or to guide each other's movements. That is why although repetition is not required to be taught until key stage 2, my experience has that it has been a necessary discussion to have in years 1 and 2.

We use repletion in programs where patterns occur, and this is the important thing for children to realise. 'Forward, forward, forward' is a pattern (of one instruction). 'Forward, up, forward, up' is a pattern of two instructions. Once we have recognised that there is a pattern, this algorithm can be more efficiently written as 'forward, up × 2'. 'Red, blue, yellow, red, blue, yellow, red, blue, yellow' is a pattern that can be written as 'red, blue, yellow × 3', once the pattern has been spotted. A pattern is where we use the same sequence more than once.

By the end of key stage 1, children should have had practice at creating algorithms to control the behaviour of each other, as well as robots and on-screen sprites. They should have encountered the fact that it is usually better to repeat instructions, rather than give the same instruction, or sequence of instructions, more than once.

Early in key stage 2, children should continue to have the opportunity to practise forming simple algorithms, realising that it is beneficial to shorten algorithms using repetition. The new versions of Beebtots, Bluebots, are programmable using an iPad app and can incorporate repetition into programs. The teacher can therefore set activities where children have to program the robots to reach a destination, similar to the activities that children might have done with Beebots/Bluebots at key stage 1. The Bluebots can also be programmed to turn using angles, making them a good tool for children to learn about this area of maths. This makes Bluebots a versatile tool for teaching in primary schools, although the initial cost of purchasing the Bluebots can be high.

Another tool suitable for years 3 and 4 to practise and demonstrate repetition is the excellent website, code.org. Code.org allows teachers to set up classes of children and set them puzzles that demonstrate coding concepts, including repetition. By watching the videos and working through the puzzles, children should develop a secure understanding of how loops are used in programs and why it is better to repeat instructions in a loop.

Once children have an understanding of how and why repetition is used in programming, a good next step for them is to use repetition to draw shapes. This can be done both on screen, and physically by programming robots such as Bluebot. Children need to be really clear about their algorithms before they start programming. They also need to be secure that they are programming from the robot, or sprite's point of view and not their own.

Children should start by giving each other instructions to move around in different shapes. These instructions can be verbal or written on paper. This will make it clear to children that there is a pattern of 'moving and then turning'. The algorithm for a square might therefore be, 'move forward, turn right 90, ÷4'. When children make a triangle, however, they might

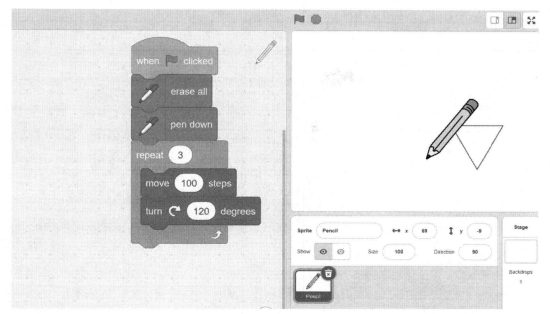

Figure 6.4 A screenshot of a 2D shape drawn using repetition in Scratch. Screenshot taken by the author. Taken from Scratch, owned by the Scratch Foundation, screenshots are used under CC BY NC 2.0 DEED.

initially way 'turn 60 degrees'. This is a common misconception that needs to be demonstrated physically. The correct instruction for making an equilateral triangle is in fact 'turn 120 degrees', as children need to consider the exterior, not interior angle of the turn. It would be a lot to ask children in lower key stage 2 to figure this out, although it might be a good challenge for years 5 or 6 children. To get over this hurdle and allow children in key stage 2 to draw shapes using angles, the teacher could provide the correct instructions, 'jumbled up' in a Parson's puzzle, for the children to arrange in the correct sequence.

Once children have an idea of the correct turning angles, they can program sprites to draw shapes using the pen commends and repetition. They will soon realise that they want to draw the same shape more than once, perhaps in another place. This will lead them to repeat sequences of code that themselves contain repetition. This is called a 'nested loop' – a loop within a loop.

Another way to demonstrate and teach repetition is through the children spotting and creating musical sequences, or sequences of dance moves. Both of these offer fun situations in which children can explore the benefits of creating a sequence and then repeating this, to create a longer piece of music or dance. Children could look at examples of music and dance and spot where patterns have been used, before writing algorithms to describe what is happening.

Musical sequences can be programmed using block-based programming environments such as Scratch. Children can use the tonal blocks to program the computer to play tunes, developing and combining their musical and computing subject knowledge.

Children who have understood how repetition is used to repeat sequences of commands in programs are ready to learn about more abstract uses of repetition in programs. Computers use repetition to 'keep checking' whether a condition is true. In this sense, repetition is closely linked to selection, as covered earlier in this chapter. Children who are creating computer games using Scratch will want their character to react if it is touching another sprite or object. To do this, they will need to learn to use 'forever if' logic. Here, the computer is constantly checking whether the sprite is touching something else. A common misconception among children while programming is to miss out the forever loop here, so that the sequence only happens once, causing their game not to work. Children who have understood conditions using flow charts are less likely to make this error and use a repeat loop here.

Nested loops

Once children are confident at using repetition in their programs, they may be able to use more complex types of loops. One example of this is a 'nested loop'. A nested loop is a 'loop within a loop'.

A good opportunity to demonstrate using nested loops is while drawing patterns. A sprite or robot can be programmed to move in a shape using repetition of commands in a loop. |Once it has executed this loop, the sprite can be programmed to move, before repeating the original loop. This can result in some interesting patterns. Scratch and Beetleblocks are ideal platforms to demonstrate this, and the children can explore some interesting designs. They may be interested in performing a web search to help them explore ideas for nested loops and patterns.

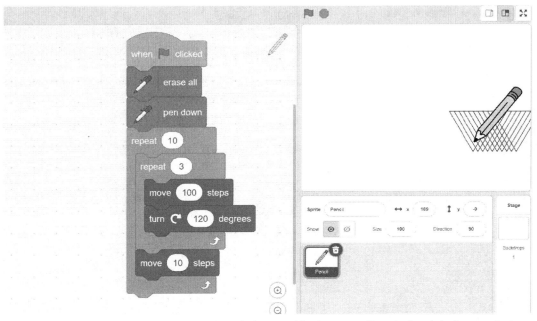

Figure 6.5 A screenshot of a nested loop being used to draw a pattern in Scratch. Screenshot taken by the author. Taken from Scratch, owned by the Scratch Foundation, screenshots are used under CC BY NC 2.0 DEED.

Teaching computer science 75

PAUSE AND REFLECT...

The national curriculum does not require children to learn about repetition until key stage 2.

- Is repetition a concept that children in key stage 1 can understand?
- Does repetition make programming easier or more difficult?

Variables

The third part of the key stage 2 programming requirement mentions variables,

> Children should use sequence, selection and repetition within programs; work with variables and various forms of input and output.

The concept of variables in computing can be linked to that of variables in science – things that we can change or keep the same in an experiment. Variables, from the word 'vary', refers to data that can change in a program. Variables are probably not necessary to teach early in key stage 2, when children are firming up their knowledge about sequence, selection, and repetition. Children can be taught to use variables late in year 4 or wait until year 5 or 6. Under a spiral curriculum, the concept is repeated each year at increasing levels of difficulty. This is because variables, like all aspects of computing, can be taught at increasing levels of difficulty.

A good way to introduce children to variables is through the concept of a score in a game or quiz. We have discussed how children can create simple quizzes using an 'if/else' structure, and it is not a huge leap to add a score to this. A teacher explaining a variable for the first time might run a class quiz and keep the score on the whiteboard, eliciting from the children when this needs to change and by how much. The teacher can make the point that it doesn't matter what this variable is called, but it is helpful to name it something like 'score', which is also good practice when programming.

Once children have understood the concept of an amount being told to change, they should be able to add variables into their algorithms when planning a quiz game, or other type of game. They can also consider that in their quiz games, the 'if answer = ...' statement is using the variable 'answer' (although this is not made obvious in Scratch, as the answer block is a different colour to the variables blocks).

Kodu is an excellent coding environment in which children can explore using variables. Kodu uses a very simple coding interface, but features use of variables which can be used for player score. In Kodu, children can think about when they want their score to change and what they want to happen once the score reaches a certain amount.

Developing children's understanding of variables

As with all aspects of programming, the important thing when children are using variables is that they are able to plan their use in algorithms. Children should, for example, be able to

76 *Teaching computer science*

write an algorithm that says 'when touching the apple, change the score by 10'. Children can be presented with games that have been created by the teacher in Scratch and shared via a VLE for the children to modify so that they have the opportunity to explore using variables without having to start a project from nothing.

Once children are able to understand and use algorithms to make variables such as score change, they can start to use variables in a more sophisticated way. One way to do this is to use variables to control the movement of sprites or devices. Creating a variable called 'speed', they can then create algorithms to tell this variable to change. They can then tell something to move 'speed' steps, an amount that could be changed, for example, by collecting a power up in a game.

When drawing shapes and patterns, children can also use variables to change the say that something moves. Instead of telling a pen to 'move 10 steps' when drawing a shape, they could tell the pen to move 'length' steps. They can then include commands in their program to change this length and create different shapes.

Another way to develop children's understanding and use of variables is to set variables to random amounts. In a game that they are designing and making, instead of telling a sprite to start at 'x' position and 'y' positions defined by coordinates, they can create variables for the x and y position and set these to random amounts. This makes the game less predictable and often more fun. In fact, any time that variables are used for unpredictability in programs, it often makes the user experience more interesting and more likely to be repeated.

Functions

Functions and procedures are both types of subroutines. A subroutine is like a mini-program within a program; a set of instructions that is remembered by the computer and can be used again as many times as necessary.

Functions are not required by the national curriculum until key stage 3, where it states that children should,

> Design and develop modular programs that use procedures and functions.

It might therefore seem odd to include functions in a book about primary computing. The reason for this inclusion is that functions are incredibly easy to use in block-based programs such as Scratch and children often naturally incorporate them into their programming.

Using functions at key stage 2

In **Scratch**, it is possible for children to create their own blocks. By doing this, they can create a section of code that is attributed to this block, before naming this block of code. In doing this, they are creating a function. This simple process can actually help children organise their code and make it easier for them to write and debug programs. As an example, when children draw patterns using the pen command and movement/turning commands, they quickly realise that they can create patterns by using the sequence of code for a shape again and again. Children could use a nested loop to do this, with the initial loop for the shape and the next loop repeating that shape several times. Alternatively, they can create the shape for their shape, attribute this to a block that they have created and then use this block as many times as they want. Children in upper key stage 2 have often prefer the second approach!

Flowol 4 is another program where children can make subroutines. In Flowol 4, the subroutines are referred to as 'sub', but they are, just as in Scratch, short sequences of instructions that can be repeated as many times as necessary. Children in upper key stage 2 often see the value of defining sequences of code in subroutines and then calling this several times, for example, to make a light flash on and off.

Some software teaches children that it is beneficial to shorten code by using subroutines. **Cargobot** is a fun coding game, where children have to program a crane to place blocks in the correct order. As the levels get harder, the children are challenged to construct more complex programs in a finite amount of space. To succeed, they have to predefine sequences of commands that they can use over and over, in other words create subroutines.

The mobile app **Lightbot** features puzzles where children have to program a robot to move and turn on all lights in a level. As with Cargobot, children quickly progress to levels where they have a limited amount of space available to construct their programs. In this way, they learn to create and use subroutines. Lightbot used to be available as a web-based application, but it is now only available as a free mobile app.

Teaching children to use functions is a tool for helping them to organise their code. Some children can easily grasp the concept of pre-made sequences of instructions. There is an excellent video, produced by **code.org**, which equates functions to pre-defined 'plays' in a basketball game. For example, when the coach says 'attack', the team know which instructions to carry out. As part of a class discussion on functions, the children could think of other occasions where one word leads to a series of actions or movements, without having to say each action individually!

Text-based programming

At which age should children begin using text-based programming to control devices? Is text-based programming appropriate for primary-aged children?

Block-based programming is used by most secondary schools into years 7, 8, and 9. Secondary schools may use Scratch, or may use block-based programming that incorporates JavaScript, or another text-based language. This is the case in the 'App Lab' in code.org.

The advantage of block-based programming is that it lets children focus on understanding concepts, separate from syntax (the rules of typing a language). This lessens children's cognitive load and allows them to experience success with programming projects from an early age.

Some children may display an interest in text-based programming. This could be because of programming they have seen in the outside world, or perhaps because they have a family member who is involved in programming. Text-based programming is eventually quicker and more powerful than block-based programming. However, children should be encouraged to use block-based programming until they have a firm grasp on principles such as selection, repetition, variables, and functions.

78 *Teaching computer science*

Networks

At key stage 2, the national curriculum for computing states that children should,

> Understand computer networks including the internet; how they can provide multiple services, such as the world wide web; and the opportunities they offer for communication and collaboration.

What is a network?

Computers can connect together to form a network. Nowadays, we take this for granted. However, it was not long ago that home and school computers operated in isolation.

Computers that are connected in a network can communicate and share information. They can also be configured remotely, using another computer.

Nowadays, networks are made of both wired and wireless connections.

The **internet** is the name for the network that spans the globe. The first version of the internet was created in the 1970's and gradually more businesses and organisations began connecting to this.

In 1990, Tim Berners-Lee invented the **World Wide Web**. The World Wide Web is system for accessing webpages via the internet. The World Wide Web is a service that uses the internet, making it possible for a wide range of people to access information online.

Two types of network connections exist: wired and wireless. Most computer networks are a mixture of wired and wireless network connections.

A computer network includes the following components:

- Devices, or 'clients' (PC's, laptops, printers, etc.)
- Switches
- Routers
- Servers
- Data centres
- The internet
- The world wide web
- IP address
- Packets

Data is created and stored on computer hard drives. This can be on client hard drives, or on powerful computers called **servers**. Major companies and organisations all have servers hosting large amounts of information. Large schools may have a server, hosting the school's information. Joining many servers together creates a **data centre**, massive structures used by some of the world's largest companies.

Information is sent around the world via the **internet**. To send information across networks, it is broken down into **packets**. A packet is a like a piece of a puzzle. A picture sent across a network will be split into many small packets. These packets are sent across the network in the most efficient way. This includes splitting them up and sending them across different routes. When a computer requests information, it sends its **IP address**, a long number which tells the receiving computer where to send the packets to. Packets are routed via the most efficient route by **routers**.

Once a data packet reaches its destination router (i.e., a school), it is sent to the correct client computer via **switches**. Sometimes, switches are part of routers. Switches can be wired, or often in schools, wireless.

The terms **cloud** and **cloud-based computing** are used to refer to computers accessing data that is stored on servers around the world. All cloud-based data is initially sent via wires around the world, often under oceans. From there, routers transmit data to the eventual user.

Teaching children about networks

Teaching children about how network work will usually start with showing the children a diagram of a computer network. There are some excellent videos online which explain how data is sent over computer networks, which can be a good starting point for lessons. The website **code.org** has a unit of work called 'The Internet', as unit 2 of their 'Computer Science Principles' course. This course features activities that the children can do to help them understand how networks work.

Schools are an ideal location for children to begin to understand networks. This is because all schools feature a network of computers which children can observe, study, and interact with.

A great activity to carry out with children is to lead them around the school on a 'tour' of the school computer network. The children should be asked to identify individual computers, network cables leading out from computers, wireless access points, network sockets in the wall and the school's switches and server (if it has one).

An easy task that children can perform is to find the IP address of their computer or device. This can be found in different ways, including through Windows settings.

Children benefit from creating models of networks, including using physical resources. They can 'act out' the journey of packets across a network that they create, helping strengthen their understanding of how a network operates.

Conclusion

Computer science enables children to understand the process that occur in the world around them. Through understanding processes that occur around them, children start to think of their own ideas for things that could work, including hardware and software.

Although a lot of what we teach children about computer science seems specific to computing, there are many opportunities for making this knowledge applicable to other subject areas. As we have seen, computational thinking and algorithm design are skills that can benefit children across the curriculum. Children can also apply their knowledge of maths and other subjects to understand computer science, for example, incorporating maths in their algorithms or using their writing skills to explain how networks work.

Note

1 https://www.appsforgood.org/.

References

Apps for Good, https://www.appsforgood.org/
Code.org, https://code.org/
Computing Programs of Study: key stages 1 and 2, National Curriculum of England, Department for Education, 2013.
Gearsbot, https://gears.aposteriori.com.sg/
Scratch, https://scratch.mit.edu/
VexcodeVR, https://vr.vex.com/

7 Teaching information technology

What is information technology?

Information technology is the second of the three strands of computing. The national curriculum states,

> Building on this knowledge and understanding, (referring to computer science), pupils are equipped to use information technology to create programs, systems and a range of content.

Information technology refers to children expressing their ideas, using their knowledge and understanding of how computers work to solve problems, design solutions, and create their own content.

The objectives that concern information technology are at **key stage 1**:

- Use technology purposefully to create, organise, manipulate, store and retrieve digital content.

And for **key stage 2**:

- Use search appreciate effectively; understand how results are selected and ranked and be discerning in evaluating digital content
- Select, use and combine a variety of software (including internet services) on a range of digital devices to design and create a range of programs, systems and content that accomplish goals, including collecting, analysing, evaluating and presenting data and information

As discussed in Chapter 2, there will be overlaps between the strands when teaching computing. When teaching children about a computer science concept such as repetition, children will usually practise making their own programs which contain loops. In this sense, within one lesson, they could be covering both computer science (understanding concepts and developing algorithms) and information technology (creating their own programs). This is fine, the purpose of the three strands of computing is not to separate teaching, but to ensure that teaching is balanced and covers different aspects of computing.

In a similar way, when teaching children to use internet services to create content, children will also think critically about technology use and online safety, covering digital literacy objectives alongside computer science and information technology objectives.

DOI: 10.4324/9781003502555-7

82 *Teaching information technology*

With regard to information technology, important phrases in the national curriculum are as follows: for key stage 1, 'purposefully' and for key stage 2, 'that accomplish given goals'. These phrases help us understand that the information technology strand relates to children going beyond knowing how digital tools work, to being able to apply them to solve problems and express ideas.

This chapter will guide teachers through some of the methods of content creation that children should use throughout key stages 1 and 2. There are some exciting and empowering tools that children can use to express their ideas and create digital content, many available for schools to use for free!

This chapter should be read in conjunction with Chapter 18, which provides a progression of skills based on the national curriculum.

Information technology skills and tools

This book advocates a 'spiral' curriculum, where children use the same creative tools repeatedly, increasing their mastery and allowing them to focus on the task and learning, as well as the tool itself.

In this chapter, we will consider some of the creative skills that children should learn to develop at key stages 1 and 2. We will also consider some of the most accessible, powerful, and best value tools that can allow them to develop the skills required by the information technology strand.

Basic computer skills

Before expecting to use computers creatively and effectively, sufficient time should be devoted to teaching the basic skills required to use a computer. Children using computers can experience increased cognitive load, especially if software and systems are unfamiliar to them.

Basic computer skills are included in the progression of skills in Chapter 18. They include:

- Mouse skills, including left and right mouse button, scrolling
- Keyboard skills, including using keyboard shortcuts and typing
- Naming, saving, organising, and opening work, including using folders
- Turning a computer on and off
- Opening programs and navigating between programs
- Windows skills, including minimising, maximising, resizing, and closing windows

The above skills can be neglected in favour of more creative use of computers in computing lessons. With time for computing limited in schools as it is, spending lesson time practising opening and closing work, or any of the above skills can seem like time lost.

In fact, the opposite is true. Spending time practising routine tasks saves lesson time in the long run. Practice of basic tasks can be done in a fun way, including giving children checklists of tasks to demonstrate linked to achieving a 'computing licence'. Teachers should make it clear which procedures children are expected to follow during lessons. In computing classrooms, this can be displayed on the walls, minimising cognitive load and helping establish independence.

Teaching information technology 83

Mouse skills

There is a range of software that can be used for teaching children mouse skills. It is important that children are taught to use a mouse correctly and that they do not get into bad habits. Children should probably begin learning to use a mouse in year 1, although this could happen earlier or later. Doing this too early will be very hard for some children and doing this too late will restrict their access to software that requires a mouse.

One piece of software that allows children to practise mouse skills is **Poisson Rouge**.[1] This software is developed by a French company and features mouse activities that do not require any reading of words. The activities help children to practise clicking, dragging and dropping, and highlighting with the mouse.

The website **tinytap.com**[2] is another resource, featuring activities that let children practise mouse skills. It features activities that include clicking, dragging and dropping, without children needing to read any words.

PBS Games[3] is another website that features activities, many of which are perfect for developing children's mouse skills. This includes the excellent **Dinosaur Train**[4] games.

The **Sesame Street**[5] website also features games that can reinforce mouse skills.

Whichever software is used, it is important that mouse skills are taught, monitored, and assessed, in the same way that handwriting skills are taught. Children should learn to use the 'rabbit ears' hold of the mouse, so that they get used to clicking with the correct finger and avoid pressing the other mouse button. Children who are not taught in this way will develop habits such as using their thumb to press the mouse button.

It is important to keep teaching mouse skills explicitly so that they do not become a barrier for learning. Highlighting text, for example, is something that needs to be taught and practised. This skill enables children to change the URL on the internet and navigate to a web page. Children will need to learn to double click in order to open programs and select whole words in a document. Teaching them to triple click allows them to select whole sentences or paragraphs. Teaching children to use the secondary mouse button allows them to copy, paste, and use other shortcuts, as well as use the spell check tool.

Keyboard skills

Typing is a skill that children will need to use computers to express their ideas. As with mouse skills, typing is a skill that children will continue to develop throughout key stages 1 and 2. Children will eventually learn to touch type and use a range of keyboard shortcuts to control the computer effectively.

Initially, children will need to learn how to press the keys gently and that the letters they press correspond to what appears on the screen. Children can start using keyboards in early years, even if they are not connected to a computer. This will enable them to learn where some of the letters are, giving them an advantage when they start entering text onto a screen. Children should then learn how to log onto a computer, pressing the 'enter' button for 'okay' and learning to type familiar words such as their name and favourite things.

A with mouse skills, there is a range of online software that children can use to learn to type. The website, **Typing Club**,[6] offers fantastic typing instructional videos, activities, and assessment data.

84 *Teaching information technology*

While learning to touch-type, children need to use the correct fingers and avoid looking down at the keyboard. To aid with this, the teacher can place a cloth over their hands, forcing them to develop and rely upon their muscle memory for typing. Children should be encouraged to develop muscle memory over accuracy, and accuracy over speed, repeating previous activities as many times as necessary.

In Chapter 18, we explore continuum of keyboard skills that children will develop throughout primary school. This list is non-exhaustive, but children should learn to use the 'enter' key, 'shift' and 'caps lock' keys, 'backspace' and 'delete' keys, and later 'home', 'end', and 'tab' keys to navigate the page. In key stage 2, they should start to become familiar with keyboard shortcuts such as 'ctrl + v', 'ctrl + c', and 'ctrl + z' to undo. They could also learn to use 'alt' + 'tab' to cycle between programs and 'ctrl' + 'alt'+ 'delete' to lock, restart, or turn off the computer. Mastering these skills could be part of a 'computer licence' scheme.

Tablet skills

Children should have experience of using mobile devices in school, whether these are tablets or laptops. The basic skills needed for using mobile devices enable children to use a device safely and carefully. Children will then progress to device-specific skills, such as opening and closing apps, navigating between apps, and combining apps to produce an outcome.

While most children pick up tablet skills quickly, these skills should be decided and monitored by the teacher, as skills for other mediums are. One way of doing this is monitoring children's skills against a progression of skills, as exemplified in Chapter 18.

Word processing

In key stage 1, children will start using word processing software to express their ideas through text, add and arrange images, and change the appearance and layout of what is on the page.

In Chapter 18, we explore is a progression of the skills that children should develop as they use word processing software. It is important that this is coordinated within a school and that these types of skills form some lesson objectives. This is so that teachers know what children entering their classroom are able to do already on the computer.

The school will choose whether children start using simpler word-processing software in key stage 1, or whether the word-processing software they use remains consistent throughout school. Most children can use tools such as **Word** or **Google Docs** if they are trained to recognise key tools.

Children can produce expressive work using word processing software. By changing fonts, font colours and font size, as well as page layout, children can use word processing software creatively, creating striking work.

Presentations

One of the most common purposes for children to use digital technology in schools has been for them to create posters to collate and present their ideas about a topic. Variations on this can include the children designing card games, board games, e-books, and infographics.

Teaching information technology 85

Traditionally, children have used desktop publishing suites to share ideas on the above types of projects. This can include them using software such as **PowerPoint** or **Google Slides**. While these are widely used tools in both schools and employment, they are not the only tools available to children for presenting their ideas at school.

For younger users of technology, the app **Book Creator** is a simple and versatile tool that children can use to create content and present their ideas. One of the reasons that Book Creator is powerful is that it allows users to combine different types of media within the eBooks that they create. This media can include children's photos, text, and voice recordings. Book Creator is an app that can be used across different subjects, such as children presenting photos they have taken in science or maths or planning ideas for a story in English.

For iPad users, Apple's **Keynote** is an intuitive app that lets children create visually striking presentations with relative ease. This includes children being able to do digital drawings and even add their own animation.

PAUSE AND REFLECT...

Under the national curriculum, children are required to present data and information.

*   How important is an audience for children when they are presenting their ideas?
*   What audience do we ask children to present their information to?

Canva is a powerful tool that is offered for free to educational institutions. Canva is very easy and intuitive to use. It allows children to quickly create beautiful digital presentations in a short amount of time. This can be very useful to teachers, as compared to using other presentation tools, children using Canva can create beautiful work within the space of a lesson. This is particularly true when children make use of and adapt the existing Canva templates.

Canva features an inbuilt huge range of images and graphics, eliminating the need for children to search for images online.

By using the templates in Canva, children can be inspired to make different types of presentations, including infographics. The good thing about the templates in Canva is that they can scaffold children's work, instead of requiring them to start from a blank slate.

'Infographics' are posters where information is presented visually. An example might be the population of different countries, where a population of a million is represented using a 'person' graphic, and this graphic is placed onto a world map. The user can see the information straight away, before reading text to accompany the graphics. There are some good examples of infographics that can be found through an internet search. A class can discuss what makes good infographics and what kinds of information might be appropriate to share in this medium. Canva is an ideal tool for creating infographics and even features infographic templates that can be used. By creating infographics, children are learning to understand a medium that is used in the real world, such as in advertising, news reporting and museums.

Teachers who decide to use Canva with children will need to set up classes carefully and monitor children's use of this tool. Canva allows users to collaborate, which can be a powerful

86 *Teaching information technology*

tool, but is something that needs to be monitored. Canva also features a tool called 'Magic Studio', an AI tool that children should not use below the age of 13.

Collecting, organising, analysing, storing, and presenting data

Collecting, organising, and presenting data are relevant to many subjects across the curriculum. The skills for doing this can be taught in computing lessons and then used purposefully in other subjects. Another benefit of this cross-curricular approach to data collection is that children can develop this computing outcome as part of other lessons.

Data collection is a key part of science. Data that children collect can include photographs, videos, measurements, and observations. In this way, young children can collect data about experiments they do, or observations of the world using digital devices.

As children move into key stage 2, they can use more sophisticated tools for collecting and analysing data. The company **Sparkvue** produces a range of sensors that can connect via Bluetooth to digital devices. These sensors are sophisticated and, in some cases, expensive, but reliable and can transform scientific experiments. The temperature sensor is perhaps the most suitable for children in key stage 2 to use.

Children can also make use of iPad apps such as **Arduino Science Journal** or **Phyphox**, which both feature a range of data collection tools. These apps generate graphs based on readings using light, sound, and movement.

WindTunnel Free is a simple, yet powerful app that allows users to simulate the effects of air resistance on drawn objects. Children can press the 'calculate' button to see how much drag and lift is created by shapes that they draw.

Sphero robots have been discussed in this book, and they have great potential in terms of children recording and interpreting data. The robots store movement data, which can be viewed once a program has run.

By key stage 2, children may start to record data using spreadsheets. Spreadsheets are able to automate tasks, as well as present data clearly and visually. By entering data into a spreadsheet, children can quickly generate different types of graphs. Children can even be shown how to use basic formulae and find, for example, the sum of a range of cells.

Collaboration

One of the most exciting benefits of online technology is its potential for users to collaborate on a task. Children can contribute to online publications, creating piece of work including class blogs and wikis.

A **wiki** is a website that many users contribute to, editing and improving each other's work to create a piece of work together. Obviously, ground rules need to be established here. Teachers can refer children to **Wikipedia's** 'pillars' and create their own pillars for creating a shared online document, including not sharing personal information, improving but not deleting the work of others, organising work into pages and subpages, etc.

Using **Google Sites** is a good way for children to contribute to a wiki and a class blog, as it allows children to easily organise their work using pages and subpages.

Other collaborative tools that children can sue include websites such as **Jamboard**, **Miro**, **Padlet**, and **Mentimeter**. These websites all allow children to collaborate and contribute to a shared document. This can be ideal for generating ideas around a topic before individual work is carried out.

Augmented reality

Creation using augmented reality (AR) is a new development in education, even within the field of computing! Children can now use a range of apps and websites to create content which can be superimposed onto reality with exciting results.

AR Makr is a simple, yet powerful AR creation tool available as an app for iPads. Using AR Makr, children can create images and videos where they superimpose photographs and digital artwork onto images of the world. In this way, children can create AR artwork about books they are reading or scientific concepts they are explaining, narrating and even acting in their AR videos!

Reality Composer is a slightly more sophisticated app than AR Makr, suitable for more advanced users. Reality Composer is exciting in that it allows children to program object in their scene, so that they move, speak, or make sounds when a user gets close.

CoSpaces is a website that offers both free and paid versions of usage. CoSpaces allows children to create 3D worlds and program the objects in the world using block-based programming. Children can then view their world using AR, as well as interacting with objects they have added into their AR world.

JigWorkshop is an iPad app that lets children construct 3D models that they can view in AR.

As well as apps aimed at allowing 3D creation, there are many apps that allow children to experience concepts in AR. Some of the best are **JigWorkshop**, **Apollo Moonshot AR**, **Monster Park AR**, and **Luke AR**.

3D design

3D design is a method of digital self-expression with that is applicable across many subjects. Children may learn to use Tinkercad in computing lessons, before making 3D models of objects for history, science, or other subjects.

One of the most popular 3D design platforms for children in primary schools is **Tinkercad**. Tinkercad lets teachers set children up in into classes in much the same way as Canva or Google Classroom. Children can then either work on templates shared with them by the teacher, follow the Tinkercad lessons or work on a blank canvas on their own design.

3D design in Tinkercad is as simple as dragging the pre-existing shapes onto the work plane. Shapes can be stretched along any of the three axes, either manually or by clicking on the white boxes in the corner of the shape and entering a precise value in millimetres. Children will need to master the concept of moving and stretching shapes in three axes, as well as rotating and moving rh camera in three axes and the Tinkercad tutorials are perfect for learning these skills.

88 *Teaching information technology*

Once children have mastered manipulating a single shape, they can add other shapes. By drawing a box around more than one shape and pressing the 'group' button, children can create compound, 3D shapes. Conversely, children can 'ungroup' compound shapes to turn them back into their elements. Children can press 'ungroup' as many times as they need until they are left with the original shapes.

As children advance with placing shapes, they may be able to use the **workplane** tool. Pressing this tool lets children work on the surface of another shape. In this way, they can add detail to the surface of their models.

As well as adding shapes, children can add 'holes' (the greyed-out version of the 3D shapes). Any 3D shape can be added as either a solid shape or a hole. Children add holes in the same way that they add 3D shapes, by dragging them onto the work plane. Once grouped together with solid shapes, holes will 'chisel' out sections of the overall 3D shape.

The teacher should demonstrate creative ways of forming complex shapes by stretching shapes and grouping solid shapes and holes together. Children who use their imagination will be able to create almost anything in Tinkercad.

3D printing has recently become much more affordable, and schools may choose to invest in a 3D printer. The company, **Flashforge**, makes good quality, reliable 3D printers and for approximately £300, a school can purchase a 3D printer that is more than sufficient to print work that the children have created using Tinkercad. The filament that goes into a 3D printer costs between £15 and £20 for a roll that will print approximately 80 models, depending on the model size and complexity. To print models on a 3D printer, the file made in software such as Tinkercad must be downloaded, usually as an STL file. This file can then be opened on a computer that has the 3D printer's software installed. The 3D printer software will then convert this into a model that can be saved onto a USB stick and plugged into and read by the printer. Some printers allow for wireless transmission of 3D models from the computer to the printer.

Sketchup, now owned by Trimble, has been used in schools for a long time to do 3D design. It allows for more precision and therefore, more complex 3D shapes to be built. It also features a much larger working environment, as opposed to the 20cm square maximum that Tinkercad uses.

Children can create amazing models with Sketchup, but this requires patience and learning. One of the key points to make to children using Sketchup is that they should move things along one axis at a time. The axes in Sketchup are represented with red, blue, and green lines, so children must make sure that they are moving objects along the correct axis with each movement.

There are some excellent video tutorials online about using the basic features of Sketchup and it is perfectly viable for primary children to progress to 3D design using this software. Once children have learned to use the basic tools in Sketchup, they will be able to create more complex buildings, models, and other objects.

Minecraft has been something of a phenomenon over the last decade. It is still one of the most popular pieces of software among primary aged children, despite its simple graphics and largely open gameplay.

There are two ways to play Minecraft, 'survival' mode and 'creative' mode. Survival has players battling the elements, growing food to survive, and crafting building, weapons, and

Teaching information technology 89

armour to defend against various enemies. Creative mode gives children access to any blocks that they need and takes away any danger or need to survive in the world.

Schools that decide to use Minecraft in lessons will opt for 'creative' mode, allowing children to focus on designing and building and not survival.

Many teachers debate the idea of children using Minecraft in lessons. Yes, children can build historical buildings or geographical features, but is the time spent really worth the educational payoff when compared to children using more traditional methods of working?

Use of Minecraft in lesson can have really positive results. Children are capable of creating buildings within lesson time, especially if they work together and plan out the foundations of their building prior to starting. By creating buildings using blocks, children are forced to think about the detail, usage and features of these buildings and some of the discussions that have been had are worthwhile. Minecraft can also be used with children to represent fractions and algebra.

Like all computer games, playing Minecraft can become addictive, and some schools may decide that it is not something that they wish to promote. Other schools may take the view that computer games can be valuable educational and creative tools and that we can teach children to use them in moderation.

PAUSE AND REFLECT...

Minecraft is a tool that children love using, with many of them having played it at home.

- Do you have any experience playing Minecraft, or using it in education?
- If you gave children access to a tool like Minecraft, what success criteria would you establish to ensure that they completed the task?

Filmmaking

Filmmaking can be one of the most powerful tools available for schools to use. Creating a film requires children to write a script, create characters and consider themes that can span subjects. Children are usually highly motivated to produce a film to a high quality, particularly if it is to be shown to an audience.

Creating a film requires planning. Planning a film requires two things: a plot outline and a storyboard. The plot outline is the script, or an outline of the events that happen in the film. The storyboard is that plan of the camera shots. This should show when the camera angle changes and what movement there is within shots. It is important that children understand this distinction. Many children will create storyboards that just show what is happening in their movie, when this is the job of the plot outline.

To create a successful film, children must have planned out how they are going to set out what is in each shot, as well as what story they are telling. Filmmaker, **Zack King** has created some excellent videos about types of camera shots which children enjoy watching. These videos explain when different shots should be used. For example, establishing, or long shots,

90   *Teaching information technology*

should be used at the start of a film to 'set the scene'. Close up shots are used to show emotion and cutaway shots are used to focus attention on important objects in the film.

The **Across Asia Youth Film Festival (AAYFF)**[7] website features some good examples of short films made by children. Children can watch and analyse these films, spotting different camera angles and talking about why these have been used, before using them in their own films. As when learning any new skill, to avoid cognitive overload, children should be given time to practise using camera angles when they are learning about them, without having to also produce an interesting film at the same time!

Other types of films that children can create can include them using a digital device and screen recording to explain a concept. This helps them by requiring them to draw upon their knowledge and understanding of a concept to explain it. Children could create individual or class banks of videos explaining concepts, for example, recording themselves using a stylus on a screen to make a video about long division in maths.

The job of a film editor is to select and order the clips of recorded film that tell the best story. There have been many films 'saved in the edit' over the years. Children should have the opportunity to select, order, and edit clips of film that they have recorded. This helps their growth mindset – that film clips do not have to represent the finished article when taken, but with work and polishing, a successful film can be made. Children should also start to make films in a logical way that saves them time in the editing process. This can include them deleting duplicate clips, or clips that are definitely not going to make the final cut and even using a clipboard prior to filming so that they can quickly identify which part of a story a clip refers to.

There are different options for film editing software. **iMovie** on the iPad is an excellent choice for schools, due to the ease at which children can add, arrange, cut clips, and add captions and special effects including greenscreen. Using iPads with iMovie has the added benefit that children do not need to transfer clips from one device to another in order to edit them. If children want to include clips from a Google Drive in an iMovie project, they can press the 'three dots' icon in Google Drive and 'save a copy' onto the iPad This adds clips to the iPad photos library and allows them to be used in iMovie.

When editing clips into a film, it is useful to teach children a logical process that they can follow. This usually involves them watching all the clips through, having a time target for the overall film, and then cutting sections of clips that are boring and do not add to telling the story. Clips in a film do not usually need to be more than a few seconds long – any longer than this and the viewer can start to get bored, particularly if someone's back is to the camera!

When filmmaking and editing, it is useful for children to watch sections of films and analyse them, in terms of the camera shots, visual effects, story, script, and direction of the film. They can experiment at creating films in different styles, including documentaries, silent films, or action films. Children can film and edit highlights of school sporting events, plays or other school events, giving them experience of real-world uses of filmmaking.

Greenscreen

Several years ago, replacing greenscreen backgrounds with other photos or videos required specialist software and was a complex process. The overall effect was worth it, with children being able to create videos of themselves on the Moon, in the rainforest, or in other locations. The impact of creating greenscreen videos is still great, and it is now much easier to replace greenscreen backgrounds.

iMovie, and many other film editing suites, have 'chroma key' features inbuilt. In iMovie, children first add photos or videos that they want the background to be (i.e. the surface of the Moon). They then add a video shot in front of a greenscreen and press the 'three dots' in iMovie, before selecting 'import as green or blue screen'. This replaces anything green or blue in the second clip with the background that already exists.

By having other objects in the filming that are covered in green, children can create some interesting visual effects. Lying on a box that is covered in green, for example, can give the effect that the child is flying when the box is removed using greenscreen. Likewise, children can use greenscreen when creating animated videos.

Animation

The word 'animate' means to 'bring something alive'. We can achieve the illusion of pictures and objects moving as if they are alive by taking photos of them in different positions and then viewing these photos as a film.

One of the best ways to introduce animation to children is by having them make physical **flip books**. Small packs of paper notes are good for this. This makes the concept of animation really clear to children – that we need to draw many pictures of the same thing in different positions. The children will discover that smaller changes in the drawings lead to a smoother overall animation.

Once children have grasped this concept, creating animations becomes an exciting and useful way for them to express their ideas. One of the easiest ways for children to create animations is using an iPad, or other mobile device and an app like **I Can Animate**, or **Stop Motion Animator**. Even children as young as reception-age can create animated versions of stories such as the 'Hungry Caterpillar' in this way, adding materials as a caterpillar gets bigger.

While it is fun to create animations using Lego, plasticine, and other objects and the results can be amazing, the process is time-consuming and requires patience. A good alternative to animating physical objects is to have a camera that points down at the table and animate 2D pictures. These can be pictures that the children have drawn, or pictures that they have found online and cut out. Children can form their animation on a background which can, again, be either drawn or printed. Purchasing simple clamps allows iPads or other mobile devices to be pointed down at the table.

As well as physical animation, children can use software to create on screen animation. A free tool is the website **Wick Editor**. This software features some powerful tools, such as the 'onion skinning' tool. The onion skinning tool allow children to see the previous drawing, or drawings that they have done, helping them to make small changes to the next image they draw. On iPads, children can use **Keynote** to draw on multiple slides, or to import pictures that they have drawn in other apps such as Sketches. Keynote then allows these to be combined into a film.

Planning is key to creating successful animations. Just as when they make any other kind of film, children should plan out a plot outline, and a separate storyboard. As discussed previously, the storyboard shows how the camera is going to be set up and what movements will take place. Another thing that is useful prior to creating any animation or film, is a time-line. Making a timeline and allocating, for example, three weeks to a project, helps children ensure they do not spend too long setting up and conversely, do not rush their filming at the expense of quality animations.

Once children start their animation, it can be useful for them to take on roles such as 'animator' and 'photographer', and even 'director'. This ensures that all children are involved and makes for an overall better piece of work. Children should try to 'frame' their animation before they start, which means decide what should be in their shot and out of it. Using masking tape on the table for the area that the camera will see helps with this.

Digital art

Teaching children to draw on a screen with a **stylus** allows them to create art in a distinct style. Drawing on a screen can save children time, as they use tools to quickly fill in areas of colour. Children can also achieve degrees of precision that are hard with physical drawing. One way of achieving this is for children to start with a low-opacity photograph and draw on top of this.

A good choice for digital drawing on iPads is the **Tayasui Sketches School** app. This app features a minimalistic interface, but still allows children to use powerful tools to create attractive digital drawings. As with teaching children to create using any media, good quality modelling is key, either as the teacher modelling use or the teacher showing children videos of how to use digital drawing tools effectively.

Photography and photo editing

Like filmmaking, photography is a means of digital self-expression and content creation with huge potential across the curriculum.

In science, children can take photos of flowers and insects. Using an iPad, children can zoom in on an object before tapping the screen to focus the camera again. In this way, children can create stunning photos of small objects, hosing, for example, the parts of the body of an inset.

It is possible to teach children some basic rules for taking good photographs. There are some excellent videos available online which demonstrate this. Some techniques include the 'rule of three', where the interesting objects in a photograph are at particular points of the photograph or taking photos from interesting perspectives and angles. Motion photographs can be exciting to take and view, particularly when combined with splashes of water. 'Painting with light' is a photography technique that children can explore, where they set the exposure of a camera to long and then take photographs of moving lights.

As with any instance of creating digital content, children will be particularly motivated if their work is viewed by an audience. Holding a school photograph exhibition to display children's photographs is an excellent way to do this, with the possibility of even raising money through sale of photographs!

Teaching information technology 93

Programming

Programming is one of the main ways that children will create digital content at key stages 1 and 2. They will design games, apps, and physical systems, applying their understanding of computer science.

Programming has been discussed extensively in Chapter 6, and we will consider projects that children can engage in in Chapter 11, 'physical programming' and Chapter 16, 'green opportunities'.

In terms of programming and information technology, we can return to the important wording from the national curriculum, discussed at the start of this chapter. This was, for key stage 1, 'purposefully', and for key stage 2, 'that accomplish given goals'. This language reminds us of the creative requirements for teaching programming. Children should engage in programming that is goal-focused and requires them to think of their own solutions and approaches to solve a problem.

Conclusions

There are so many opportunities for children to create their own content, collect, and present data and information and express their ideas. As with all aspects of teaching computing, schools should start with the skills that they want children to develop, before considering the types of projects they will complete and technology they will use. Consideration of a progression of skills, such as that found in Chapter 18 will help with this.

With the huge range of technology available for children to use, schools can fall into the trap of constantly introducing new tools to children. As explained previously in this book, a 'spiral' approach is often preferable, giving children the chance to become familiar with tools and having the opportunity to master them. This can sometimes involve some difficult choices for schools, which must select which platform to use with children.

The good news for schools is that, with well-planned work, children will succeed and have fun whichever projects and technologies are chosen! In choosing which technology to use, schools should consider their ethos, the wider curriculum, and staff expertise.

Notes

1 https://www.poissonrouge.com/.
2 https://www.tinytap.com/content/.
3 https://pbskids.org/games.
4 https://pbskids.org/dinosaurtrain/games/.
5 https://www.sesamestreet.org/.
6 https://www.typingclub.com/.
7 https://www.aayff.com/.

References

Across Asia Youth Film Festival website, https://www.aayff.com/
Computing Programs of Study: key stages 1 and 2, National Curriculum of England, Department for Education, 2013.
CoSpaces, https://www.cospaces.io/

94   *Teaching information technology*

Miro, https://miro.com/
Padlet, https://padlet.com/
PBS Games, https://pbskids.org/games
Poisson Rouge, https://www.poissonrouge.com/
Sesame Street, https://www.sesamestreet.org/
Sketchup, https://www.sketchup.com/en
Tinkercad, www.tinkercad.com
Tiny Tap, https://www.tinytap.com/content/
Wick Editor, https://www.wickeditor.com/#/
Wikipedia, https://www.wikipedia.org/

8 Teaching digital literacy

What is digital literacy?

Digital literacy is the third strand of the computing curriculum. The national curriculum states,

> Computing also ensures that pupils become digitally literate – able to use, and express themselves and develop their ideas through, information and communication technology – at a level suitable for the future workplace and as active participants in a digital world.

Digital literacy aims to ensure that children use technology appropriately. This includes children making decisions about which technology to use, deciding when it is appropriate to use technology and knowing how to use technology safely.

For key stage 1, the objectives that concern digital literacy are,

> Pupils should be taught to:

- Recognise common uses of information technology beyond school
- Use technology safely and respectfully, keeping personal information private; identify where to go for help and support when they have concerns about content or contact on the internet or other online technologies

For key stage 2, there is one objective that concerns digital literacy,

- Pupils should be taught to use technology safely, respectfully and responsibly; recognise acceptable/unacceptable behaviour; identify a range of ways to report concerns about content and contact

This objective, from the key stage 2 information technology strand also closely relates to children's digital literacy,

- Use search appreciate effectively; understand how results are selected and ranked and be discerning in evaluating digital content

The digital literacy strand requires children to think not just about what they *can* do with technology, but what they *should* do. They use the knowledge from computer science and

DOI: 10.4324/9781003502555-8

96 _Teaching digital literacy_

information technology to be express their ideas, with the added emphasis on making good decisions with technology.

As with all the strands, there is overlap between digital literacy and the other two stands. At key stage 1, children 'recognising common uses of technology beyond school', will include discussion about how the technology works along with children evaluating its use. At key stage 2, children understanding how to keep safe will also involve them understanding what the internet is and how it works, drawing on aspects of computer science. Safety is a key part of using online creative tools, meaning that digital literacy is also closely linked with information technology.

In this chapter, we will consider ways that we can teach children to use technology responsibly, appropriately, and safely. In Chapter 19, we will explore how schools have further responsibilities, beyond teaching, to ensure that children use technology safely.

Resources for teaching digital literacy

As with other aspects of computing teaching, the digital literacy strand of computing benefits from some excellent materials available for teaching and wider use in schools. In this book, we have already discussed the excellent **Teach Computing curriculum**,[1] produced by the National Centre for Computing Education. This curriculum provides a good way to ensure that E-safety is taught comprehensively across the whole school. The curriculum can be modified by schools, according to their strengths and requirements.

Another fantastic resource for planning E-safety teaching and provision for the whole school is **Project Evolve**.[2] This is an amazing initiative, featuring questions to ask children, lesson plans, and resources for all aspects of E-safety. Using Project Evolve provides a comprehensive grounding for teaching E-safety across key stages 1 and 2.

In addition to resources for teaching children, Project Evolve also features resources for ensuring whole school digital safety. These are discussed further in Chapter 19.

Digital literacy at key stage 1

Following rules

One of the most important aspects of children's E-safety in school is learning to follow rules for ICT use. This is effectively achieved through a discussion about E-safety rules at the start of the year, followed by children agreeing to follow E-safety rules.

E-safety rules for key stage 1 will be simpler than for key stage 2 but will cover many of the same principles. They should involve children agreeing to follow instructions, asking if they feel concerned and looking after equipment.

Separate to E-safety rules, which apply to all uses of technology in school, the teacher might also establish **routines** for using digital technology. For children in key stage 1, this should involve sitting sensibly with digital devices, logging on, logging off, and saving work. Children should also learn to navigate to resources that are reliable and to navigate away from resources that they do not want (either by closing an app or pressing the 'back' button).

Reliable sources of information

It is very difficult for young children to distinguish between true and untrue information. It is equally difficult for children to avoid clicking on links, pictures, or videos that they see. For young children, the fact that something is available to them gives it legitimacy.

Instead of framing this in a negative way for young children, we can talk about websites and apps that we trust and can rely on. Children should get used to navigating to websites that are used frequently, either through opening shortcuts or typing in a web address. By the end of key stage 1, children should be able to list websites and tools that are useful to them and that they can trust. These are easier concepts than the concept of unreliability.

Keep information private

Children are familiar with the idea of privacy. They understand information that is personal to them and would be reluctant to divulge this to strangers. (A good activity for lesson is to act this out and explore questions that ask and do not ask for personal information.)

It is the job of the computing teacher at years 1 and 2 to help children equate this personal, private information with their conduct online. Even young children are increasingly engaged in online activities, including games and platforms where they might have contact with strangers. Children should be trained that they should walk away if they are asked personal information online and tell an adult.

Other types of personal information that children might give out online include information relating to shopping or online purchases. Children should learn to equate online shopping with real shopping and understand that giving money or address out online is the same as spending money in a physical shop.

Being kind

As with handling personal information, children in key stage 1 need to learn to equate online behaviour with how they behave offline. This can usually be explained to children in key stage 1 as 'being kind' when working with technology, with year 2 progressing to use the term 'respectful'. Children might practise typing nice comments online to each other, giving positive feedback or contributing kindly to a collaborative piece of work such as Padlet.

With all types of E-safety teaching, a good way to approach this topic is through discussion of situations and how characters should react. When children observe the consequences of saying mean things online, they are much less likely to engage in this kind of behaviour themselves.

Manage inappropriate content

It is a sad reality that many children in key stage 1 will be exposed to content that is inappropriate for their age, and in some cases, harmful. This can be through advertising, watching older family members view content, having unrestricted access to content at home, or accidentally viewing such content online while using the internet.

98 *Teaching digital literacy*

While we cannot completely prevent children from viewing inappropriate content, we can teach them to recognise content that is not suitable for them. We can also give them the vocabulary to talk about such content, their feelings, and the procedures that they should follow.

In school, children should be clear about what to do if they view inappropriate content. This usually involves them turning off the screen or pressing the 'back' button online and telling the teacher.

Again, discussion of fictional situations is useful for giving children the vocabulary and framework to handle viewing inappropriate content. Children should recognise when content is 'scary', 'nasty', 'violent', or 'rude' and be decisive about informing an adult straight away.

Reporting concerns

For key stage 1 children, their main method of reporting concerns relating to technology use will be through face-to-face conversations. It is important that the children have the chance to talk regularly about what they do online, which for some children is a major part of their lives.

Some classes have a 'worry box', or similar system, as a way for children to report concerns in a discrete way. Whether this is appropriate or not will depend on the dynamic of the teacher and the class, as well as the ethos of the school.

As already stated, a highly effective way to promote E-safety among children is through regular reading of stories and situations that promote discussion. Literature can play a part in this, with stories such as **Chicken Clicking**[3] forming the basis of situational discussion about E-safety.

PAUSE AND REFLECT...

Children have varying degrees of access to technology and the internet at home.

- How can schools teach children to use technology safely both in and out of school?
- How can we give children regular opportunities to discuss safe internet use?

Digital literacy at key stage 2

Children at key stage 2 will display a huge range of technology use. Some children will have limited access to technology at home, whereas some children, especially by year 6, may have their own mobile devices with the potential for freer access to the internet.

Effective teaching about E-safety is therefore vital to guide children to make good decisions while using technology. The importance of this is recognised with the inclusion of E-safety in health and relationships education, which is discussed in Chapter 23. E-safety teaching should operate in conjunction with wider school practice on internet safety, which is covered in Chapter 19.

Teaching digital literacy 99

Following rules

As with children at key stage 1, effective E-safety teaching in school starts with children agreeing to follow school rules for technology use. At key stage 2, these rules will be more comprehensive than at key stage 1. An 'I will always' and 'I will never' structure is a clear way to present E-safety rules to children, who can sign rules either physically, or via a digital form. Including children in developing the wording of these rules can be beneficial and give them a sense of ownership, although it should also be clear that there are some rules that are non-negotiable.

Rules that can be included in an acceptable use agreement are:

'Always'

- Follow teacher instructions
- Be respectful and considerate when communicating online
- Use online resources that are trustworthy or provided by the teacher
- Keep personal information secure
- Respect copyright and ownership
- Follow school rules, terms of use and laws
- Report messages or content that makes me feel uncomfortable

'Never'

- Access someone else's account or modify their work
- Behave in an unkind way while using technology
- Take photos, videos, or recordings of someone without permission, or share images, videos, voice recordings, or other media depicting someone else online
- Attempt to access parts of the computer system that I don't have access to
- Attempt to modify computers belonging to the school

This is a non-exhaustive list. Discussion about which of these, or other provisions to include in a key stage 2 acceptable use agreement is a highly beneficial activity for teachers to engage in. When presented to children, this should be done with an explanation that these rules are to keep everyone safe and ensure that technology is used positively.

Reliable sources of information

Children in key stage 2 will begin to build up a bank of resources that they can use across different subjects and even year groups. Children should be taught the value of some of these tools, including features that make them secure and reliable sources of information. Children can keep track of reliable websites through organising their own bookmarks, once signed into a platform that hosts a web browser.

Teaching children to recognise unreliable sources of information is difficult. Even adults find it hard to know what to believe online and can fall victim to misinformation. A good first step is to discuss with children that all content online is created by a person, which

100 *Teaching digital literacy*

might seem obvious. Creating online materials such as wikis and blogs with children helps them to understand that information on the internet is user-created, and therefore subject to individual opinion. Discussion about the difference between fact and opinion is also crucial.

Inappropriate content

As is the case with children at key stage 1, children in key stage 2 will unfortunately, encounter inappropriate content online. As with key stage 1 children, to help children deal with this, they should be taught to recognise where content is appropriate and use vocabulary when reporting this. Children at key stage 2 can also be given a greater range of ways to report content online.

Children using many games and web services can be taught to 'block' users who are saying inappropriate things online or asking inappropriate questions. This is a far better strategy than trying to communicate with such people. Blocking inappropriate content should always be followed by children telling a trusted adult.

Children should be given the opportunity to discuss why content online is inappropriate. This is part of their wider mental health education. This type of discussion is the only effective way of stopping children from accessing content that is inappropriate, as children must realise that it is in their interest not to access content that is violent, explicit, illegal, or otherwise harmful to themselves or others.

As with all aspects of teaching E-safety, a highly effective way to deal with most topics is through children discussing hypothetical situations relating to E-safety. Putting themselves in the position of others helps them to things processes through and emphasise with others.

Children can also engage in anonymous surveys about E-safety, contributing to shared, collaborative documents using tools such as **Padlet** or **Mentimeter**. These can be a great way to start lesson on E-safety, asking questions such as 'what should, this person do?'

Copyright and ownership

Children should be taught that all content, even digital content online, is produced and owned by someone. Sometimes individuals give other people permission to use their content, such as sharing it under a Creative Commons licence.

While it is unlikely that children will get into trouble for using someone else's content shared online in their own work, it is increasingly possible, as more children start blogging and creating videos shared online. Teaching children to respect copyright is also, however, a key part of teaching them to be respectful in general online, follow rules and laws and treat people as they would wish to be treated.

When children are searching for images online to use in their own work, they should be directed to use websites such as **Pixabay**, which features millions of images featuring permission to use, or **Wikipedia**, which features images shared under a Creative Commons licence. Children can also use the 'tools' menu when performing a web search to search for images that have been shared under a similar licence.

Digital footprint

A 'digital footprint' is the record of a person's online activity. This includes searches, content created, comments posted, websites viewed, and information shared. Even when users delete content, in reality, it remains stored online, on servers around the world, or on the computer it was created on.

Many companies nowadays carry out online searches for prospective employees. Although this might seem like a long way away to children in primary school, they should start to consider that some of the things they post online might be regrettable one day. Children could consider the things that they might have said years ago, when they were younger, and how embarrassing some of these things might be if they were recorded and replayed now.

Children in primary school should have a more limited digital footprint since they should not have access to social media at primary age. However, they will still have a much larger footprint than they think, and it can be interesting to explore this with children. Their internet search history, YouTube viewing history, contents of online drives are all aspects of their digital footprint. Connected to this area are 'cookies', information gathered by websites as we use them.

We do not want children to worry about a digital footprint and it is important to present the internet to them as the technological marvel that it is, allowing for communication and information retrieval on a scale unparalleled in history. Teachers can discuss having a 'positive digital footprint' with children, talking about ways that we can use the internet is a positive, legal, and responsible manner, respecting copyright, being respectful and creating and sharing content in the right way.

Digital citizenship

The term, 'digital citizenship' refers to users of the internet acting responsibly, following laws and contributing to a positive environment, just as in physical society. The term is a useful one to use with children as it encourages them to take on a sense of ownership for the online environment that they are contributing to.

It is a good idea to hold discussion with children equating online behaviour to offline behaviour. This will hopefully, encourage safe and responsible behaviour online. A good way to begin practising safe and responsible behaviour is through children contributing to the school's VLE. Here, children can engage with each other in a positive and monitored environment. They can also do things like hand work in time, organise their work and respond to feedback. These small actions help build responsible and positive use of the internet.

Being able to follow rules online means being aware of rules online, and it is important that all schools have a clearly defined **ICT acceptable use agreement**. A good way to organise this is with 'things we always do' and 'things we never do'. There can be one version for younger children and one version for older children in the school and it should be displayed prominently and referred to frequently. It is also important that children sign and agree to follow the rules at the start of every school year. This can be through an online form, with children typing their name and the date at the bottom of the form.

102 *Teaching digital literacy*

Digital citizenship should be a positive concept. It envisions children engaging in a digital world, using the amazing tools available to them. They can access materials posted by the teacher through VLE's such as Microsoft Teams or Google Classroom, respond to teacher feedback, and make improvements to their work. They can collaborate on documents or piece of work, using tools such as Google Docs, Slides, and Tinkercad. They can share their work with an audience using platforms for sharing work agreed in the class by the teacher. They can even communicate with other children around the world, using email and voice calls. Of course, as with being a citizen of any environment, there is the opportunity to make bad choices, which is where schools must help guide children.

PAUSE AND REFLECT...

'Digital citizenship' refers to children contributing to a positive online environment.

- What opportunities to children in school have to do this?
- What kind of positive online behaviour is exemplified or modelled for children?

Cyberbullying

Bullying is defined as targeted and repeated behaviour that seeks to cause harm to another person. Cyberbullying is where bullying happens using a digital device, usually involving the internet. Cyberbullying is particularly harmful since content created is viewable by a large audience and hard to erase, sometimes with the effect of it seeming permanent.

As we will see in Chapter 19, the effects of cyberbullying on mental health are recognised through teaching in relationships and health education.

Forms of cyberbullying include:

Harassment – could include sending messages directly, sending images or videos, posting rumours about someone online

Flaming – sending unkind messages or content to someone in order to provoke a reaction from them

Outing – sharing personal or private information online about someone else

Impersonating – Acting online as if you were someone else. This could include hacking into their account via their password and posting messages or other content

Masquerading – creating a fake account with a different name to harass someone online

Exclusion – Not permitting someone else to join in games, chat groups or other activities.

It is important to note that in some cases, cyberbullying may constitute breaking the law. This is particularly the case in terms of harassment or sending explicit photos to another person.

Schools should discuss cyberbullying with each year group, at a level appropriate to the children. Children should be taught vocabulary relating to cyberbullying so that they can use this if they encounter it and recognise this wrong behaviour if they are tempted to engage in it.

Although prevention of cyberbullying starts with modelling positive behaviour, teachers should always remain vigilant for signs of cyberbullying, including through the methods listed above. Schools should make it clear to children that there is a zero-tolerance policy relating to cyberbullying, whether this takes place inside or outside of school.

Use of AI

As we will discuss in Chapter 21, artificial intelligence (AI) is likely to transform many aspects of society. Children are increasingly aware of AI tools and many will have experience of interacting with them at home.

Generative AI creates new content. Examples of generative AI include Chat GPT, Midjourney, and Canva's Magic Tools. All of these tools have a lower age limit of 13 years old, with many requiring adult supervision between the ages of 13 and 18.

As with all aspects of teaching E-safety, effective provision for AI begins with appropriate dialogue with children. This will be far more effective in the long run, than ignoring tools and letting children discover them by themselves.

That is not to say that we should introduce tools to children that they are not ready to use. Instead, discussion of AI with children might be more general at primary level, talking about concepts like trustworthiness of online tools, reliability of content and the importance of not sharing personal data online.

Reporting concerns

While we can teach children ways to stay safe online, inevitably, they will encounter situations that make them feel uncomfortable. Key to children being able to deal with these situations is that:

- Recognising situations
- Knowing the vocabulary to describe online behaviour or content
- Having an immediate procedure to follow
- Being able to report concerns

The national curriculum requires that children in key stage 2 'identify a range of ways to report concerns and contact'. The primary way for children to report concerns is for them telling a trusted adult at home or at school. This should always be part of the procedure that children follow when they encounter inappropriate contact or content online. Additional ways that children can learn about are reporting through websites themselves, or through services such as Childline, which runs a helpline for those under 19.

Conclusion

E-safety should be discussed as regularly as possible, in the same ways that other aspects of children's health and wellbeing are. One of the most effective ways to discuss and teach E-safety is through exploring fictional scenarios. This can include reading literature, such as **How to be More Hedgehog**, by Anne-Marie Conway,[4] which can form nice crossovers between English and computing.

104 *Teaching digital literacy*

E-safety should be celebrated within school. This can include children producing work on the theme of E-safety through animation, filmmaking, art, graphic design, music, and writing, including poetry.

It is well worth considering how most other subjects in the curriculum can be adapted to celebrate this crucial topic, particularly as the school looks to celebrate events such as **E-safety week** each year in February.

Notes

1 https://teachcomputing.org/curriculum.
2 https://projectevolve.co.uk/.
3 Wills, Jeanne, *Chicken Clicking*, Andersen Press, 2014.
4 Conway, Anne-Marie, *How to be More Hedgehog*, UCLan Publishing, 2022.

References

Canva, https://www.canva.com/en_gb/
Computing Programs of Study: key stages 1 and 2, National Curriculum of England, Department for Education, 2013.
Conway, Anne-Marie, *How to be More Hedgehog*, UCLan Publishing, 2022.
Mentimeter, https://www.mentimeter.com/
Padlet, https://padlet.com/
Pixabay, https://pixabay.com/
Teach Computing curriculum, https://teachcomputing.org/curriculum
Wikipedia, https://www.wikipedia.org/
Wills, Jeanne, *Chicken Clicking*, Andersen Press, 2014.

9 Computing and ICT in early years

Introduction – rationale for using ICT in early years

From September 2021 onwards, the **early years foundation stage (EYFS) framework**[1] applied, and the current framework does not include any mention of children using ICT. Yet there is a strong case for teaching children in early years to use digital technology and for using ICT across the early years areas of learning.

As with children of all age groups, for children in early years, technology forms an important part of the world around them. Children will see people they know, including teachers and relatives, interacting with technology. They should have opportunities to discuss, replicate, and understand these kinds of activity through their own play and development.

Even young children will have to make decisions about safe use of technology, when to use or not use technology and what to do if they feel concerned. By teaching children in early years about ICT, we help them develop a positive and safe attitude towards technology. Teachers are often surprised by how much access even young children have to technology and, as with other safety topics such as road sense, we should teach young children how to avoid risks and what to do if they encounter them.

The early years framework requires children to develop in **seven areas of learning**. This chapter will explore ways that ICT can facilitate development in each of these areas. In many cases, considered use of ICT can allow for enhanced development within each area, as well as enabling children to learn how to use ICT tools.

The primary goal for early years teachers is to ensure that children meet the required standards in these areas, not that they develop ICT use. Accordingly, only examples of ICT that offer the potential to develop children's skills in each of the areas of learning will be discussed in this chapter.

Finally, while use of ICT is not a statutory requirement for children in early years, it is required in year 1. As far as possible, we would hope that children enter year 1 with skills to build upon, as they start year 1 computing lessons. Through planning opportunities for ICT use into early years learning, this progression can be ensured.

DOI: 10.4324/9781003502555-9

PAUSE AND REFLECT...

The early years framework does not mention use of digital technology.

* Should children's early years education include them learning to use technology?
* How can children using technology benefit them in the seven early years area of learning?

Early years area of learning – 'communication and language'

To say that using computers and technology can support the development of communication and language might seem counterintuitive. Children at school undoubtedly need as much face-to-face communication as possible, with opportunity to develop their speaking, listening, and language skills. Many children receive a lot of screen time at home, and it is certainly not suggested that early years children spend a lot of time looking at screens in school.

The early years framework states that children should,

> Participate in small group, class and one to one discussions, offering their own ideas using recently introduced vocabulary.

Taking turns using resources like **Beebots** and the **Duplo Coding Express** set offers exciting and stimulating situations for children to get involved in discussions, share ideas, and use technical language. Even electric trainsets or other toys offer these kinds of communicative opportunities. Toys like this often require an element of planning, prediction, and problem-solving. Through using electronic toys, children will also automatically start using some of the logical language relating to computing and problem-solving, including language such as 'if' and 'when'.

Some of the simplest uses of technology encourage children to notice and talk about things in the world around them. By **taking photos** with an iPad or digital camera, children are able to share images that interest them and talk about what they have noticed. Children could take photos about a topic they are studying, take photos on a school visit, or take photos of people in their school. 'Shape safaris', where children take photos of 2D shapes around the school offer a great way for children to notice shapes around them, as well as verbalise their justifications to why certain objects meet the criteria for different shapes. By opening their photos in apps such as **Chatterpix**, children are able to add 'mouths' and 'eyes' to inanimate objects and photographs, bringing pictures and objects to life and thinking about the types of things they might say! This can be a great way to develop children's vocabulary around a topic, as well as explore the characters in stories that children are reading. The app **Puppet Pals** allows for similar possibilities in animating objects and adding speech to their actions.

Other simple forms of technology can also stimulate children's discussion and communication, often in contexts that fit other topics chosen by the teacher. Children can press buttons on tills, pretend computers and use phones and cameras. Use of this kind of equipment will involve instruction, negotiation, and other forms of communication.

Early years area of learning – 'personal, social, and emotional development'

The early years framework states that children should,

Be confident to try new activities and show independence, resilience and perseverance in the face of challenge.

These skills closely resemble those required for **computational thinking**, required for key stages 1 and 2 computing.

Programmable toys such as the **Beebots** and **Duplo Coding Express** sets are ideal for allowing children to develop problem-solving skills required by this area of learning, including perseverance, resilience, and independence. Teachers can set goals for children to achieve, such as programming the Beebot to reach a destination, or allow the children to negotiate and design their own challenges. Many of the challenges that children complete will involve elements of mathematics, discussed in more detail below. While teaching children to solve challenges, teachers can model strategies, such as breaking the problem down and tackling it step by step. The teacher can also model what to do if an approach does not work and emphasise that this is a normal part of the process of solving problems, further building resilience and perseverance.

Development of these types of skills will take place when the children are working on both electronic and non-electronic challenges. In both cases, children will build their computational thinking skills, which are a key part of technology use at all ages. As examples, children working on jigsaw puzzles and building structures will benefit from being taught logical approaches, such as looking for pictures in the pieces of a puzzle or building the base of the tower larger than the top of the tower. These approaches teach children the basics of pattern spotting, an aspect of computational thinking that will allow them to become much more effective problem solvers and users of technology, as well as meeting the requirements of the early learning area above.

There are apps and websites available which offer problem-solving opportunities to early years children. Much of the time, these apps are more abstract than their physical equivalents. Some good examples to present to children include the iPad app **A.L.E.X.**, where the robot receives instructions to navigate a maze and the **Beebot app. Scratch Junior** is an app that my own daughter enjoyed when she was in reception. This app allows children to program simple situations to occur using a range of sprites and backgrounds. Children can record their voices, allowing them to tell stories.

Some teachers may decide to save these slightly more abstract, on-screen activities until key stage 1, which is a valid choice. Other teachers might offer these types of apps to children who would enjoy the challenge of writing their own on-screen programs to solve a problem.

Early years area of learning – 'physical development'

In the fine motor skills section of this early learning area, the framework states that children should,

Use a range of small tools, including scissors, paint brushes and cutlery.

108 *Computing and ICT in early years*

While the framework does not mention digital devices here, children learning to press buttons accurately is another means of developing their fine motor skills and coordination. Learning to switch devices on and off, press the correct button to make a device move, handle electronic devices carefully, and connect things to electronic devices are all practises that will help develop children's fine motor skills, as well as teaching them how to use the technology in the world around them.

Combined with use of iPads or other tablets, **styluses** are a tool that children can use in accordance with the physical development objective. Styluses allow children to draw and write precisely on iPads and other touchscreen devices. In this way, children can achieve results that are comparable to their writing and drawing using physical media such as pencils and pens. In fact, through working with a stylus, children can access tools specific to digital drawing and writing, such as changing the colour and type of brush and copying and pasting aspects of their drawing.

Digital art and writing are likely to become increasingly widespread in schools and teaching children to become familiar with stylus use in early years could be a good investment of time. While official iPad styluses may prove prohibitively expensive for a class set, there are styluses available for around £20 that are functional, precise, and even feature the crucial 'palm rejection' feature. The most basic tool for digital drawing or writing is the app **Draw and Tell HD**, which allows for basic mark making and digital art. Children in early years could also be encouraged to use apps such as **Tayasui Sketches**, which is a minimalistic, but powerful app that can be used well into key stage 2.

Early years area of learning – 'literacy'

The framework states that children should,

> Demonstrate understanding of what has been read to them, by retelling stories and narratives in their own words and recently introduced vocabulary.

Providing technology that records children's voices is a good way of encouraging children to verbally retell stories in their own words. Children can use apps such as the excellent **Puppet Pals (with Director's Pass)** to create puppet versions of stories that they have read. If doing this, the teacher should set up this activity by placing photographs of characters and scenes within the app for the children to use, prior to them using it. The app **Toontastic** is another lovely app to use with children of this age, although as of now, it is only available on Android devices.

Scratch Junior is another app with great potential for children to use to retell stories. Children can create scenes from stories they know, using either the backgrounds and sprites in Scratch Junior or by adding their own. To add their own backgrounds, children need to select the 'background' tool, then the 'paintbrush', then take a photo. The teacher could set up iPads with backgrounds and characters from a book already loaded, so that children can concentrate on coding the characters to move and recording their voices to tell the story. While Scratch Junior is used in computing well into key stage 1, children in reception can learn to use it quickly. It is particularly helpful to emphasise that all actions need to start with a 'green flag' and encourage children to test out the algorithms for their characters one at a time.

Children can use technology to tell stories by using cameras to make short films, or animations of stories they have read. Creating films is easier than creating animations, as the children can talk at the same time as moving the objects in the film. In an animated film, children would have to add in the voice narration once the film has been compiled, which they would need more support with.

The literacy early years goal also states that children should learn to

Write recognisable letters, most of which are correctly formed.

While most of this learning will take place using pencil and paper, children can also use a stylus with the free app, **Draw and Tell HD**. This app allows teachers to set up paper featuring different types of lines and offers children an enjoyable medium to practise forming letters. Children can also decorate their letters using the various stickers and images available in the app.

Early years teachers will give careful consideration to the stories that they choose to read to children, choosing stories that are memorable, enjoyable, and support topics that children are learning about. There are now stories available for young children that feature messages about technology use and E-safety, presented in ways that children can understand and engage with. **Chicken Clicking**[2] is a story about a chicken that clicks on things online without thinking, with the result of shopping for the entire farm. The story is perhaps more suited for slightly older children, but could be used as a cautionary tale of thinking before clicking on things with a computer.

Early years area of learning – 'mathematics'

The framework states that children should,

'Have a deep understanding of number to 10, including the composition of each number.' It also states that children should be able to, 'verbally count beyond 20, recognising the pattern of the counting system.'

At early years age, the primary method of understanding numbers will be through physical or concrete resources, supported by pictorial and written resources where necessary. The **MLC Maths** apps provide excellent, clear pictorial representations of many mathematical concepts, including number bonds, number lines, number frames, and shapes. To compliment these apps, the MLC website has a teacher tool for demonstrating use of these apps to the whole class. In this way, children could either explore numbers to ten using these apps or be set tasks around using these apps by the teacher.

Using programmable toys like **Beebots** is another context in which children can use and explore numbers. Beebots move in clearly visible, single movements. Programming Beebots to reach destinations requires them to count the number of these movements the Beebot needs to make, even if the children are only telling the Beebots to move forward.

As well as programming physical Beebots children can also program simulations of Beebots using the Beebot app, or other similar apps such as 'A.L.E.X.'.

Children using other electronic equipment, or simulations of electronic equipment, such as tills, phones, and computers exposes them to a variety of situations where numbers will

110 *Computing and ICT in early years*

be used. Children will get used to pressing buttons to make numbers appear on a screen. Providing children with calculators is another way that many children enjoy exploring numbers through ICT.

Early years area of learning – 'understanding the world'

The framework states that,

> Children will talk about the lives of people around them and their roles in society.

Many jobs that children will see people around them performing use ICT and machinery of some sort. Children will engage in roleplaying, being doctors, nurses, shopkeepers, scientists, teachers, builders, and other jobs that they have witnessed people doing. Having ICT tools, or pretend ICT tools available for this roleplay enhances this roleplay and allows children to explore the devices that these professions use. Children roleplaying being a shopkeeper, for example, will benefit from having a till and calculator to include. Children pretending to drive around roads will benefit from having toy traffic lights that can change when someone presses a button.

Using ICT might also allow children to speak to adults in these professions. Adults could conduct video calls with a class and children could ask adults questions about the role they work in. This is a use of ICT to do something that might not otherwise be possible.

This section of the framework also states that children will,

> Explain some similarities and differences between life in this country and in other countries, drawing on knowledge from stories, non-fiction texts and – where appropriate – maps.

As well as using **Streetview** to explore other counties, children can use an iPad and use the **Google Earth** app to explore parts of the world, helping them to understand the geography of the world and the position of countries. Children in reception enjoy turning the world around in the Google Earth app, as well as zooming in and out to see different locations.

In the natural world section, the framework states,

> Children will explore the natural world around them, making observations and drawing picture of plants and animals.

Children in early years can use **iPad cameras**, or other types of digital camera to take pictures of plants, insects, and animals that they observe. This often aids discussion after the fact and allows the teacher and children to point out details that they might have missed at the time. Children can even be shown how to 'reverse pinch' and zoom in using the iPad camera, tapping the screen to focus on a small detail, before taking a photo. Using this method, children in early years can take incredible photos of insects, spiders, and plants, which they are delighted to share and talk about in class.

Schools can set up **time lapse cameras** to observe animals and the weather. This could even include 'nature cams' – cameras set up to record bird boxes or the behaviour of animals at night time. There are websites where children can observe animals in feeding locations around the world in this way, a Google search provides many examples at home and abroad!

Early years area of learning – 'expressive arts and design'

The framework states that,

> Children will safely use and explore a variety of materials, tools and techniques, experimenting with colour, design, texture, form and function.

'Materials, tools, and techniques' likely refers more to physical tools, to develop children's motor and practical skills. However, children could also use ICT here to explore concepts like colour and design. There are many iPad apps that allow children to experiment with colour through digital drawing and photography. Apple's **Photobooth** app allow children to take photos and see these in a range of different styles, colours, and effects. Children could also use apps such as **Tayasui Sketches** to explore mixing colours on a screen, without having to get paint sets out and the set up/cleaning up that accompanies that!

Conclusion

The primary focus of early years teachers is on ensuring that children complete nursery and reception years happily, safely, and in accordance with the early years goals. Technology should be introduced only where it contributes to these aims, although, as we have seen, there are many opportunities for technology to facilitate and even enhance achievement of the early years goals.

Technology use is also inevitable, part of children's consciousness, even at early years age. Children should have opportunities to discuss and explore technology use in the world around them, as with other aspects that make up their lives. Investing in digital literacy in early years can be done without disrupting the rest of the early years curriculum and will in fact, pay dividends as children enter year 1.

Notes

1 Early years foundation stage statutory framework, for group and school-based providers, Setting the standards for learning, development and childcare for children from birth to five, 2023, Department for Education.
2 Wills, Jeanne, *Chicken Clicking*, Andersen Press, 2014.

References

Computing Programs of Study: key stages 1 and 2, National Curriculum of England, Department for Education, 2013.
Early years foundation stage statutory framework, for group and school-based providers, Setting the standards for learning, development and childcare for children from birth to five, 2023, Department for Education.
Wills, Jeanne, *Chicken Clicking*, Andersen Press, 2014.

10 Robotics

Robotics in context

The word robot comes from the Slavic root word 'robota', meaning 'to work'. The first use of the word 'robot' is attributed to Czech playwright, Karel Capek, in his play 'Rossovoni's Universal Robots', published in 1920.

One hundred years later, robots are a part of our lives, performing jobs with a level of accuracy that makes them ideal for certain types of work. Not all robots have arms and legs, and children must learn to overcome this anthropomorphic view. This is because when children are asked to build a robot, they need to be able to imagine all sorts of devices, from colour sorters to name pickers. When children are presented with a building set, they must see past building a vehicle with wheels and consider other types of robotic devices that they can build. This understanding comes from being exposed to and discussing different types of robotic devices.

The case for featuring robots in education

It is certainly possible to incorporate robotics into the computing and wider school curriculum. But what are the merits of teaching children about robotics?

Teaching children about robotics allows them to see actions relating to principles of mathematics, science and computing. Children are much more likely to understand angles if they program something to rotate 80 degrees clockwise, than if they imagine this. Similarly, children are more likely to comprehend the process of input → process → output if they can see this in action.

Robotics can lead to some fascinating and important discussions at all ages. These can be discussions about the nature of being alive, being 'clever' and the ethical implications of robotics. As with all technology, we should teach children to think critically about robotics, the key point being 'just because we can do something, it doesn't mean we should do it!'

There is a strong case for planning a robotics teaching topic for at least one year group. Children could explore literature regarding robots, examine how robots are used around the world and think about how robots will shape their own lives.

DOI: 10.4324/9781003502555-10

Teaching children about robots

There are so many interesting discussions that can be had with children about robots. These can include discussions about how robots work, how intelligent robots are, whether robots are a good thing and even whether robots are alive. There are some great books, including fiction books that support discussion about robotics. Many schools read the **Iron Man**,[1] which is an excellent text to stimulate discussion of robotics, the nature of robots and how robots work. Children can build a giant Iron Man out of cardboard boxes and (a lot of) aluminium foil. They can make the eyes light up using an electrical circuit and incorporate other electronic components into their model.

There are some great videos to show children to get them thinking about robotics. Videos about robotic distribution centres always amaze children, as they see robots selecting products at high speed.

In Thailand, there is a hospital featuring robotic nurses (with red eyes), which is viewable via a video on YouTube. Children enjoy watching videos about drone deliveries and drone security (see the new Amazon 'Always Home' drone). There is a new robotic chess set that has just been released which provokes good discussion among children. Schools in South Korea have even experimented with robotic teachers, a topic that children find very stimulating indeed.

The key to useful discussion about robots is decomposition of how they work. This mostly comes down to sensors, programs and motors (input, process and output), which is how all computers work. It is good to challenge children to decompose the actions of robots as much as possible, which really gets children thinking about what robots are and how they function.

Decomposing the way that robots work prepares children to build their own robots. Children can then be presented with motors and sensors, forming ideas for their own robots to solve problems. This can be through robotics sets, such as **Lego Spike Prime**, or separate motors and components, such as **Crumble** sets and **Arduino** sets. We will discuss Lego Spike Prime more in this chapter and Crumble and Arduino in Chapter 11, on 'physical computing'. The more discussion that children have had about how robots perform jobs and solve problems, the more imaginative they will be when building their own robotic systems.

Robots and robotics sets for school

Beebots and BlueBots

Robot sets are expensive and represent a significant investment for schools. As discussed in previous chapters, **Beebots** are a good tool for children in early years and key stage 1, not just for learning about computing, but also for applying concepts in maths. We should not underestimate the impact that even simple use of robots has on children and the collaboration and discussion that children have when controlling robots can be fantastic. The newer version of Beebots, Bluebots, are programmable using block-based coding and angles, extending their possible use into key stage 2 computing and maths.

Sphero Robots

Another programmable robot suitable for use in schools is the **Sphero** robot. These are durable, waterproof robots that can either be driven directly, or programmed using block-based programming. As well as for teaching children about programming, the Sphero robots are great for application of maths. This is because they are controlled using the parameters, 'power, heading and duration', with heading being measured in degrees and duration in seconds. Children can therefore create programs to make the Spheros travel in shapes or through mazes. The Spheros can even drive over paint and create robotic artwork! As with learning about all robots, children starting to use the Spheros should aim for precision in simple tasks. This could be a task such as making the robot drive and stop on a target with the extension of driving back again). The progression from this activity could be for the robot to drive in a rectangular shape, which allows the task of navigating a racecourse around the room!

The other attraction of Sphero robots is their data collecting capability (tested on the Sphero Bolt). These robots store data as they move, which can be accessed by pressing the 'view sensor data' button in the Sphero app. This shows data about location, distance travelled, velocity and acceleration, all displayed on line graphs. This is a really engaging way to get children to look at graphs and interpret data, in other words, 'tell the story' of the line graph.

Ohbots

Ohbots are robotic heads that can either be bought as kits to be assembled, or ready-made. For most cases, it is strongly suggested buying the robots ready-made, as the process of putting them together is complex. Many schools will likely prefer to have something that works and can be programmed out of the box.

Children program the Ohbots using Ohbot's own block-based interface, which closely resembles Scratch. Children should be encouraged to discover for themselves what commands like 'set top lip to 1' and 'set top lip to 10' do (more the lip up and down, with 'set top lip to 5 being in' the middle. Of course, the program for the bottom lip will be the opposite, with the numbers being reversed for up and down. This is a good exercise for pattern recognition, as children realise parts of their program that can be reused with parameters changed.

The OhBot robots are capable of speech and of moving lips in time with speech, by setting the position of top lip to the variable 'top lip' and setting the position of bottom lip to the variable 'bottom lip'. The robots can be fitted with webcams, giving them the ability to detect faces and respond accordingly. The robots also feature voice recognition ion their programs and can supposedly be programmed to respond to voice inputs, although this can be hard to activate.

The Ohbot robots have great potential for teaching children to decompose actions and behaviours. This can include decomposing facial expressions into individual actions and decomposing sequences of speech, such as jokes or songs. It is quite funny to get the robots to 'talk to each other', that is to program one to tell a joke and the other to respond, or to sing in unison.

Robotics 115

A downside of Ohbots is that they lack flexibility. They are built for one type of function and cannot be disassembled in the way that other robotics kits can be. In this respect, while Ohbots are impactful and educational, they may represent less overall value than more flexible robotics sets.

Lego Spike Prime

Spike Prime is a powerful, although expensive, choice for schools wishing to teach robotics. Alternatives to Lego Spike Prime include physical computing sets such as Crumble or Arduino, which are covered in the next chapter. These sets offer children the chance to experiment with robotic inputs and outputs to create their own solutions to problems. They allow computing and programming to be applied to solve real problems and this practical context stimulates children and makes clear some of the programming principles that they are learning.

Lego Spike Prime sets are the successor to the Mindstorms series of Lego sets. This started with the NXT sets, which featured a programmable brick and sockets for inputs and outputs. It featured Lego's own programming environment. The next major development in this series was the EV3 set, which featured more advanced inputs and outputs, but continued to use Lego's own programming interface. Most recently, the Spike Prime set features the same type of brick, inputs and outputs, but has adopted a block-based programming environment similar to Scratch. There are also major aesthetic improvements in the set, such as the ability to program lights to turn on in a matrix display on the Lego brick.

Lego have released a simpler Spike Essential set, with a similar range of simple motors and sensors. This set can be programmed with a picture-based language similar to Scratch Junior.

Overall, the standard Spike Prime sets represent good value for schools. They can be programmed with three types of programming languages, **picture blocks**, **word blocks** and **Python**. This means that they can be used by children from key stage 1, all the way through to key stage 2 and beyond.

There is a large community dedicated to use of Lego in schools. One exciting application of this is the **First Lego League**, a national and international competition where children earn points by completing challenges with Lego robots. Events are held annually across the country.

A good way to teach children to use robotics is to teach them component by component, only presenting them with a new component when they have mastered control of the previous one. Children should initially, be set very simple tasks, such as making a colour sensor turn the motor one way or the other. Other tasks could include an alarm that goes off when a hand gets close to an object. These types of tasks teach children to decompose simple tasks into code and teach them to control the inputs and outputs with precision. Only when children have mastered making motors turn precisely, should they incorporate them into more complex systems such as vehicles.

The other point worth making here, is that Lego feature some excellent building resources, lesson plans and materials on their website. Children will learn a lot by following some of these instructions to build and program devices. These projects will, however, take several

116 *Robotics*

lessons and depend on not having to deconstruct the robots at the end of each lessons. These resources are a good safety next for children and teachers who are not sure where to begin with using Lego robotics sets.

PAUSE AND REFLECT...

Robotics sets usually represent a significant investment for schools.

- What objectives form the national curriculum would benefit from schools using robotics sets?
- What kinds of events at school could we create for children to aspire to when building robots?

Simulations of robots

There are several excellent robotics simulations available. These allow children access to problems featuring robots, even if schools do not have robotics sets available. These simulations are also useful even if schools do have robotics sets, as they encourage children to think about problems, prior to trying out their solutions with actual robots.

There are several major categories of robotics challenges that roboteers are often tasked with. These are:

- Course plotting challenges. These are the simplest type of challenges and require children to plot a predetermined course through a maze.
- Obstacle avoidance challenges. Children program robots to avoid bumping into obstacles, turning when they get close to them. There is a competition called the 'Micromouse challenge', with videos available online, where contestants program robots to navigate mazes in the quickest time possible. This is an excellent stimulation for these types of challenges.
- Line following challenges. These are challenging, as they require the robot to continually detect whether there is a line below it and to adjust its movement accordingly. The video of robot nurses in a Thai hospital is a good stimulus for why robots might need to follow lines!
- Object retrieval challenges. These types of challenges feature programming a robot to drive somewhere, pick something up or do another task, and drive back. It is good to equate these type of challenges with robots that enter emergency zones, or deliver objects.

Children who can logically approach these types of challenges are doing very well indeed. Remember that the first stage of programming any robot should be to make its motors function precisely. The first challenges that children should do with any robot should therefore be making it move to a point, or a certain distance. Once children have mastered control over robotic motors, they can start incorporating sensor inputs into their programs, i.e., 'keep driving until you get to a black line'.

As mentioned already in this book, two of the best websites for online robotics work are Vexcode VR and Gears Bot.

Vexcode VR[2] is an amazing robot simulator, featuring an easy-to-use interface and a wide range of challenges. It has both a free and premium edition, with the premium edition featuring more challenges, Python programming and some other improvements.

In Vexcode VR, the children select a 'playground' with the button at the top of the screen. The then code the pre-built robot to solve the challenge.

Some of the best challenges are the maze challenges and the 'disk mover'/'disk transport' challenges. There is both a fixed maze and a dynamic maze, which changes each time. Solving the dynamic maze requires the children to use the robot's ultrasonic (distance) sensor to detect the walls. Lots of discussion can be had with children about how close the robot should be before it reacts, and what the reaction should be. The disk mover challenges require the children to use the robot's 'down eye' sensor (colour sensor) and to turn on the magnet when it needs to pick up a block (energise magnet command).

Children should think about these challenges prior to programming them. They should decompose the problems and think through algorithms. They should spot where patterns can allow them to repeat code, or cerate functions, such as with the 'disk mover' challenge, which is essentially repeating the same set of actions three times in three different locations.

VexcodeVR also features some tutorial videos to help children grasp basic concepts without the teacher having to explain all of them.

One thing missing from Vexcode VR is a line solver challenge. Fortunately, Gearsbot offers such a challenge!

Gearsbot[3] is a free robot simulator with many similarities to Vexcode VR. It features a wide range of challenges, featuring all of the popular types of robotics challenges outlined earlier in this chapter. It does feature a line following challenge, which is often a mainstay of robotics competitions and a great task to get children thinking about the most efficient way to tackle this kind of problem.

The main difference between Gearsbot and Vexcode VR is that in Gearsbot, the children must use slightly more complex commands to move the robot forward. The basic movement block features the language 'move tank with left speed' and 'right speed...'. In other words, children must control each wheel motor separately, rather than just saying 'drive forward', as in Vexcode VR. Incidentally, Lego Spike Prime sets allow for both types of movement commands, the 'pink' blocks allow for simpler movement commands, whereas the blue movement blocks allow for control of individual motors.

The more complicated movement blocks are a barrier to children who are less confident with robotics or percentages. When controlling the sensors, children also have to select the correct port, adding another layer of complexity. This is good practise for children though, as it gets them ready for programming real robots.

Overall, both Vexcode VR and Gearsbot are amazing resources to support and enable teaching of principles of robotics. As with all computing teaching, the value of these simulations will depend on how well the concepts behind programming are taught, with the simulators being excellent tools in which to apply these concepts.

118 *Robotics*

Beebot emulators

Beebots, the mainstay of robotics before key stage 2, can also be simulated. Again, this may help schools where sufficient numbers of Beebots are available, or where the teacher wants the children to do a coding activity without getting the equipment out.

The **Beebot app** on the iPad features several interesting Beebot challenges, ranging from straight lines, to more complex courses. Children need to understand the gateway concept of creating algorithms from the robot's point of view, so that 'left' means 'turn left' and not 'go left'. Children should also be familiar with a process of tackling challenges step by step and testing as they go. It is good practice for the teacher to print out some of these challenges and support children by giving them a small model Beebot to move around the maze as they develop their algorithms.

The Bluebot app allows for similar tasks, with the advantage that children's algorithms are clearly displayed as they enter them, allowing for easy debugging.

Conclusion

Robotics can represent a big investment for schools. However, teaching about robotics can also be achieved for a much lower budget.

Some robotics sets and kits, such as Lego, are quick to set up, configure, and pack away, making them ideal where large numbers of children are going to use them. Other sets, such as Crumble sets (from which robots can be built) are cheaper but require closer supervision, since connection of components is slightly more technical.

Even moving away from robot sets, children can still learn about robots through reading well-chose books, watching and discussing videos and using robot emulators.

Whatever medium the school uses to teach children about robots, having an understanding of robots in the world around them will help children make more sense of their environment.

Notes

1 Hughes, Ted, *The Iron Man*, Faber and Faber, 2005.
2 https://vr.vex.com/.
3 https://gears.aposteriori.com.sg/.

References

Computing Programs of Study: Key stages 1 and 2, National Curriculum of England, Department for Education, 2013.
Gearsbot, https://gears.aposteriori.com.sg/
Hughes, Ted, *The Iron Man*, Faber and Faber, 2005.
VexcodeVR, https://vr.vex.com/

11 Physical computing

What is physical computing?

Physical computing is a term that refers to creating a program to see something happen physically in front of you, rather than on a screen. This can be by programming a pre-built robot, such as a Beebot, but the term 'physical computing' usually refers to children designing, building, and programming their own systems and devices.

Physical computing has gained prominence in schools in the last few years. Teachers are becoming more confident with programming and are now looking for ways to move beyond on-screen programming. Physical computing also allows schools to address design and technology objectives with computing objectives as children work on projects that require physical design, building, and programming. This is explored further in Chapter 24.

Another reason that physical computing has gained popularity is the availability of simple, accessible sets that primary children can use. Electronic sets can be very intimidating to those unfamiliar with them. However, sets such as **Crumble** and **Arduino** are learnable and accessible by primary teachers and children.

The benefits of physical computing

One of the main benefits of physical computing is that it combines design technology with computing. This means that the programs that children write have a real purpose – to control something they have designed and built.

Physical computing is also often far less abstract than on screen coding. There is a real tangibility about an LED coming on, or not, or a motor turning one way or the other. Children are often far more motivated to fix programs with physical results, rather than programs that have on-screen results.

Physical computing also helps children to think about and understand how the devices in the world function. This demystifies technology and ultimately, empowers children as they become creators as well as users. By starting to design, build, and program their own devices, some children may be taking their first steps on a path that might lead to engineering and entrepreneurship futures.

DOI: 10.4324/9781003502555-11

120 *Physical computing*

Physical computing is better than on-screen coding. While there is undoubtedly, a magic about seeing something happen on the table in front of children, simulated, on screen outcomes are just as important. As with many choices between possibilities, the best option is that children have experience of both onscreen and physical programming.

Electronics sets

Crumble

Crumble electronics sets have become the mainstay of physical computing in primary schools. Designed and manufactured by **Redfern Electronics**, Crumble kits have several key advantages:

1) Crumble kits are **affordable**. A basic starter kit, containing everything that children need to build and program their first device costs around £20 from the Redfern website.
2) Crumble kits are **customisable**. Schools can choose to purchase individual components including light strips, motors, distance sensors, and switches, all at affordable prices. In this way, schools can customise the equipment they make available to children based on the amount that they want to spend.
3) Crumble kits are **simple**. The basic component is the Crumble controller, which plugs into a laptop or desktop PC via a USB cable. Children can plug in other components, such as LED strips and motors and write programs to control these components using a programming environment which is very similar to Scratch.
4) The amount of **educational material available**. The Crumble website features tutorials for both basic and complex systems, which will get children going with their first projects. Because Crumble is in such widespread use in primary schools, there are video tutorials on YouTube, CPD courses offered through organisations like Computing at School and examples featured on websites and Twitter.

Simple Crumble projects are perfect for five or six-week designing and programming projects. Children can be tasked with designing and building simple devices, such as advertisement boards featuring flashing lights, fairground rises and moving vehicles. Crumble also offers excellent links to science, requiring children to connect components in circuits, with positive and negative connections.

Microbits

Microbits are tiny computers, resembling small, black rectangles. They feature temperature and tile sensors, as well as a matrix of led lights.

Microbits are programmable using through the excellent website, **Makecode**. This website features a simulation of a Microbit, on which children can practise running code. Makecode also features some good ideas for starter projects to inspire children.

Microbits are probably suitable for use by children from about year 3 upwards. The hardest part about using Microbits can be sending the code to them from a computer, as this requires connecting the Microbit via USB cable and dragging the code into the Microbit via Windows File Explorer.

Physical computing 121

Arduino

If Crumble electronic sets are suitable for years 3 to 6, **Arduino** is suitable for about years 5 to 9. Children who have had experience with Crumble sets will take to Arduino sets quickly. The amount of different sensors inputs, switches, and outputs that can be controlled by Arduino gives children incredible possibilities once they are ready to start using these sets.

Like Crumble sets Arduino sets are affordable and highly customisable. A basic Arduino set costs around £25, although different manufacturers will offer Arduino sets at different prices.

Children starting out with Arduino will spend several weeks making simple things happen, such as turning on one LED, or several LEDs in a sequence. Motors and buzzers can then be substituted in for LEDs as children experiment with different circuits. Children should then be introduced to using a breadboard, so that they can connect lots of components. This is done by having a wire come out of the 'GND' (ground) socket into the negative bus on the breadboard. Components can then be connected to the negative bus, with their positive connections going straight into one of the digital pins on the Arduino to be programmed.

Arduinos are connected to PC's or laptops via USB cable. The Arduino IDE must then be downloaded. Older versions of the IDE can sometimes work if the newer version does not, but it is worth trying both the latest version and an older version of the IDE to see which is best.

Once the IDE has been opened and the Arduino has been connected to the computer, in the IDE, select 'Tools', the 'Port' and choose the option that is not 'COM1' (usually COM13, or another number). Code can then be pasted into the IDE and run by pressing the arrow at the top of the screen.

Arduinos run code written in C++, which is a challenging, text-based language to learn. Fortunately, **Tinkercad**[1] offers a simulation of an Arduino system and the option to program in blocks, which can then be converted into text-based code to be pasted into the Arduino IDE.

Tinkercad also features some great tutorials to get children used to using the Arduino in a simulated environment. Children can also simulate other types of circuits (connecting potatoes together to power a light is always a favourite).

If setting up and programming Arduinos sounds complex, it is, but it is learnable. Children in upper key sage 2 may relish the challenge of building Arduino systems, once they have successfully connected the Arduino a few times and run a simple program to make an LED blink on and off. Incidentally, Arduino programs usually feature resistors. This is because the current from the Arduino without an LED will burn out an LED eventually. This is not as dramatic as it sounds and for the very low cost of a few LEDs, children can initially forgo adding resistors to their circuits, even if the LEDs won't last quite as long.

As with all electronic components, safety and common sense should be taught and referred to; 9V batteries can give a shock, crocodile clips can give a nasty nip, and some components or solder might contain metals that we do not want to get in our mouths. Schools should do their own risk assessment when using electrical components and make sure that all children follow class rules.

PAUSE AND REFLECT...

Crumble sets, Microbits, and Arduino sets are all viable options for physical computing in schools.

*   Is there space for physical computing in your school curriculum?
*   Have you had the opportunity to try out these types of sets?

The engineering process

Teaching children about design and building physical systems is a good way to introduce the engineering process. This is a logical process of starting with a problem, narrowing down a concept, testing, and improving.

The engineering process is usually expressed as:

Ask a question, **research** ideas, **imagine** solutions, **select** a solution, **create** a prototype, **test**, **improve**, **ask** a question, etc.

In this way, children develop a logical, step-by-step process that they can apply to any design problem, and in fact, many types of academic problems too.

Through following the engineering process, children realise that there are often many solutions to a problem. They also realise that failure is often a necessary step to eventual success. The famous quote by Thomas Edison, "I have not failed. I have just found 10,000 ways that won't work", should be on the wall of every design classroom.

The engineering process is an example of metathinking, where children learn to talk about the thinking process. They should be able to make comments like, "let's brainstorm different solutions", or "I think we are not ready for the 'choose' stage", which show that they are aware of a process of thinking through a problem. Children will soon start to apply this logical process to other areas of the curriculum.

Example physical projects

When doing physical computing projects with children, cognitive load is an important consideration. If children are using new equipment, they will need time to learn how to operate this equipment effectively. The teacher should therefore plan activities for them to learn to connect components and control inputs and outputs precisely. This is a far more effective way to manage physical equipment with children, than to present them with new equipment and expect them to solve complex problems straight away.

For this reason, the first lessons in a series of physical computing lessons might involve setting the children challenges that involve connecting one or two components. The teacher can even lead the class in 'class building' exercises, where the class connect components at the same time, modelled by the teacher. Children will have the opportunity to modify and extend the system that they build, and all children will experience success.

Once children are familiar with the components and programming interface of a physical system, the teacher can ask them to think about more open challenges. There is no point in

Physical computing 123

the teacher doing this until children have demonstrated the ability to control components they are using with precision.

As an example, giving children a controller, some wires and a motor will immediately prompt some of them to build a car, or similar vehicle. They may well be able to make all the motors operate by connecting them to the battery. However, they will not be able to build a vehicle or device with any kind of controlled motion until they are able to make a motor turn precisely in both directions, at an appropriate speed, for an appropriate length of time.

Some of the example projects explained below are suitable for beginners, such as making lights flash on and off with a Crumble. Others presuppose an understanding of how the device and its programming interface work, which should be taught discretely in prior lessons.

Example Crumble project – advertising boards

One of the first things that children will learn to do with Crumble sets is to make single lights flash on and off. Using the simple circuit and program for this, they can create posters and advertising boards for topics or issues that are relevant to them. Children could, for example, create an advertising board to raise awareness of an issue that they were studying, or that was important to them.

Arduino projects

Arduino sets offer great flexibility in the types of projects that can be accomplished with them. Projects can be as simple as children connecting up LEDs and program these to flash. LEDs can be replaced by motors or buzzers, extending the possibilities with even simple circuits. Children can incorporate sensors into their systems, triggering outputs to turn on. This leads to some exciting and useful possibilities for devices that can be constructed!

Example Arduino project – plant watering system

Building plant monitoring and watering devices is an exciting and cross-curricular project that Arduinos are perfect for. Moisture sensors can be connected to the Arduino and programmed to trigger an output when the level gets too low. It is therefore possible for a water pump to be activated when the moisture level in the soil gets low, creating an automatic watering system. An easier alternative would be for an LED to turn on when the moisture level was too low, or a green and red LED to be turned on when moisture level was too low or just right.

The best types of moisture sensors to buy are capacitive moisture sensors which are resistant to corrosion. The moisture sensor is plugged into the analogue in socket and the negative and positive power sources, as shown below. By running the simple code below, children should be able to see a moisture reading given on the serial monitor of the Arduino IDE. It is then fairly simple to modify the code so that an LED turns on when the moisture reading reaches a certain amount. The moisture reading needed to turn on the LED will need to be determined by the children, as the sensor has a range of about 295 (dry) to 590 (moist).

124 *Physical computing*

To program the Arduino to turn on a water pump, a relay switch must be used. In effect, the Arduino turns on the relay switch which turns on the water pump (as in a relay race). Water pump kit sets including relay switches can be bought cheaply online. In setting up this system, the relay switch is plugged into the analogue output on the Arduino. The positive connection of the water pump connects to the 'com' connection of the relay switch, while the negative connection of the water pump connects to the negative connection of a 9V or 12V power supply. The positive connection of the 9V or 12V power supply connects to the 'no' connection of the relay switch. Powering the pump can be an issue; it either needs a mains supply with a transformer, converting the mains supply to 12V, or another power supply. I have found that 9V batteries drain very quickly when connected to the pump and cannot be left indefinitely. Water and mains electricity are obviously a dangerous combination, so the teacher will have to think about ways to provide power safely. Solar power, wind power, or rechargeable batteries might be suitable solutions.

Example Crumble, or Arduino project - self-driving cars

The self-driving car project is a nice project to do with children for several reasons. Self-driving cars are often in the news and children will likely have heard of this concept and have opinions about it. Building a self-driving vehicle with Arduino is, in fact, a fairly straightforward project (initially, at least!). Children need to connect motors to the Arduino and then either program them to drive around a course, or use an ultrasonic sensor to trigger the motors when the sensor is not too close to an object. Children could take this project as far as they wished, including other outputs such as LEDs and buzzers on their car and programming more intelligent behaviour.

Children who have programmed other vehicles, such as Lego SPIKE Prime vehicles, or virtual robots in Vexcode VR, will benefit from this prior experience. They will then be able to focus on the design and building aspect of this challenge.

Conclusion

Physical computing combines computing with design and technology, as well as engineering, maths, and art. This combination is often referred to as 'STEAM'. Ideally, when working on physical computing or STEAM projects, children are applying their skills, rather than learning entirely new skills. Children should have the opportunity to revisit systems such as Lego Spike Prime, Crumble, and Arduino, so that they become familiar with the equipment and are able to use their cognitive power to create new designs, rather than figure out how a new system operates.

Children should also be given chances to apply coding knowledge that they have previously gained in a physical setting. This will happen naturally, but should also be planned in by the teacher, which should make it clear to the children what programming concepts they have available to help them solve the problem – even if it is just placing commands in the correct sequence.

Any teacher considering doing physical computing projects with children should keep the project and range of equipment simple to start with. Children should demonstrate complete mastery and control over one piece of equipment, before they ask for more. Having trays with one or two piece of equipment, a few wires and a controller helps keep children focused on controlling the equipment they have and thinking carefully about whether they really need extra components. This leads to much more focused and systematic work and ulti- mately, more success for children.

Note

1 https://www.tinkercad.com/.

References

Computing Programs of Study: Key stages 1 and 2, National Curriculum of England, Department for Education, 2013.
Tinkercad, https://www.tinkercad.com/

12 'Unplugged' activities

What are unplugged activities?

Unplugged activities are activities where children explore computing concepts while away from a screen or computer. Children may take part in whole class activities or demonstrations led by the teacher. They may take part in activities where they work in pairs or groups to simulate aspects of a computer system or network. One of the children may pretend to be a robot, for the other children to give instructions to. Alternatively, children may control 'fake' bots; models of robots that they need to construct algorithms for before they or their partner moves them.

Rationale for using unplugged activities in computing lessons

Children should have a good understanding of concepts before they sit down and use them, through programming or any other activity on a computer. By removing the computer from children, physical computing activities focus on the concept itself, exploring this through discussion, questioning, and exploration.

In maths teaching, teachers talk about moving from concrete → pictorial → abstract. Ideally, the calculations that children write down in their maths books are based on a solid understanding of what is happening mathematically. This understanding can be gained through manipulating concrete objects, then drawing this out as diagrams, before finally writing calculations. This is true at all levels of maths, although more commonly happens in earlier stages. Children who learn to divide by placing Cuisenaire rods on a number track are much more likely to be able to solve harder divisions, such as 165 divided by 13, as they will have the process of multiplying 13's until they get to 165 firmly engrained in them.

Thanks to block-based coding, programming is already very visual for children. They can see things like loops and sequence and this can help them to program and identify errors. However, even with block-based coding, some concepts such as conditions, variables, and broadcasts are still very abstract for children who are learning to code.

Unplugged coding activities make these concepts more real and more concrete for children. Through exploring these concepts in unplugged activities, children know where and why they need to use them in their programs.

DOI: 10.4324/9781003502555-12

Unplugged activities also offer children a good bridge between their ideas for a program and planning out their program using pseudocode. Pseudocode is where children write down what is going to happen in their program in 'computer style' language, which may very closely resemble a computer language such as Scratch or Python. By taking part in well-planned unplugged activities, children will naturally use pseudocode, making it easier to plan and ultimately write programs to express their ideas.

Examples of unplugged activities

Parson's puzzles

Parson's puzzles, named after computer science professor Dale Parson, involve the teacher giving children the code that they need to solve a problem, but it is jumbled up. This could be through providing the children with cut cards with code written on the cards, or simply by cutting and pasting code onto a document in the wrong order.

Children placing the code in the correct order encourages them to read and discuss the code, talk about what it will do and examine the effects that ordering the code differently will have. Once children have completed a Parson's puzzle, they can either run the code and check whether they are correct, or the teacher can lead a demonstration and discuss different outcomes with the class. This method of teaching also fits the PRIMM methodology – Predict, Run, Investigate, Modify, Make.

Parson's puzzles work well with code written in a block-based language such as Scratch, text-based code, or even simple pseudocode (instructions written in English, but using computer words and phrases).

Parson's puzzles are so powerful that they should be used in some form whenever children are planning to create their own code to solve a problem.

PAUSE AND REFLECT...

Parson's puzzles help children to scaffold their own coding.

- What are some ways that we can present jumbled up code to children?
- In what ways can children collaborate and communicate while solving Parson's puzzles?

Dance routines

Dance routines are a perfect way to demonstrate sequence, different types of repetition, functions, and variables. Dance routines can be run as independent unplugged activities or linked to programming a real robot (physical or onscreen) to do a 'dance'. Because dance involves so much physical activity, they are a fun, non-threatening way to explore what can otherwise be abstract computing concepts.

Children can be presented with movement cards to arrange into routines or can make up their own movement cards. A teacher-provided example would be useful at the beginning

128 *'Unplugged' activities*

which will also help to establish the level of abstraction. The level of abstraction is the level at which we need to 'break commands down' – can we say 'forward step', or do we need to say 'right leg extend, body forward, left leg extend', etc. The teacher can also model how routines can be made more efficient by using repeat loops and even functions, where whole blocks of commands are grouped under a word and then repeated.

Once children have finished creating their algorithm, the real test occurs when they give it to another group to perform. This will expose (often hilariously) any bugs in their algorithm and highlights the importance of sequence, which an activity such as this might be used to teach about.

If the children have access to real robotics, such as Lego Spike robots, Beebots, or even simulations of robots such as Vexcode VR, children can write dance routines to control these robots, having first tested the routines on themselves. Putting the routines to music adds even more fun. Alternatively, **code.org** has an excellent dance routine activity where children can program animals to dance on the screen. Having thought carefully about the sequences and timings that they want to use will make this activity much more meaningful.

'Fakebot' exercises

Prior to programming any robot, whether onscreen or real life, it is beneficial for children to have 'acted out' that robot, ideally from the robot's point of view. One of the biggest hurdles that children encounter when programming Beebots is giving instruction to the robot from its point of view and not theirs. Accordingly, a common misconception is for children to say 'forward, left', when what they want the robot to do is go 'forward, turn left, go forward'. Before programming the Beebot therefore, children should have had practice at ordering instruction cards for a Beebot and following them without the real Beebot. To do this, they could use any appropriately sized object, or even their finger.

As children progress to programming more advanced robots, whether real or though simulations, they will still benefit from programming 'fake' versions of the robots, which again, could be models, or any other physical object. This will encourage children to think about how the robot works and the algorithms that it needs, which will be given via programs. Children programming a 'line following' robot will benefit enormously from moving a physical object along a line and discussing the algorithms needed. They will quickly start using words like 'until' and 'if' which will help them to build and understand the algorithms they will need to program the robot.

When teaching children to program OhBot robotic heads, children can program the robot to show facial expressions, such as happiness or surprise. This is a great activity for teaching children to decompose commands, as 'smile' is a command that humans can follow, but means little to a robot. Children must think about what the elements of 'smile' are – how do eyes, lips, and eyebrows move when we smile. Children can make these expressions at each other with the OhBot also in front of them and to then consider how the parts of the OhBot would need to be programmed. This is an unplugged activity which takes place before programming, but which is crucial to successful coding afterwards.

Physical copies of games

Planning and programming computer games is a popular activity when teaching computing at primary age. Children are usually highly motivated to produce working games that they and others can play. These types of projects can usually be accomplished within a half-term of about five or six weeks. We have talked about ways that children can be supported on these types of projects, including giving them games that are partly made by sharing projects with them in Scratch and making sure that they decompose and plan their games before programming them.

Another way that teachers can support children is by encouraging them to 'act out' their games using either physical models, or even by acting out the elements of their games themselves. In both of these unplugged activities, children will be forced to think of algorithm to control the many elements of their games.

When devising algorithms for the physical aspects of their games, children should think in terms of event, outcome. The teacher should model the type of language that the children should use, including language that resembles programming terms such as conditions (if/else), waits, repeat loops, and use of variables.

The good thing about modelling their work physically is that children realise that nothing in their game will happen unless they tell it to. So, if they want a heart to appear on the screen, they need an algorithm to tell it where to go and when to appear.

The teacher may provide the children with premade, printed sprites for their game, or ask the children to draw and cut out their own. Clear success criteria to achieve by the end of the lesson are key here, to ensure that children manage their time well and do not spend 20 minutes drawing one sprite!

Whatever the physical outcome of the children's work in this lesson, the exercise will be beneficial, if children have explored and recorded algorithms that they will use in their programming.

Marshmallow tower/weight bridge

There are a wide range of physical, problem-solving activities available which help children develop their computational thinking and metathinking (thinking about their thinking). As children do these types of activities, the teacher can help them to realise some of the principles of computational thinking. These are:

1) decomposing a problem
2) spotting patterns
3) abstraction (deciding what is important to focus on in the problem
4) algorithm design (thinking of instructions to solve the problem)
5) debugging (following a logical process when things do not work)

Teachers can include generalisation within computational thinking - realising that an approach from a previous problem fits this one too. This idea could also fall under pattern spotting.

The marshmallow tower involves giving children a bag of marshmallows and a bag of toothpicks and asking them to build the tallest, self-supporting tower possible. The first time that children do a physical task like this, they could be left to themselves and will enjoy the task, possibility with some degree of success. The plenary of this initial lesson should involve discussion of the principles of computational thinking. Did the children build and test the tower in a modular way? (decomposition) Did they consider shapes that real towers use? Did they repeat any strong shapes in their designs? (pattern spotting) Did they test and improve their tower in stages, or test it at the end by simply letting go of it? (debugging).

In subsequent tasks, children will hopefully employ a greater degree of computational thinking to physical problems that they approach. The teacher will then help children to make the link between using computational thinking to solve physical problems, and other types of problems in computing, such as graphic design, robotics tasks and coding.

Other physical tasks that children can prates using computation thinking to solve include:

- Building a bridge out of toothpicks, straws, Lego or other materials to hold the greatest weight possible
- Building the tallest possible tower out of everyday materials, such as newspaper and tape
- Building a device to protect an egg from breaking out of straws or other materials

Other physical tasks

Computational thinking can be employed to solve problems and be successful in nearly any physical task or game. The more we point out to children when they are, or should be doing things like decomposing a task or spotting patterns, the more that they will start to think logically about tasks. This approach will aid them in all tasks, especially in solving problems in computing.

Chess is a great physical activity where children can look for patterns and follow algorithms. For example, openings in chess are patterns of moves that children can learn and sue depending on the situation, often achieving more success than just moving pieces in isolation would.

Even when children are taking penalties in football, they may be able to decompose this process, practising their run up, strike of the ball, follow through, etc. Story writing in English clearly follow elements of computational thinking, with children decomposing stories into opening, build up, etc.

Conclusion

In maths, it is common for teaching to move from concrete to pictorial, to abstract. It is much easier for most children to work in the abstract if they have had physical experience with the concept they are describing.

The same is true in computing. Presenting children with opportunities to explore concepts physically helps them when they come to program these elements. The more contexts in which we can allow children to explore coding concepts, the deeper and more secure their understanding becomes.

Reference

Code.org, https://code.org/

13 Debugging

The need to teach debugging

Debugging is mentioned in the computing national curriculum at both key stages 1 and 2.

For key stage 1, the national curriculum states:

Pupils should be taught to

- *Create and debug simple programs*

For key stage 2, it states:

Pupils should be taught to

- *Use logical reasoning to explain how some algorithms work and detect and correct errors in algorithms and programs,*

Despite being mentioned in the national curriculum, it is easy to treat debugging as an afterthought when planning a computing scheme of work. Lessons can instead focus on creative elements of computing, such as program design, writing, multimedia, and data handling.

This is a mistake for several reasons. As any computer programmer will agree, debugging usually takes at least as long as writing programs. The reality of coding in the classroom is the same; the children will spend at least as long fixing code that does not work as writing it in the first place. Failing to teach children to debug effectively transfers this task to the teacher – an impossibility when there are thirty children with significant amounts of code to debug!

PAUSE AND REFLECT...

The national curriculum for key stages 1 and 2 requires that children debug their code.

- What processes should we give children when their code does not work?
- Do we teach debugging as a process, or is it seen as an afterthought?

DOI: 10.4324/9781003502555-13

132 *Debugging*

Progression of debugging skills

As with anything they learn, children should progress in their understanding and ability to debug as they practise it throughout academic years. In Chapter 18, we consider progression of skills across all areas of computing. In this chapter, we will just consider progression of skills in debugging, and explore what debugging should look like at each year group. This is one interpretation of the national curriculum intended to demonstrate how a key stage objective can look in different year groups. As with the progression of skills in Chapter 18, children may or may not be assessed against all skills. Children's debugging could be assessed against certain 'key skills', or the skills could simply form lesson objectives, with children being assessed on their debugging, in general.

Debugging at key stage 2

For the skills shown in Tables 13.1 and 13.2, there are two types of knowledge needed for successful debugging. These are:

1)   knowledge and understanding of programming.
2)   knowledge and understanding of the debugging process.

In other words, as children become more knowledgeable and experienced programmers, they will find it easier to spot bugs in code. This comes with creating programs, but also reading and discussing code – a vital piece of the education process for computing.

Table 13.1 Debugging skills at key stage 1

Year 1	Year 2
• When given a choice, spot and correct common mistakes in algorithms • Choose the correct algorithm to accomplish a task • Recognise common types of error, including counting the square a robot starts on • Show resilience when a program doesn't do what it is expected to and try again	• Talk about common errors prior to programming (i.e. not considering the point of view of the robot) • Watch the behaviour of a device and associate this with commands in an algorithm • Identify the type of bug – whether it is a missing command, wrong value, or the wrong sequence of the instructions • Use the word 'bug' to describe mistakes in programs

Table 13.2 Debugging skills at key stage 2

Year 3	Year 4	Year 5	Year 6
• Debug algorithms where commands have been repeated incorrectly • Spot errors caused by missing 'wait' commands	• Debug algorithms where the conditions have been used • Observe behaviour and point out the section of code likely to contain bugs	• Debug errors caused by mathematical symbols ($<$, $>$, $=$) • Debug errors caused by incorrect numerical values (i.e. distance) • Run programs section by section to help identify bugs	• Debug programs containing nested loops and nested conditionals • Debug code containing variables • Identify the type of bug: logical, syntax, numerical

Debugging 133

The debugging process is something that children are familiar with and can turn to when they have errors in their programs. This process may develop over years, but should retain some key elements. We will consider the debugging process in the next section.

The debugging process

Teaching children to be independent benefits them, the teacher, and the rest of the class. Children who raise their hand straight away when they are stuck demonstrate dependence on the teacher and inability, or unwillingness to help themselves. Children demanding the teacher's time in this way leads to disjointed lessons and children who do not feel responsibility for correcting their own work.

As adults, we usually know where to turn when we are stuck with a task – this rarely involves asking directly for support (at first, at least). Adults have a process of trying themselves, looking on the internet, reading books, looking through policies, and watching videos, which they will follow in the event of not being able to do a task.

The debugging process should be on the walls of their classroom and present in children's books, along with examples of code and other helpful materials. If children are using a VLE, the teacher may post informative videos and examples there.

Jim Smith has written an excellent book called the **Lazy Teacher's Handbook**.[1] In this book, it turns out that teachers are not lazy at all, but by putting in significant work to setting up their classroom and procedures before the lesson, they can then take on a different role during the lesson, with children who can help themselves.

One effective debugging process for use with children is this:

1) Run the code and observe the outcome.
2) Read the code. Do we need to read all of the code, or can we identify the section of code that causes the problem?
3) Change something in the code and retest.
4) If you don't know what to change, work out which code definitely works and separate that.

This process works well for any age group, although the language might be modified for younger children. Older children could be prompted with questions linked to the skills on the progression grid above. For example, year 5 could be asked to consider whether errors are caused by mathematical operators or values.

PAUSE AND REFLECT...

Teaching children to follow a process helps them debug independently and effectively.

- Try debugging some code yourself. What process do you follow? Does the process above help?
- As well as posters displaying a debugging process, what other resources can we give children to help them debug? Can we set the room up to help children with their debugging, or can we use a VLE to provide help?

Pattern spotting

In Chapter 2, 'computational thinking', we explored how debugging can sometimes be thought of as the fifth aspect of computational thinking, following decomposition, pattern spotting, abstraction, and algorithm design.

Patterns spotting is also an important part of debugging. Children should be trained to look for patterns in their algorithms and code, not just so that they can use loops, but also to help them realise where code is wrong, or where they have omitted code. This is a skill that will serve them well with both block-based code and, eventually, text-based code.

How to teach debugging

As stated in the opening to this chapter, debugging can be an afterthought, something that is only covered and discussed if or when errors arise. This is a mistake, since debugging will inevitably take at least as long as programming itself and time spent on teaching debugging should reflect this.

A simple, but effective way to practise debugging is to give children broken code to fix. By doing this, children get to read code without needing to write it – something they will learn immensely from. Children also get to practise going through the steps of the debugging process that has been agreed upon by the class. The concept of cognitive load also comes into play here. Very often, debugging happens and is therefore practised late in a lesson, after significant cognitive load has already been spent on creating the program. By placing debugging activities at the start of the lesson, children can devote their full cognitive power to the debugging and are therefore, more likely to experience success.

Teachers can give children broken code to fix in several ways. For younger children, they could be given a choice of algorithms to select from to accomplish a goal, such as drive a robot to a goal. With older children, the teacher could share a Scratch project with them by creating a piece of work with broken code and sharing the link with the class via a VLE.

Presenting children with some broken code to debug can be a good five-minute starter activity to lessons, even lessons where programming is not being taught. To keep this activity interesting, code from different contexts can be presented to children, such as code from Scratch, Scratch Junior, Vexcode VR, Cargobot, or even Python.

The website **code.org** has excellent units of work which teach debugging. Courses on code.org presents children with ten challenges of increasing difficulty, where part of the program is given, and children have to correct and finish the program to make it work.

Instead of giving children small pieces of code to debug, teachers could give children whole projects to debug and then improve. This has the added benefit that all children will have the basis for a piece of work, rather than having to start from nothing. There could be a variety of bugs to fix, from missing code to code in the wrong sequence, to gameplay bugs, where the program works but not as intended.

Resilience and growth mindset

Growth mindset has gained prominence in schools. Many schools have adopted a mantra of 'I can't do it – yet', or 'I don't know – yet'. Growth mindset teaches that ability is not just dependent on talent, but also on effort and time spent on something.

Debugging compliments this philosophy, removing the expectation that something should work first time and instead emphasising the time spent grappling with a problem and equating this to success. For this reason, any school that emphasises growth mindset in its school philosophy has a good opportunity to put this into practise though computing, problem-solving and debugging.

Conclusion

Debugging should be taught as prominently as other aspects of computing. A good process of debugging can be followed not only when coding, but also when designing, composing or film making, as children ask themselves, 'which parts work and which parts don't work?'

In fact, a debugging process can extend outside of computing. Framed more generally, a process of debugging can be a process of being independent, keepings parts that work and changing parts that don't work. This can apply to all subjects across the curriculum.

Note

1   Smith, Jim, *The Lazy Teacher's Handbook*, Crown House Publishing Ltd., 2017.

References

Code.org, https://code.org/
Computing Programs of Study: Key stages 1 and 2, National Curriculum of England, Department for Education, 2013.
Smith, Jim, *The Lazy Teacher's Handbook*, Crown House Publishing Ltd., 2017.

14 Inclusion

Inclusion in computing

Inclusion is concerned with making sure that all pupils can access opportunities and learning in school, are engaged with learning, feel as though it relates to them, and are able to develop their skills. Barriers to inclusion can include special educational needs, gender, sexuality, race, religion, ability, economic background, family situation, and other factors.

There is evidence that computing and other STEAM subjects have been dominated by a limited demographic over the last century. This is a tragedy for both students and for society. There have been attempts to address this, including **President Obama's Computer Science for All**[1] initiative, celebrities giving their support to materials on **code.org**, and a UK government initiative launched in February 2023 to bring more women into STEM.

There are things that schools can do to ensure that children start their lives interested in computing and able to experience success, whatever their background. In this chapter, we address some of the potential barriers to success in computing and explore ways to ensure that these do not stop children from reaching their potential.

PAUSE AND REFLECT...

All children should be included in computing lessons, having equal opportunities for learning.

- What are the potential barriers to learning in computing faced by children you teach?
- Are there unique aspects to computing that can present barriers to children?

The purpose of SEND provision

The purpose of special education needs and disabilities (SEND) provision is to remove barriers to learning caused by special educational needs. These needs could include conditions such as autism spectrum disorder (ASD) conditions, attention deficit hyperactive disorder

DOI: 10.4324/9781003502555-14

Inclusion 137

(ADHD), dyslexia, dyscalculia, physical disabilities, and sensory impairment. Children with these and other conditions should have the same opportunities to learn, participate, and develop their skills as children without these conditions.

Autistic spectrum disorder (ASD)

Autistic spectrum disorder (ASD), sometimes called autistic spectrum condition (ASC), refers to development of the brain, resulting in difficulties with communication and some behaviour. This can include difficulties with social behaviour and communication, repetitive behaviour, difficulties when routines are not followed, and feeling overwhelmed by environmental factors.

Throughout this book, we have talked about the need to **reduce cognitive load** when teaching computing. This is particularly important for children with ASD.

There are many ways that we can minimise cognitive load. One way is presenting technology to children one step at a time, such as presenting one type of electronic component at a time for children to learn to use, before moving onto the next. This approach can benefit all children but is useful in avoiding feelings of being overwhelmed by stimulus.

Another way that teachers can reduce cognitive load is through classroom organisation. Resources should be organised and accessible, and spaces can be provided for planning, testing, and thinking. Digital resources should be similarly organised, including setting up bookmarks for useful websites. In some cases, the teacher may set up resources prior to the lesson, allowing children to use their cognitive capacity on problem-solving and not collection of resources.

Children with ASD can benefit from structured, online resources. Websites such as **code. org**, **Blockly games** and **Typing Club** offer step-by-step, levelled learning with immediate feedback. Code.org has a huge range of courses, covering most aspects of the computing curriculum. Children with ASD should not rely entirely on these types of courses and should still be given opportunities for creative expression, such as applying learning from code.org courses from in the code.org **App Lab**, or **Game Lab. Flowol 4** is software that simulates programming of a range of physical systems, including traffic signals, train sets, and home devices in a structured and manageable environment.

Attention deficit hyperactive disorder (ADHD)

Children with ADHD show behaviours including having difficulty paying attention to a particular input, beyond what is expected from children of their age. Children may also experience other behaviours, such as hyperactivity and difficulty sleeping.

Many children in schools will have received an ADHD diagnosis. Behaviours associated with ADHD will affect children in all subjects at school, as well as situations outside school. Teachers must, therefore, have strategies for ensuring that children with ADHD can be successful in computing lessons.

Some of the strategies to help children with ASD conditions will also benefit children with ADHD. **Reducing cognitive load** is also crucial for children with ADHD. Teachers of computing

138   *Inclusion*

will need to consider how exhausting it may be for children with ADHD to pay attention to lengthy or detailed instructions. Instead, teachers will need to find ways to make instructions concise. Teachers will also need to take into account that children need to dedicate significant brainpower to what can seem simple tasks, especially when they are new to children.

Dyslexia

Dyslexia is a condition that makes reading and spelling much harder for children. According to the **NHS website**,[2] 1 in 10 people in the UK are affected by some form of dyslexia. However, as the **British Dyslexia Foundation website**[3] points out, people with dyslexia often display strengths in other creative areas.

To assist children with dyslexia, we need to find ways to prevent reading difficulties becoming a barrier to learning in computing. Digital tools, such as **Microsoft's Immersive Reader** can be used to present text and websites to children in ways that assist reading. Sharing of video instruction and examples can also benefit children with dyslexia. The website, **code.org**, has some excellent video materials available, including to support the excellent 'App Lab'.

Dyscalculia

Dyscalculia affects children's comprehension of mathematical concepts. According to the **British Dyslexia Foundation**, dyscalculia affects 6% of people.[4]

Children with dyscalculia may have excellent ideas for work in computing but be held back by application of maths. To support them with this, the teacher might provide resources to help with mathematical concepts. This might include resources to help with angles for turning, use of coordinates when using Scratch, aids for calculating distance while programming robots or other devices or measurements and conversions of time. As with all special educational needs, key to providing for children with dyscalculia is recognising the types of situations that will cause barriers for them so that these can be provided for.

Physical disabilities

Physical disabilities cover a huge range of conditions including vision impairment, hearing impairment, difficulties with mobility, coordination, and speech. Teachers will need to consider the needs of the children in their class alongside the requirements for learning and activities in computing lessons.

Use of technology presents unique challenges in terms of motor skills and coordination. It is also likely that children with physical disabilities will learn to use technology to help them overcome barriers. These tools can include speech control of computers, voice dictation tools, text to speech tools and reading tools, such as Microsoft Immersive Reader.

Teachers will develop strategies for helping children overcome barriers caused by physical disabilities by conversing with the school special educational needs coordinator (SENCO), the parents of the child and the child themselves. Many of the strategies put in

Inclusion 139

place to assist children across the curriculum will apply, but teachers must also be aware of the unique challenges that children may face while using computers, equipment and reading from screens.

More able pupils

There will be children in computing lessons who can work at a level above other children in the class. These children have may an interest in computing and work on their own projects outside school. They may have relatives who work in IT-related professions, who have taught them about concepts prior to them being covered in school. They may receive extracurricular tuition, such as attending after school clubs. Or these children may just pick up concepts quickly, understand them in depth, and be ready for further challenge.

The word 'depth' is important here. Teaching has, in general, moved away from extending children simply by giving them access to harder work. Instead, children who understand a concept are encouraged to explore it fully, including different interpretations of the concept and some of its applications to different problems. Once children have demonstrated this, they might be offered concepts 'above' what is required for that year group.

Particularly able pupils should be just as much a consideration for inclusion as any other group. On the face of it, these pupils can access lesson content, and so can seem less of a worry in terms of being included. However, this only tells half the story. These children should also be able to access _learning_ in the lesson, which means offering them, challenge, and the capacity to grow their learning and understanding in the same way that other children do.

One strategy that is an effective way to ensure that more able pupils are stretched and continue learning is to encourage them to **collaborate on projects**. Able children who work together will learn from each other's ideas and experience, often creating an exciting dynamic.

It is important for the teacher to identify these children and communicate with them. Children can help **set their own success criteria**, identifying goals that they are excited about, and which feel challenge them.

Nowadays, it is also a lot more possible to offer more able pupils access to resources and even instruction that challenges and extends them. Using a VLE, teachers can post materials, including video instructions from third parties for able pupils to view independently of the rest of the class. Teachers could even **subscribe to separate courses** on websites such as code.org, particularly for more able pupils to follow.

Examples of external courses that can be set for able pupils can include lessons on Tinkercad, where particularly able 3D designers or programmers can be set harder courses to follow. The same can happen with the excellent website, code.org, where different lessons or courses can be set for able pupils. Even skills such as touch typing can be differentiated like this through typing websites, where harder courses can be set for children who are already able to type well.

Finally, more able pupils might be encouraged to **enter competitions** such as the **BEBRAS**[5] problem-solving competition, or the **First Lego League** competition. These competitions can

140 *Inclusion*

provide an opportunity for able pupils to showcase their skills, show their work and meet other children who are interested in the same topics that they are.

English as an additional language

Children with English as an additional language (EAL) might find it hard to access learning in computing lessons. The vocabulary of computing is unique, and terms may be unfamiliar to children with limited English vocabulary.

And within any subject, pre-teaching vocabulary and lesson content can help these children and allow them access to lessons. Technology can also help children to access lessons. **Google Translate** on mobile devices allows for real-time speech translation and translation of text. Many computing websites, such as **code.org**, also feature translation of content into many languages.

Diversity – race, gender, sexuality, religion

As with subjects across the curriculum, children should not feel excluded from computing based on any characteristic. Teachers must strive to ensure that children feel included in lessons, but also in the wider context of the subject. This means being conscious of the role models chosen for the subject, the outcomes, and the learning materials provided.

The materials on **code.org** do an excellent job of providing learning materials delivered by people from a diverse range of backgrounds. This includes programmers, athletes, scientists, and entrepreneurs. The effect of this is that all children see themselves as potentially successful users and creators in terms of computing.

There are also **role models** in computing coming from a diverse range of backgrounds. Children should have heard of Ada Lovelace, Katherine Johnson, Grace Hopper, Alan Turing, Shigeru Miyamoto, Tim Berners-Lee, Charles Babbage, Robin Li, Lov Grover, Steve Jobs, and Margaret Hamilton. These pioneers of computing are all an excellent focus for lessons, assemblies, reading tasks, and project work.

Economic background

Children who are from poorer backgrounds will have more limited access to technology use at home than children from wealthier backgrounds. This is not just in terms of hardware, such as computers and tablets. Children from poorer backgrounds might not have internet access at home, might not be able to afford subscriptions to online services, software, or be able afford to join extracurricular clubs relating to computer use.

Schools will need to consider how they can support children with computer use outside of school. One way to do this is through **provision of lunchtime, or after school clubs**. Lunchtime computer club might be an opportunity for children to use the schools' computers and technology in a relatively free way, with children having some freedom over how they use the internet and what they choose to create. After-school clubs might have more focus and encourage children to work on specified projects. These could include coding projects, animation projects, photography, filmmaking, physical computing, or 3D design projects.

Schools can also support children by **creating sign ins for free-to-use services**, such as **code.org** and **Tinkercad**. These services both feature in-depth tutorials, examples, and support materials, ensuring that children can work independently as long as they have access to a device and internet access. The school should also set up a VLE, such as Google Classroom, so that children can post their questions and work even when they are outside of school.

Conclusion

All teachers will be very aware of the needs of the children in their class and will have ensured adequate provision for them. Teachers also need to be aware of the unique challenges of a subject like computing.

Fortunately, use of technology also offers opportunities to children in terms of inclusion, both in lessons and in the wider world. Because of this, children may go onto be very successful at using and creating with computers, if appropriate provision is made to ensure inclusion in computing at school.

Notes

1 https://obamawhitehouse.archives.gov/blog/2016/01/30/computer-science-all.
2 https://www.nhs.uk/conditions/dyslexia/.
3 https://www.bdadyslexia.org.uk/dyslexia/about-dyslexia/what-is-dyslexia.
4 https://www.bdadyslexia.org.uk/dyscalculia/how-can-i-identify-dyscalculia.
5 https://www.bebras.uk/.

References

Bebras, https://www.bebras.uk/
British Dyslexia Foundation, https://www.bdadyslexia.org.uk/dyslexia/about-dyslexia/what-is-dyslexia
Computing Programs of Study: Key stages 1 and 2, National Curriculum of England, Department for Education, 2013.
NHS website, https://www.nhs.uk/conditions/dyslexia/
The White House President Obama, https://obamawhitehouse.archives.gov/blog/2016/01/30/computer-science-all
Tinkercad, www.tinkercad.com

15 STEAM

What is STEAM?

In the early 21st century, the term 'STEM' began to be used in relation to preparing the future workforce. The goal was to ensure that enough children were graduating with skills and knowledge in subjects that led to careers in engineering, science, and related industries. 'STEM' stood for **science**, **technology**, **engineering**, and **maths**. The acronym was later changed from STEM to STEAM to include **art**. This was to ensure that creativity and expression were given suitable prominence, alongside the STEM subjects.

STEAM in schools can best be described as **making links between the five subjects**. Through making these links and using skills from other disciplines, children are using and applying their knowledge from STEAM subjects. This makes their learning in these subjects useful to them, embeds and deepens their knowledge and allows them to use their knowledge to work on meaningful projects.

STEAM work does not have to include all five subjects, although there will often be opportunities to use skills from more than two of the five subjects. Any piece of work or project that combines skills from any of the other subjects can be considered a STEAM project or piece of work.

PAUSE AND REFLECT...

'STEAM' is a term used for work with a basis in more than one of the five STEAM areas.

- What links do you make between STEAM subjects in your own lessons?
- What are the benefits of STEAM work?

STEAM and computing

Computing falls into both the 'technology' and 'engineering' sections of STEAM, teaching children about how devices and digital content operate in the world around them. Accordingly, all computing lessons have elements of STEAM in them. Children will use their maths skills to program robots to move accurately, they will draw pictures and use computers to animate them, and they will use technology to create and run simulations of scientific processes.

DOI: 10.4324/9781003502555-15

Physical computing projects, such as those covered in Chapter 11 will combine more than two of the STEAM disciplines. For example, using an Arduino set to create a plant moisture sensor will use programming, engineering to build and test the device, maths to calibrate the device, science to install the device to monitor growing plants and may even involve art to design a casing for the device. Even simple Lego projects, such as building a bridge that opens when a ship gets close will combine maths for measuring distance, programming, and engineering.

Computing is an ideal subject in which to promote STEAM through links to other subjects. This is because in most computing lessons, we aim to go beyond the theoretical teaching of concepts. Whereas in other subjects such as maths, we may teach and practise skills more in isolation, in computing, we tend to achieve more of a mix of teaching and practising skills explicitly, with using these skills to create exciting outcomes. For this reason, it is easy to plan STEAM opportunities into computing lessons, including use of other subjects to achieve project outcomes.

Incorporating STEAM into a primary curriculum

STEAM projects have the potential to enthuse children in school and present opportunities for them to apply and embed knowledge from other subjects. For STEAM to effectively take place in schools, it will be necessary to coordinate teaching in other subjects, so that children learn the skills that they will need to apply in their STEAM project prior to undertaking the project.

A good way to ensure this is to **start with a desired outcome and then work backwards**, considering what skills would be necessary to be taught for students to achieve this outcome. For example, children might decide to improve the variety of birds that visit the school garden. Children would combine their science and maths skills to count and record types of birds. They could use computing skills to create a spreadsheet to organise and analyse this data. Children could then combine their art, technology, and computing skills to build devices that attracted, fed or counted birds.

The difficulty with projects such as this is that learning can seem sporadic and even diluted. Teachers are under pressure to ensure that children acquire and can demonstrate knowledge and skills across the curriculum. Time spent working on projects such as this is time spent away from practising key skills.

STEAM projects, such as the example outlined above, require significant curriculum design and planning, even though they may seem 'freer' than more structured activities. Teachers must ensure that the children learn and apply the skills needed to progress their learning. This can be achieved through 'non-negotiable' success criteria established, stating that work must contain particular elements.

While working on cross-curricular, STEAM work, teachers must also ensure that there are still opportunities for direct teaching and practice of skills. This could come before a freer activity, or as a result of it, when the teacher suggests ways that children's work could be improved.

STEAM projects in computing

While STEAM projects can be grand in scope, they can also be smaller and achievable in a lesson. As we have seen, any piece of work that involves design, science, maths and other areas

144 *STEAM*

Table 15.1 Possible STEAM projects incorporating computing

Project	STEAM elements	Time needed
Children use the **App Lab** in **code.org** to program an app about climate change. They submit this into the **Apps for Good** showcase.	Science (climate), engineering, technology (coding), maths (statistics)	six-eight weeks
Based on the story of 'The Iron Man' by Ted Hughes, children build models of this robot using **Crumble** sets.	Science (circuits), engineering, technology (programming Crumble sets), art (designing the robot)	one-two lessons
Children plan and hold a photography sale, based on nature photographs they have taken	Maths (money) technology (photography), science (nature)	one-two lessons

is a STEAM project. Making a 'balloon powered car' would be a STEAM project, if it included consideration of the science and maths needed.

In terms of computing, we are looking for projects that make use of digital technology. This will likely involve an element of programming, but it could also involve 3D design, animation, filmmaking, digital art, or data collection.

We have considered several STEAM projects throughout this book. Table 15.1 shows a recap of some of them, as well as other possible projects!

Conclusions

STEAM teaching resembles projects in the real world, which combine elements of different subjects to achieve an outcome. Children love solving problems, especially when they are working in a context that is real and meaningful to them.

Presupposing any STEAM project is children having the knowledge to apply in order to tackle the problem. Therefore, some lessons will still need to be skills-based, with other, STEAM focused lessons giving children the chance to use and combine their knowledge. Teachers will often find that the learning that ensues is worth the experiment of planning at least one cross-curricular project with a STEAM focus into the year.

References

Apps for Good, https://www.appsforgood.org/
Computing Programs of Study: Key stages 1 and 2, National Curriculum of England, Department for Education, 2013.

16 Green opportunities

Changing the world

The opening sentence in the purpose of study of the national curriculum for computing states,

> A high-quality computing education equips pupils to use computational thinking and creativity to understand and change the world.

This makes sense when we consider the ways that technology is already changing the world. Through using technology, children learn to be creative and solve problems in new ways. Technology enables children to express their ideas where they would not have been able to before, whether through digital design, programming, or simply using a device to type. Technology offers new possibilities for communication, collaboration, understanding each other and the world we share.

Computing and green technology

There is a push to live in a more environmentally friendly and sustainable way. This recognises the need to lower energy usage, emissions, and pollution over the coming years.

This focus extends into schools. The children in our schools will experience the world that we shape today. It is crucial, therefore, that children learn about sustainability, the environment, and ways that they can improve the world around them.

Computing is an ideal subject to incorporate green thinking into. Computing contains many objectives, at key stages 1 and 2, that fit perfectly with opportunities for green thinking and problem-solving. These are:

Key Stage 1

- 'Use technology purposefully to create, organise, store, manipulate, and retrieve digital content'.
- 'Recognise common uses of information technology beyond school'.

Key Stage 2

- 'Design, write, and debug programs that accomplish specific goals, including controlling or simulating physical systems; solve problems by decomposing them into smaller parts'.

DOI: 10.4324/9781003502555-16

146 *Green opportunities*

- 'Select, use and combine a variety of software (including internet services) on a range of digital devices to design and create a range of programs, systems and content that accomplish specific goals, including collecting, analysing, evaluating, and presenting data and information'.

Coupled with the statement at the start of this chapter, which sets out the requirement for high-quality computing as offering the possibility to 'change the world', the objectives above give us not only the possibility, but the requirement, to teach computing in a way that encourages children to think about how technology can improve their world.

'Apps for Good'

Of all the resources, schemes of work, and initiatives available, **Apps for Good** may be the one of the most powerful and significant for schools.

Apps for Good is a UK-based charity that aims to empower young people to make change to the world through technology. The charity runs courses that teach children to make a mobile app with the potential for changing the world. The charity has recently launched new courses, including one with a focus on creating an app to address climate change, and one with a focus on an app to address a social justice issue.

Teachers can sign up to the charity via the website for free. Teachers can then view teaching materials, videos, and lesson plans to support them in delivering this scheme to their class. Children complete the course via filling in a workbook, which can be distributed in digital format.

Through taking one of the courses, children are encouraged to go through a logical design process before creating their app. This involved looking at other mobile apps, considering a wide range of issues, designing their app on paper, and even speaking to experts in the technology industry, which Apps for Good supports schools with. Teachers should create logins for children to use the website, **code.org**. Once this is done, children can sign into code.org and use the **App Lab** to create their app. These apps can then be submitted to Apps for Good for a showcase.

The App Lab in code.org can seem complex at first. The blocks of code are written in Java programming language, making them harder to understand than a language such as Scratch. However, the concept of dragging blocks of code should be familiar to children. It is possible to create a fully functioning app with just two blocks of code, the **on event** block and the **set screen** block. In this way, children can program their app to change screen when buttons or screens are clicked.

Prior to working on their real app for the Apps for Good scheme, children could follow the **Intro to App Lab** course on the code.org website. To do this, the teacher must put children into classes on code.org and then assign this course, which is in the 'Hour of Code' section. The good thing about children following this course is that they can work through it at their own pace, supported by text instruction, videos and examples. At the end of the course, children can build a practice app.

In the app lab, the 'design' tab allows children to add in the elements of their app, including buttons, text boxes and images. Using just these three elements, a fully functioning app can be created, although children may wish to experiment with charts and checkboxes, etc.

Green opportunities 147

> **PAUSE AND REFLECT...**
>
> Apps for Good is an initiative with the potential to inspire children to code for a real purpose.
>
> - Have you visited the Apps for Good website?
> - Have you tried out the 'App Lab' in code.org?

Children who have planned their app should be able to construct their app in the design tab easily. They can then code the elements that they have added.

Children should follow convention of naming their elements, including screens, buttons, and images. Adding images is also a good opportunity to discuss copyright and to ask children to sue images with creative commons licences (in Google search, use the 'tools' to find these images, or use a website with royalty free images, such as **Pixabay**.

The Apps for Good course could be taught in computing lessons; children need about ten lessons to work through the course, design, and build their app. Schools could take this further, incorporating work from other subjects into the app design unit. Children could research climate issues, do pieces of writing about them, collect data for their app and even create pieces of art that they could use in their app.

It is recommended doing the course with children who are already familiar with app design in code.org so that they can use their cognitive power on designing an app to address climate change, and not on learning to use the software. Teachers could do the 'Intro to App Design' course with children prior to them doing the Apps for Good course or teach children to create a basic app in a previous term, or year group.

Collecting, analysing, evaluating, and presenting data

Technology offers unique examples for collecting, storing, and interpreting data relating to the environment. This can include children collecting data first-hand about their local environment or using data collectors set up by others.

The website **waqi.info** allows children to view air quality readings from around the world. Clicking on a location on the map allows children to view readings for markers relating to air quality, including ozone, PM2.5 and nitrogen oxide. This data could be tracked over time, for example, by children entering the data into a spreadsheet and creating graphs.

Costal Climate Central is a website where children can see visual representations of the effects of changes in temperature, and other factors, on maps of places around the world. This visual data can be quite striking, showing, for example, the potential for flooding with a change of just a few degrees in global temperature.

Google Earth Engine allows children to see timelapse photos of any location on the planet. This data shows children how the environment is changing, including forests shrinking, rivers and lakes changing and cities growing. I have found this a powerful tool to use with children, particularly when they create their own explanations of what is happening in greenscreen videos or other types of films.

148   *Green opportunities*

Enroads is a website that shows the effects on the planet, based on variables that users change. These variables include use of different energy types, change in land usage, and population.

World Weather Map is a website with a visual representation of weather around the world. It features current temperatures, wind speed and direction and weather types. Clicking on any location also generates graphs showing change in conditions over time.

Children can collect their own data using technology available to them in school. A simple way to do this is through photography. Using most cameras, including an iPad camera, children can set up **timelapse videos** which could show changes in clouds, growth of plants, or movement of animals over time. Some schools have positioned **permanent cameras** outside or in bird boxes to show activity of animals – these cameras can even link directly to the school website or class blog! Even by their own **photographs** of nature helps children to stop and appreciate the nature, or problems around them. Children could even print and showcase their photos in a photo display or take this further by composing music or writing to accompany them. I have taught children about the ethics of photo editing by asking children to take photos of locations, or choose photos other have taken, before using editing tools to 'erase' aspects they don't like.

There are tools that children can use to collect precise data about the environment around them. Both the **Phyphox** and **Arduino Science Journal** apps allow children to collect data and view graphs about light, sound, movement, temperature, pressure and other indicators. The **Sparkvue** sensors and app are the best data collection equipment that I have used with children. Although expensive, the sensors allow children to collect precise data about pH levels, CO2 levels and temperature and view this using the Sparkvue apps, which creates precise tables and graphs about this data.

Physical computing and engineering

Physical computing and engineering can provide children with the opportunity to use technology to approach real world problems. Physical computing, by its nature, is concerned with problem-solving and it is usually a logical step to make when designing systems, to design a system to solve a real problem, including problems relating to the environment.

As discussed above, schemes like Apps for Good and websites like code.org offer children ways to address real world issues using on-screen technologies.

Microbit

Microbits are good solutions for physical computing in primary schools. Previously, a scheme aimed to issue all UK children with a Microbit. In 2023, a similar scheme was launched where teachers can register for a pack of 30 Microbits to enable physical computing teaching. This scheme can be accessed by teacher through the BBC website, or by searching online for 'Microbits for UK teachers'.

The **Do Your Bit** challenge encourages children to use Microbits to design solutions to problems relating to UN Sustainable Development goals. The 'Do Your Bit' website has some truly inspirational examples of how children have approached environmental goals through creating systems based on Microbits.

Photography

Photography is a skill that is accessible to all children but can be developed and mastered with practice. Children can learn techniques for taking good photographs, such as the 'rule of thirds'. Using this, children can create digital content about the environment around them. This can be for the purpose of showcasing nature or highlighting problems.

Photographs can be edited using simple photo editing apps and photographs can even be displayed in school events or on the school website.

Writing, blogging and communicating

Most children love problem-solving and collaboration. Communicating and collaborating to address environmental problems is an exciting use of technology that can achieve many computing objectives.

Using Google Sites, children can easily set up a blog, recording the environmental actions they are taking. The school must decide whether this is to be seen only in school, or in the wider world.

Children can communicate with each other, or even with outside schools via email or voice chat, supervised by teachers. In this way, children start to realise that there are other children around the world dealing with similar environmental issues as they are.

Conclusion

Most schools now have green initiatives, whether it involves gardening, recycling, energy saving, or wildlife conservation. Technology is already playing a role in solving some of the problems the world faces from pollution and it is good if schools can mirror this, incorporating use of technology into their green initiatives.

References

Apps for Good, https://www.appsforgood.org/
Code.org, https://code.org/
Computing Programs of Study: Key stages 1 and 2, National Curriculum of England, Department for Education, 2013.
Do your Bit Microbit Challenge, https://microbit.org/teach/do-your-bit/
Enroads, https://www.climateinteractive.org/en-roads/
Google Earth Engine, https://earthengine.google.com/
Pixabay, https://pixabay.com/
UN Sustainable Development Goals, https://sdgs.un.org/goals
World Weather map, https://map.worldweatheronline.com/
World's Air Pollution: Real Time Index, waqi.info.

17 Evidencing and feedback

Evidencing and feedback in computing

As with any subject, children's work in computing should be accessible so that it can be discussed with children and assessed. This can be challenging in computing since work done is often saved locally on a device or done within a specific app. This work is then not easily viewable by the teacher. Asking children to share their work with a teacher by printing it, screenshotting it or another means adds a layer of complexity to lessons where children are already grappling with complex tasks.

As we have discussed in this book, time for computing is usually limited within schools and asking children to take time in lessons to reply to teacher feedback, improve their work and submit work to the teacher can impact upon children's time spent practising use of technology.

The key for effective evidencing and feedback in computing is having clear expectations. Teachers and the school should have clear expectations of how much work computing children should submit, how this is submitted, how often this is submitted, how this is fed back upon and assessed and how this process impacts learning in computing. Children should know the expectations of them of how much work they should produce within a lesson and how they should share this with their teacher, including time spent to respond to their teacher's feedback.

Ultimately, although time spent submitting work to the teacher can detract from time using technology, effective submission of work and action based upon teacher upon feedback will make the work that children do of a higher quality, even though children might spend slightly less lesson time on it.

Using a VLE for evidencing

Setting up a virtual learning environment (VLE) is perhaps one of the most important steps a teacher can do to prepare for the year's computing lessons. A VLE can be thought of as being a digital classroom, somewhere for the teacher to post resources, for students to post work, view feedback and for the teacher to conduct assessment.

Examples of VLE's include **Google Classroom**, **Microsoft Class Teams** (including Class Notebook), **Seesaw,** and **Moodle**. An alternative to using a VLE might include setting up a class website with a blog section, where children can post their work.

DOI: 10.4324/9781003502555-17

Evidencing and feedback 151

Setting up a VLE for children to use serves a much greater purpose than children evidencing their work. A properly set up VLE is a place where children can see materials that the teacher has posted, receive log in links for websites and share their own interests and ideas, in addition to what is done in class. A VLE could operate alongside a class blog, with children posting their completed work on a class blog and using the VLE to share ongoing work with the teacher.

Both Microsoft and Google offer free access to schools through their educational programs, making these obvious choices for schools looking to use a VLE. The advantage of other platforms, such as Seesaw, is that they can offer slightly more child-friendly environments, such as children being able to sign into the VLE using a QR code instead of typing in an email address and password. The disadvantage of these other VLE providers can include the costs associated with them, having a separate service that is not connected to other applications that the children might be using.

Google Classroom is perhaps the easiest to use VLE 'out of the box'. Classes are easy to set up, assignments are easy to post and the whole experience is simple and usable with a minimum amount of time spent. There are some basic assessment tools and Google Classroom links directly to Google apps, which are similarly simple to use. Google has also introduced a **rubric** tool, making it quick to assess children's work and clear for children to view feedback.

Microsoft Class Teams usually takes more work to set up than Google. Microsoft applications are more complex than Google, but give users more control, with even simple things like the possibility of adding text boxes easily being possible in Microsoft apps. Microsoft Class Teams can carry out a similar function to Google Classroom and resembles Google Classroom in many ways. It includes Class Notebook, a digital notebook where the teacher can set up folders containing copies of documents for children to work on digitally.

In computing lessons, children should have clear expectations about what is expected of them in terms of using a VLE. Are children expected to sign into the VLE at the start of the lesson and do some independent work set by the teacher? Are they expected to sign in and reply to feedback? Are children expected to photograph their work and upload it to the VLE with a comment about what they have achieved? Will the children complete planning work digitally in computing lessons via digital documents? These are the questions that teachers of computing need to consider.

For children in key stage 2, signing into the school's VLE should be the first thing that children do in their computing lesson. Children can then respond to comments and access lesson material at the start of the lesson. Most children should be able to log into a service using their email address quickly from about year 3 onwards. If children are doing practical work, they might be able to take a photograph of this with a table and upload it to their VLE for evidence. If children are working using an external website, they could screenshot this and upload it to their VLE with a comment about what they have done.

For children in key stage 1, the situation is harder. Asking children in key stage 1 to log onto a computer, navigate to a VLE and log into it with an email address will challenge many children at this age. Some teachers may choose to invest the time into training children to do this, and this will be a school decision. Other schools may choose to sue a simple VLE,

152 *Evidencing and feedback*

such as Seesaw, for younger children. The basic version of Seesaw is free for schools to use, although doesn't feature some of the tools such as assessment tools. As stated, the advantage of Seesaw is that it is child friendly; children can sign in quickly with a QR code and upload their work in a very easy way.

Another possibility to help children log into a VLE is to set up devices as shared devices. For example, iPads feature the 'shared iPad' tool. In this way, children log into the same device every lesson by tapping on their portrait and entering a short code, with the device then remembering all their settings and passwords.

Computing exercise books

There are times when using a pencil and paper is a desirable method of working. This is true in all subjects, including computing.

Schools may, therefore, decide to issue children with computing exercise books. As we have seen throughout this book, there are times when children need to plan out their work, whether this is designing the layout of an app, drawing a storyboard prior to filming, or recording ideas in pseudocode prior to coding. Schools that incorporate engineering and physical computing will also benefit from children drawing diagrams and planning their work before building and testing systems.

Another advantage of computing exercise book is that they allow for quick comments about lesson work, without having to navigate to a VLE or digital journal. Children can quickly self-assess themselves against the success criteria at the end of the lesson and provide a comment about what they have achieved.

Furthermore, although photocopying is something that schools are rightly trying to reduce, there are times when the teacher wishes to give children a printed resource to annotate. This may be code to read, annotate discuss or a piece of technology to label.

The decision to issue paper books for computing will need to be carefully considered by schools. Sets of workbooks are added costs for schools, yet the benefits of using them in other subjects also apply to computing. Computing should be a subject where children primarily use digital technology to work, developing their digital skills and being able to use the power of technology to express their ideas. However, there is clearly a case for some paper-based work in computing and organising this in an exercise book may be suitable for some schools.

External websites

Many of the websites that facilitate work in areas of computing enable children to organise their work and teachers to view and assess children's work.

Code.org is one of the most useful resources available to computing teachers. Teachers can create log ins for children and place children into classes. This allows teachers to assign courses to children to carry out. Children can use the excellent videos and other learning materials throughout the course and work independently at a pace that suits them. Teachers can view children's work and monitor their progress on the course they are doing. Children can apply their knowledge by working in the various labs, including the **App Lab** and the **Code Lab**.

Evidencing and feedback 153

Tinkercad, in a similar way to Code.org, is a website that lets teachers set up classes and view children's work. Using Tinkercad, children engage in 3D design, programming, and electronics work. Children can also learn at their own pace using the excellent courses and teaching materials on the website. Once classes are set up, teachers can quickly view children's work, although there is no capacity for assessment or feedback.

There is a strong argument that all children should learn to touch type, since an increasing amount of schoolwork is being done with a keyboard. A good website for children to learn and develop touch typing skills has been **Typing Club**, which is part of **EdClub**. The paid version of this allows teachers to set up classes and track children's progress in typing, using a variety of metrics.

These three websites are examples of online platforms that facilitate evidencing of children's work by virtue of the children being placed into classes and storing their work on the websites. The feedback is not necessarily present in all websites such as these, although Typing Club does provide precise feedback to children about which keys and fingers they are using to type accurately.

PAUSE AND REFLECT...

Evidencing in computing can be challenging, especially if children are using a range of digital resources.

- Would you rather that children evidenced all of their computing work in one place, or are you happy for them to store it in different locations?
- What process of feedback and improvement will you establish in your computing lessons?

Providing feedback in computing

Feedback provided by teachers for children should have a positive effect upon their learning. It should also give children a clear picture of things that they are strong at and areas for development. Feedback should be specific, linked to the learning objective and success criteria for the lesson. It should provide clear, actionable steps for children so that they can improve and hopefully, receive different feedback the next time they work on a computing task. Feedback should also encourage children and recognise their hard work and successes.

Providing feedback can be very time consuming, particularly in primary education, where teachers provide feedback across multiple subjects. Schools should therefore have realistic expectations for feedback that teachers are required to give. Teachers should also ensure that any feedback they take the time to give is read and actioned by children. This can include setting aside time in lessons for children to read and respond to feedback that is given.

Teachers of computing in primary schools need to find ways to provide feedback that satisfies the requirements above, in a way that is realistic in terms of time spent. As in other

154 *Evidencing and feedback*

practical lessons, much of the feedback given in computing lessons will be verbal, taking place during the lesson to help improve children's work. If verbal feedback is specific, addresses the learning intention and success criteria and has a positive impact upon children's learning, it is just as valid as written feedback.

It is possible for teachers to provide digital feedback, providing either typed or spoken comments about work that children upload to a VLE such as Class Teams or Google Classroom. As discussed, children should be trained to evidence their work at appropriate points in their learning. Younger children might use platforms such as Seesaw, where the teacher can also provide typed or voice feedback.

Schools that provide exercise books for computing can also use these as ways for teachers to provide feedback at relevant points in the learning journey. A good system to follow is for children to self-assess their work against success criteria in these exercise books, with teachers acknowledging, agreeing, or disagreeing with this assessment and providing suggestions where it is beneficial.

Conclusion

Evidencing and feedback in computing presents unique challenges and opportunities. Without a well-established system, children's digital work can become disorganised and difficult to manage, assess and feedback upon. With a good system in place, feedback can be quick, even automated in some cases.

Children need a place to store their creative work. This can either be through a VLE, or in a digital portfolio. Schools can use slides for this, or even apps such as Book Creator for younger children or movie making apps for older children.

Children should become used to a routine of checking their work for feedback and improving it. It is worth establishing this routine at the start of the year, saving lesson time in later lessons.

References

Apps for Good, https://www.appsforgood.org/
Code.org, https://code.org/
Computing Programs of Study: Key stages 1 and 2, National Curriculum of England, Department for Education, 2013.
Tinkercad, www.tinkercad.com
Typing Club, https://www.typingclub.com/

18 Assessment and progression

Types of assessment

Assessment is important for several reasons. These include:

- Enabling children to know whether their work has reached or exceeded an appropriate standard.
- Ensuring that teaching content and methods are effective.
- Ensuring that children are always working at a level that moves them into the next phase of their understanding (referred to by Vygotsky as the 'Zone of Proximal development').
- Providing parents and those outside the school with a way to objectively understand the success of children in the school.

There are two main types of assessment: formative assessment and summative assessment. **Formative assessment** occurs during the learning process and helps adapt teaching and learning according to needs. It also provides feedback to learners, so that they can address areas for development. Formative assessment is often referred to **assessment for learning (AFL)** in schools. **Summative assessment** takes place at the end of a lesson, topic, or period, often through some sort of testing, and creates a snapshot of a children's knowledge and understanding. As with formative assessment, summative assessment should be used to identify and address areas for development.

In computing, as in all subjects, teachers need to find ways to assess children that are effective and satisfy the goals above. Assessment should also be realistic, without placing extreme additional work burdens upon teachers or children. For this reason, several different types of assessment should be used, including:

- Children's **self-assessment** against the success criteria, during and at the end of the lesson
- **Peer assessment** gives children the chance to evaluate the work of their peers. This is a particularly valuable tool as the assessor learns from the assessment process, seeing the work of another learner and considering whether this has met the success criteria.
- Children's self-assessment against the overall assessment criteria for a topic, so that children know what they need to focus on with their work.

DOI: 10.4324/9781003502555-18

156 *Assessment and progression*

- Use of **computer-assisted assessment tools**, including platforms such as Quizziz, Kahoot and websites such as Typing Club. As will be discussed in Chapter 22, artificial intelligence is expected to play an increasing role in assessment in the future.
- **Teacher assessment** of children's work. This is important at all stages of the learning process. During lessons, formative assessment, or AFL will alter the course of children's learning to ensure they succeed. Summative assessment, in the form of quizzes, assessment at the end of lessons or assessment at the end of units of work will provide a snapshot of children's understanding and ability and help provide next steps.

Methods of assessing in computing

An effective and time-saving method of assessment in computing is through a **rubric**. Both Google Classroom and Microsoft Class Teams both feature rubrics which can be used to assess children's work and provide feedback. Teachers must spend time setting up rubrics. They must also spend lesson time explaining a rubric to the class. However, once a rubric is set up, it can be a time saving and clear way of providing feedback and string assessment. Rubrics should match up to children's success criteria for pieces of work or projects.

Quizzes

Another effective (and fun) way of assessing children in computing is through quick quizzes. These can present children with questions and ask them to demonstrate their understanding. Children could be presented with a piece of code to explain or answer simple 'yes/no' questions to demonstrate their understanding.

Within a VLE such as Google Classroom or Class Teams, children can answer questions in digital forms that the teacher sets up, using Google Forms or Microsoft Forms. The advantage of these is that they can be reused as many times as needed and they generate instant assessment data when children answer them.

Progression in computing

The national curriculum specifies computing objectives by key stage and not by year group. Schools, therefore, need to interpret this and decide what children should achieve each year in computing. Ready-made schemes of work can help with this, setting out lessons and learning objectives that cover the national curriculum. However, the school will have the final say in deciding, within the bounds of the national curriculum, which computing skills should be learned each year.

There are two approaches we can take to progression in computing. The first is to split the objectives for a key stage across year groups, allocating more challenging objectives to higher year groups. The second approach is to revisit key stage objectives each year, ensuring that children gradually reach the key stage objectives at more sophisticated levels.

This book favours the second, spiral approach. This is on the grounds that skills can be taught at different levels of complexity. An example of this is division in maths, which is taught from year 1 to year 6. By year 6, children are working at a higher level of complexity and in a more abstract way, but they are familiar with a concept that they have learned in previous years.

Assessment and progression 157

PAUSE AND REFLECT...

There are two ways to interpret key stage objective in the national curriculum. We can 'save' the harder ones for later years, or we can cover objectives in each year at different degrees of complexity.

- Which approach does your school follow?
- Which approach do you think is more effective for computing teaching?

In the following section, the national curriculum computing objectives have been separated and interpreted for each year group. This might be helpful for setting lesson objectives, and it is only one interpretation. Schools may decide to use this interpretation, use some of it, or devise their own.

For each key stage objective the question 'what should this National Curriculum objective look like at this year group level?' has been asked.

For example, the National Curriculum states that at KS1, children must 'understand what algorithms are'. Arguably, there should be a difference between this in years 1 and 2 and a development in ability between year groups, although this distinction is not statutory.

There are also some skills which are not mentioned in the national curriculum, but which can be useful to develop skills from the national curriculum objectives throughout year groups.

For example, for key stage 2 includes the objective 'use repetition'. While children in year 3 may use loops to repeat their code, it is suggested that children in year 6 should be able to use different types of loops, including while loops and nested loops.

There are several alternatives to assessing each child against each of these objectives. The teacher may decide to do this, although it is a lot of work. Alternatives might be the children self-assessing themselves against these objectives, with the objectives being printed and stuck into a book for them, or in digital format. Another alternative might be the teacher choosing several objectives per year group to be 'key objectives' which the children are assessed against, and which indicate the overall progress of the child.

Even if detailed objectives are not used for assessment, they might still be sued to inform planning and make sure that lessons in each year progress children's understanding.

Suggested computing objectives for each year group

Table 18.1 Key stage 1, computer science – 'Understand what algorithms are'

Year 1	Year 2
• Use the word 'algorithm' to refer to instructions to perform a task	• Recognise that different algorithms can accomplish the same task
• Include a starting event and movement instructions in an algorithm, controlling from the point of view of another	• Recognise that algorithms can be made more efficient by spotting patterns and repeating sections
• Reorder algorithms and explore the importance of sequence	• Use computational language such as 'if', 'x times' and 'until' in algorithms

158 Assessment and progression

Table 18.2 Key stage 1, computer science – 'Create simple programs'

Year 1	Year 2
• Use the word 'program' to describe instructions for a computer • Use an event command, such as a green flag, to start a program • Place block-based movement commands in sequence to control a device • Use counting to decide the movement commands required • Use commands to control the appearance or sounds of a device	• Use different events to start a program • Use repetition in programs to repeat either single commands or patterns • Program sprites and devices to move precisely, using maths and showing awareness of the situational requirements • Create programs that demonstrate understanding of needs, such as programs that 'wait'.

Table 18.3 Key stage 1, computer science – 'Debug programs'

Year 1	Year 2
• Show resilience when a program doesn't do what it is expected to and try again • Talk about common types of error, including counting the square a robot starts on	• Use the word 'bug' to describe mistakes in programs • Identify the type of bug – whether it is a missing command, wrong value, or the wrong sequence of the instructions

Table 18.4 Key stage 1, computer science – 'Use logical reasoning to predict behaviour of simple programs'

Year 1	Year 2
• Recognise examples of programs written using block-based commands • Recognise common features of programs including a 'start' event, movement blocks, looks blocks and loops • Read programs in sequence and make a prediction about what will happen	• Read programs that contain loops and make predictions about their behaviour • Read programs that contain simple conditional elements

Table 18.5 Key stage 1, information technology – 'Create and manipulate digital content'

Year 1	Year 2
• Use a keyboard to type words and sentences • Use the buttons on a mouse to click on icons, select objects, use tools and open programs • Know, select and use from a range of programs to express ideas, i.e. for drawing and note taking • Be able to take photos and videos using digital devices • Use graphical design tools to create digital artwork, adding text and shapes where appropriate	• Use the main keys on the keyboard • Change the layout of text on a page • Create documents that include a mixture of text and other media • Select programs and apps for more complex activities, such as stop motion animation and music making

Assessment and progression 159

Table 18.6 Key stage 1, information technology – 'Organise, store and, retrieve digital content'

Year 1	Year 2
• Name and save a piece of digital work • Open and continue a piece of work done using a digital device	• Use formal commands, such as 'file', 'save', and 'open' and recognise where these are on a screen • Use naming conventions to save work, such as person's name and work description • Log onto a computer and locate work independently

Table 18.7 Key stage 1, digital literacy – 'Recognise uses of technology beyond school'

Year 1	Year 2
• Talk about how devices in the world around them act when buttons are pressed • Give examples of technology that is helpful in their life • Recognise the need to handle technology carefully to keep it and us safe	• Recognise devices in the world around them that contain computers • Give examples of sensors and buttons used by computers • Give examples of outputs, including motors, lights, and sounds • Construct algorithms for how everyday devices work, such as hen the button is pressed, ...'

Table 18.8 Key stage 1, digital literacy – 'Use technology safely'

Year 1	Year 2
• Handle electronic devices carefully and safely • Recognise and suggest websites that we can trust to go to for information • Locate the KS1 school rules on ICT use	• Care for and maintain electronic devices • Recognise unreliable information online • Follow the KS1 school ICT Rules

Table 18.9 Key stage 1, digital literacy – 'Use technology respectfully'

Year 1	Year 2
• Recognise kind and unkind behaviour online	• Communicate positively with someone online

Table 18.10 Key stage 1, digital literacy – 'Know what constitutes personal information and how to keep this private'

Year 1	Year 2
• Give examples of personal information that we would not share with strangers	• Recognise examples of online situations where we would not share personal information

160 Assessment and progression

Table 18.11 Key stage 1, digital literacy – 'Identify where to go for help and support when they have concerns about content or contact on the internet or other online technologies'

Year 1	Year 2
• Explain the process of telling an adult if they feel worried while using a computer	• Suggest different people that they can talk to about worrying online behaviour

Table 18.12 Key stage 2, computer science – 'Design and create a range of programs, systems and content that accomplish specific goals'

Year 3	• Design and create content that meets a simple design brief, modelled by the teacher
Year 4	• Design and create content that uses several features of a specific platform
Year 5	• Design and create content that uses a wide range of features of a particular platform
Year 6	• Design and create content according to an exact brief, using measurements or precise outputs

Table 18.13 Key stage 2, computer science – 'Control or simulate physical systems'

Year 3	• Connect a physical system to a computer via USB. • Program simple and precise operation of motors, lights or other outputs in a physical system.
Year 4	• Program sensors to trigger outputs using 'wait until' logic
Year 5	• Program sensors to trigger outputs based on conditions and variables
Year 6	• Create physical systems to address real world needs

Table 18.14 Key stage 2, computer science – 'Solve problems by decomposing them into smaller parts'

Year 3	• Decompose and solve problems involving simple movements
Year 4	• Decompose and solve problems involving patterns and repetition
Year 5	• Decompose and solve problems involving conditional logic
Year 6	• Decompose and solve problems involving variables

Table 18.15 Key stage 2, computer science – 'Use sequence in programs'

Year 3	• Place a range of different types of coding blocks in the correct order
Year 4	• Explore sequence with code that uses repetition
Year 5	• Explore sequence with code that uses conditions, and nested conditions
Year 6	• Explore sequence with code that uses variables

Assessment and progression   161

Table 18.16 Key stage 2, computer science – 'Use variables in programs'

Year 3	• Recognise variables in programs • Alter programs that control variables
Year 4	• Create and name a variable • Set a variable to an initial amount • Program a variable to increase or decrease, depending on a condition met • Program events to happen when a variable amount is reached
Year 5	• Create programs that use variables from sensor input • Use Boolean logic with variables (i.e. if answer = … **or** …', **not**, **and**).
Year 6	• Program something to move by a variable amount, or to variable coordinates

Table 18.17 Key stage 2, computer science – 'Use selection in programs'

Year 3	• Recognise and use 'if touching' blocks, or equivalent
Year 4	• Recognise and use 'if /else' logic
Year 5	• Recognise and use and 'if/elif' structure
Year 6	• Recognise and use conditions with different operators (or, and, not)

Table 18.18 Key stage 2, computer science – '*Use repetition* in programs'

Year 3	• Recognise and use loops in block-based programming, where a pattern is spotted
Year 4	• Reorder code to use loops and make it more efficient
Year 5	• Recognise and use nested loops
Year 6	• Use loops until a condition is met

Table 18.19 Key stage 2, computer science – 'Work with various forms of input and output'

Year 3	• Understand the terms 'input' and 'output' and give examples of these in a physical system.
Year 4	• Suggest algorithms for inputs and outputs in the real world
Year 5	• Program an input sensor to trigger an output
Year 6	• Program more than one type of sensor to trigger more than one type of output

Table 18.20 Key stage 2, computer science – 'Use logical reasoning to suggest how algorithms work'

Year 3	• Read and make predictions about algorithms that contain movement, or other simple commands
Year 4	• Read and make predictions about algorithms that contain 'if/else' logic
Year 5	• Read and make predictions about algorithms that contain variables • Make predictions about algorithms that control sensor input
Year 6	• Read and make predictions about algorithms that contain 'while' loops and nested loops

162   *Assessment and progression*

Table 18.21 Key stage 2, computer science – 'Detect and correct errors in algorithms and programs'

Year 3	• Observe a bug in a program and describe the behaviour that is incorrect
Year 4	• Observe a program running and point out the section of code that might contain the error
Year 5	• Follow an established debugging process
Year 6	• Describe and recognise different types of bugs, such as errors in the order of code, errors in syntax, omission of code and numerical errors

Table 18.22 Key stage 2, computer science – 'Understand computer networks and including the internet'

Year 3	• Name devices that connect to the internet
Year 4	• Connect a device to the internet and explain common online terms
Year 5	• Name and explain the functions of a school network
Year 6	• Explain how data packets travel from a server to a personal computer

Table 18.23 Key stage 2, information technology – 'Use search technologies effectively, appreciating how results are selected and ranked'

Year 3	• Use keywords when searching online
Year 4	• Select results discerningly, reading web addressed before clicking
Year 5	• Be discerning in searching and demonstrate efficient strategies
Year 6	• Explain different searching algorithms and how results are ranked

Table 18.24 Key stage 2, information technology – 'Collect, analyse, and present data and information'

Year 3	• Use digital devices to collect and record data
Year 4	• Use apps that collect data and data loggers to collect data precisely
Year 5	• Create a spreadsheet and use it to organise and present data, including using graphs
Year 6	• Use formulae on a spreadsheet to interpret data

Table 18.25 Key stage 2, information technology – 'Select, use and combine software (including internet services) to create programs, systems and content'

Year 3	• Use a combination of apps or programs to create a document
Year 4	• Create an online, collaborative piece of work
Year 5	• Create a piece of work, combining multimedia tools
Year 6	• Create a piece of content, showing awareness of the needs of a user

Table 18.26 Key stage 2 digital literacy – 'Be discerning when evaluating digital content'

Year 3	• Use trusted websites for information
Year 4	• Recognise websites that are unreliable
Year 5	• Recognise information online that is misleading or unreliable
Year 6	• Show an understanding of bias and give examples of this

Assessment and progression 163

Table 18.27 Key stage 2 digital literacy – 'Use digital technology safely and responsibly'

Year 3	• Give examples of reliable websites to use for information
Year 4	• Search safely using key words and selecting safe results
Year 5	• Follow copyright rules by selecting images with appropriate licences
Year 6	

Table 18.27 Key stage 2 digital literacy – 'Recognise acceptable/unacceptable behaviour'

Year 3	• Explain the effects that unkind online behaviour can have
Year 4	• Demonstrate positive online behaviour
Year 5	• Recognise behaviour that constitutes cyberbullying
Year 6	• Name more than three types of cyberbullying and describe what these involve

Table 18.28 Key stage 2 digital literacy – 'Identify ways to reports inappropriate content and contact'

Year 3	• Explain the process of reporting content or contact to an adult
Year 4	• Explain the effects of not reporting inappropriate content or contact online
Year 5	• Give examples of content or contact that is inappropriate
Year 6	• Know ways to report online and block contact

Conclusion

Key to any successful lesson is the teacher being clear upon the skills that are being learned. The skills developed in the lesson should enable children to progress their learning from where they have been previously. This is why a well-thought-out progression of skills is important.

Most children only have one computing lesson per week, not a lot of time to develop and embed computer skills. Even so, it should be possible to demonstrate progress from year 1 to 2, or from year 3 to 6. Whether this is done by teaching 'harder' key stage objectives later in the year group, or by teaching objectives at different levels is a decision for schools to make.

References

Computing Programs of Study: Key stages 1 and 2, National Curriculum of England, Department for Education, 2013.
Kahoot, https://kahoot.com
Quizziz, https://quizziz.com
Typing Club, https://www.typingclub.com/

19 E-safety and digital citizenship

Aims of this chapter

As explored in Chapter 8, E-safety is part of the computing curriculum, forming the 'digital literacy' strand of computing teaching.

This chapter is concerned with the wider need for E-safety, in computing lessons, across the whole school and at home.

In this chapter, we will explore the reasons that it is important to protect children online. As we will see, the computing coordinator and teachers of computing make an important contribution to ensuring E-safety. However, like physical safety, E-safety is considered the responsibility of all staff in the school, overseen by the school's designated safeguarding lead(s) (DSL) and school management.

Requirements for teaching E-safety

For computing, the national curriculum for key stage 1 states,

> Pupils should be taught to use technology safely and respectfully, keeping personal information private; identify where to go for help and support when they have concerns about content or contact on the internet or other online technologies.

For key stage 2 computing, the national curriculum states,

> Pupils should be taught to use search technology effectively, appreciate how search results are selected and ranked, and be discerning in evaluating digital content.
>
> Pupils should be taught to use technology safely, respectfully and responsibly; recognise acceptable/unacceptable behaviour; identify a range of ways to report concerns about content and contact.

E-safety objectives also feature strongly in relationships education and health education. These are compulsory subjects set out by the 2019 government publication, **Relationships Education, Relationships and Sex Education and Health Education**. According to this document, relationship education must teach primary children about online relationships, stating,

DOI: 10.4324/9781003502555-19

E-safety and digital citizenship   165

Pupils should know:

- That sometimes people behave differently online, including by pretending to be some-one that they are not.
- That the same principles apply to online relationships as face-to-face relationships, including the importance of respect for others online when we are anonymous.
- The rules and principles for keeping safe online, how to recognise risks harmful content and contact and how to report them.
- How to critically consider their online friendships and sources of information including awareness of the risks associated with people they have never met.
- How information and data is used and shared online.

In the 'Being Safe' section of this same document, there is the additional objective:

Pupils should know what sorts of boundaries are appropriate in friendships with peers and others (including in a digital context.)

Also contained in the 2019 publication, 'Relationships Education, Relationships and Sex Education and Health Education', health education contains a section entitled 'Internet safety and harms', which states,

Pupils should know

- That for most people, the internet is an integral part of life and has many benefits.
- About the benefits of rationing time spent online, the risks of excessive time spent on electronic devices and the impact of positive and negative content online on their own and others' mental and physical well being.
- How to consider the effect of their online actions on others and know how to recognise and display respectful behaviour online and the importance of keeping personal information private.
- Why social media, some computer games and online gaming, for example, are age restricted.
- That the internet can also be a negative place where online abuse, trolling, bullying and harassment can take place, which have a negative impact on mental health.
- How to be a discerning consumer of information online, including understanding that information, including information from search engines, is ranked, selected and targeted.
- Where and how to report concerns and get support with issues online.

In addition, the section of health education entitled 'Mental wellbeing', states.

Pupils should know that bullying (including cyberbullying) has a negative and often lasting impact on mental wellbeing.

The objectives for relationships and health education are useful as they expand on the objectives for teaching E-safety specified by the national curriculum for computing. It is likely that lessons and activities planned for teaching children about E-safety would meet objectives form both computing and from relationships and health education. As with

166 *E-safety and digital citizenship*

computing, the objectives will need to be taught at a level that is appropriate to children in the year group.

What is clear from the E-safety objectives contained in relationships and health education is that E-safety is more than just a requirement for computing lessons. Like physical safety, E-safety is something that all members of staff in school have a responsibility for ensuring, all the time. Safe and appropriate use of digital and online technology should be clear, discussed, and prevalent in school all the time, across all subjects and activities. One of the clearest ways to ensure this is to have an ICT acceptable use agreement that all children agree to and that is displayed throughout the school.

Due to the possibility of harm occurring to children, digital and online activity is considered a safeguarding matter. Children who have experienced or are at risk of harm due to digital or online activity would be dealt with according to child protection procedures.

While the computing coordinator and relationships and health coordinator in a school will organise E-safety teaching and resources, **all staff members are responsible for ensuring that children's use of technology in school and at home is monitored and is safe**. Concerns related to online safety should be recorded and dealt with according to school safeguarding and child protection policies. Ultimate responsibility for monitoring children's online safety lying with school management and the school designated safeguarding lead (DSL).

E-safety is covered by the 2023 statutory guidance, **Keeping Children Safe in Education**[1] **(KCSIE),** which, as stated in this document, schools, 'must have regard to when carrying out their duty to safeguard children'.

According to Keeping Children Safe in Education, online safety is a safeguarding requirement. Page 10 of this document states,

> Technology is a significant component in many safeguarding and wellbeing issues. Children are at risk of abuse online, as well as face to face. In many cases abuse and other risks will take place concurrently both online and offline. Children can also abuse other children online, this can take the form of abusive, harassing, misogynistic/misandrist messages, the non-consensual sharing of indecent images, especially around chat groups, and the sharing of abusive images and pornography to those who do not want to receive such content.

In October 2023, the **Online Safety Act 2023** became law. This bill aimed to offer protection to children and young people by requiring technology companies to regulate online content, balancing this need with the need for freedom of expression.

According to the Online Safety Act, technology companies have a greater duty to remove **illegal content** from online platforms. Content containing child abuse, promotion of suicide and terrorism, for example, as well as 'deep fake' pornography and included in this. Online platforms are required to detect and remove such content.

Companies have a duty to prevent children from accessing **content that is harmful**. Content that promotes eating disorders, self-harm, pornography, extreme violence, and bullying all fall into this category. Companies are not required to remove such content but are required to take steps to deal with it, including placing it behind an 'age wall', and giving parents tools to filter out such content.

The effects of this bill will include OFCOM having greater powers, requiring technology companies to undertake reviews of their compliance with this law and imposing fines where companies fail to meet its provisions.

Since primary school children are below the age of 13, they are not, according to the terms of service of most social media platforms, allowed to set up and use accounts. YouTube has a lower age limit of 13 years old, as does WhatsApp messaging service. The reality is that some primary children will have access to these tools, with and without the knowledge of their parents. In terms of the effect on primary schools, we should expect children to receive clearer age-limit prompts when using online services, as well as having clearer ways to report harm when using them. Teaching children to recognise age limits and ways to report harm are actions that primary teachers can take, now with the support of this new law.

PAUSE AND REFLECT...

E-safety has received a lot of attention recently, with health and relationships education, computing and KCSIE all providing guidance on E-safety provision.

- How can schools ensure a coordinated approach to E-safety?
- How can schools best engage with parents and educate them about E-safety?

E-safety and artificial intelligence (AI)

In Chapter 22, we will explore some of the effects that AI is having on education and is likely to have in the coming years. As with any technology, children need to be aware of AI, be able to discuss its use and learn how to use it safely. Failing to do any of these things can expose them to risk of harm.

When we talk about risk associated with children's use of AI, there are several areas to be aware of. These include:

- Respecting copyright and ownership.
- Protection of personal data and information.
- Recognising where information created by AI tools is false, unreliable, or biased.
- Knowing when AI should and should not be used as a substitute for human work.
- Being aware of ethical and legal use of AI tools.

Most generative AI tools require children to be older than primary age in order to use them. Chat GPT, for example, requires that users be at least 13 years old, and that users between 13 and 18 require parent or guardian permission to use the platform.

The 2023 government publication, **Generative Artificial Intelligence in Education**[2] contains the section entitled, **Protecting pupils, data and staff**, which sets out considerations relating to safe use of AI in schools. One of the statements is that, "Any data entered should not be identifiable". Personal information includes anything that can be used to identify a child, including their photograph, name, or email address.

168 *E-safety and digital citizenship*

The importance of teaching E-safety

The inclusion of provision relating to E-safety in *Keeping Children Safe in Education*, the provision in relationships and health education and the inclusion of E-safety as one of the three strands of the computing curriculum demonstrate the level of potential harm to children if E-safety considerations are not to be met.

Keeping Children Safe in Education uses the term 'abuse' when talking about some of the things that children might encounter online. 'Abuse' is a term that relates to the most severe types of harm that children can encounter. Even if abuse has not taken place, it is clear that Keeping Children Safe in Education regards E-safety as a safeguarding consideration.

The objectives relating to relationships and health education recognise the effects that online activity can have on children's physical and mental health.

According to the UK government **Online Safety Data Blog**,[3] 80% of children aged 12-15 have had potentially harmful experiences online. According to the **NSPCC website**,[4] from April 2021 to March 2022, there were 42,503 crimes against children recorded by the police, compared to 3,706 ten years ago. There are a multitude of statistics relating to online safety, but these statistics serve to highlight the scale of the problem. In the next section, we will look at some of the specific challenges that children, teachers and parents face concerning online safety, before considering ways that primary schools can act to address these.

E-safety challenges

The internet is an incredible resource, which has changed education and provided amazing opportunities to young people. A lot of this book is about the wonderful tools and resources that are available, many online. However, internet use presents significant challenges and risks. In this section, we will explore some of these risks, before considering ways that schools can act to address them.

Cyberbullying

Bullying is defined as repeated harmful acts, targeted at someone. In Chapter 3, we defined cyberbullying and the different forms that cyberbullying can take. These include harassment, exclusion, flaming, masquerading, outing, and impersonating.

Online bullying, or cyberbullying is particularly harmful for several reasons:

Once content is on the internet, it is very difficult, if not impossible, to erase it. This is particularly true when content has been shared. **Childline** produced an impactful poster with the slogan, 'Once it's on the internet, there's no undo button'. (This poster and others are available via the **LGFL website**.[5])

Cyberbullying, unlike physical bullying, is viewable by a large audience. This is particularly true if photos or videos are shared via platforms, including video platforms. Whereas physical bullying might concern individuals or a group, cyberbullying can extend to much larger groups, leaving victims feeling hopeless.

E-safety and digital citizenship   169

Another reason that cyberbullying is particularly harmful is the potential to hide, or disguise bullying that takes place. As we saw in Chapter 3, purposefully excluding an individual from a group, forum, chat group, or game could be considered to by cyberbullying. However, since most children who use these services would do so outside of school on their own devices, it can be difficult to prove that bullying of this sort has taken place. The factor of online anonymity adds to the potential difficulty in dealing with cyberbullying.

Violent movies and gaming

There is strong evidence suggesting that individuals who play violent games experience a reduction in empathy when witnessing other violent acts. Adults have the experience, strategies, and capacity to balance any dip in empathy caused by violent media. Children do not have this available to them. This dip in empathy may manifest itself in repetition of the violence the child has observed, or more commonly, through lower level, but still concerning behaviour showing a lack of empathy.

An added concern for children playing or witnessing violence in games or other media is the potential for children copying the violent actions they witness. Much of children's development is based on imitation of the language, actions, and behaviour they observe, and it is highly likely that this would include violence.

Put simply, children are damaged through exposure to violent content. The Online Safety Act 2023 is, in part, a response to this, requiring companies to prevent children from viewing harmful content, which includes extreme violence.

Misinformation

Most primary teachers will have been faced with a comment along the lines of, "But I saw it online". As with violence, children do not possess the life experience and critical thinking skills to balance the persuasive, yet often false information that they may encounter online. This can result in children believing that events occurred which did not, or the opposite, believing that events which are well documented did not take place. Children can subscribe to and repeat views that are articulate and persuasive, but promote violence, misogyny, excessive materialism, and other undesirable views.

Commercial activity

With many families using shared devices, it is likely that, intentionally or unintentionally, children will have access to logins that include their parents' bank information. Many shopping websites save payment information and some online services automatically fill this in, even when using a new service.

The potential for harm is significant. Children can purchase items or digital content that is unsuitable for them. They may be lured into purchasing content for games that they own, with progressing in many games being locked behind a 'pay wall', which makes progressing with payment hard, or impossible. Children have also run up large bills for

170 *E-safety and digital citizenship*

their parents through online shopping or payments to games, causing financial hardship and arguments.

Contact and grooming

With the internet, the potential for strangers to contact children is higher than it has ever been. Most children who play games online will experience contact with people they do not know, often in the form of typed messages or voice chat.

The risks around online contact with strangers often results from perpetrators 'tricking' young people into revealing more information than they should. A simple example of this can be through arguing, or trolling, where 'trolls' attempt to provoke a reaction by posting negative things online. Many children will suggest what they consider to be apt responses, not realising that the best response possible is no response at all, to block the user and to tell an adult.

Radicalisation

Under the **Counter Terrorism and Security Act 2015**, organisations including schools have a duty to take steps to prevent terrorism through young people becoming radicalised. Schools' responsibilities are clarified in the 2024 statutory guidance, **Prevent duty guidance: for England and Wales.**[6] This states that the objectives of prevent are to,

> Tackle the ideological causes of terrorism, intervene early to support people susceptible to radicalisation and to enable people who have already engaged in terrorism to disengage and rehabilitate.

As this guidance makes clear, vulnerable people may be at greater risk of radicalisation although people may also be radicalised without vulnerability being evident.

Where signs of radicalisation or a risk of radicalisation is noticed, it will usually be the school DSL who decides whether to refer this to the police, who will perform a 'gateway' evaluation to determine whether further support is required.

Mental health and body image

A phenomenon relating to online content is that people very rarely portray themselves in a negative light. Images shared online are often carefully selected and edited to portray success, happiness and conform to an idealised version of appearance. It is easy for internet users to negatively compare themselves against a vision of others that is unrealistic. This can lead to feelings of inadequacy and a perceived need to conform to this unrealistic portrayal of peers online.

While most adults have developed a resistance to this, becoming confident in their own strengths and aware that it is not necessary to conform to other people's online portrayal, children have not developed the same critical capacity.

Children's mental health is at risk as they compare themselves to peers online, who may display more wealth, success or a different body image to them.

This risk is recognised and addressed by the objectives for primary health education, which states that pupils should know,

> About the benefits of rationing time spent online, the risks of excessive time spent on electronic devices and the impact of positive and negative content online on their own and others' mental and physical well being.

Extreme manifestations of a negative view of body images can lead to problems with mental health, eating disorders and additional time spent online.

Illegal behaviour

Laws relating to online behaviour deal with areas such as online content, online behaviour, copyright protection, and commercial activity. Schools will decide whether to include discussion about the law with primary children. If schools do not include discussion of the law, then the school's teaching about use of ICT at school and at home should ensure that children's use of ICT conforms to legal requirements. The school ICT acceptable use agreement should reflect relevant laws and children should understand that their conduct outside of school should conform to the same requirements.

A common misconception among children is that because they 'can do' something, it is 'okay to do it'. This misconception relates to children's more literal view of the world than adults and the experience and critical thinking that they are yet to develop. Using the internet, it is possible to download and access content, guess passwords, and otherwise cause harm to others. Children need to understand that their behaviour online should mirror expectations offline, with some additional rules that need to be followed online.

Adult content

As we have seen, the Online Safety Act 2023 confirms on companies a greater duty to remove illegal content and restrict access to content that is harmful. This includes companies setting up parental restrictions to access such content.

The reality is that most children have easy access to content online that is violent, explicit, or otherwise harmful. Even if children cannot themselves buy games or videos, they are able to search for them online, including on popular video streaming platforms. Many websites remember passwords, making it challenging to restrict what children view. This becomes particularly difficult when children are given their own, internet-capable device.

Personal information

Personal information includes any information which can be used to identify an individual. This includes, but is not limited to children's name, birthday, email address, telephone number, address, photograph, video recording, and voice recording. From key stage 1, children should be taught to keep this information safe.

It is common for individuals online to ask questions such as 'What is your name?' and 'How old are you?' These can be followed by, 'Where do you go to school?', 'What are your hobbies?', etc. Children should be trained to react to questions such as these with at least the same level of vigilance as if they were questions from a face-to-face stranger. Dangers include impersonation or prolonged, unwanted contact which could include the sending of files or messages that are harmful.

Digital footprint

An individual's digital footprint is a record of all their online activity, whether or not they realise that this is being recorded or shared. It is important that children realise that everything they do online is logged and permanent. Comments made, images shared, and content viewed or shared remain in logs, even when deleted by a user. Screenshots can be taken of any activity that children engage in – another reason that online content is more permanent than its offline equivalent.

As children get older, they may come to regret content that they, or others, have shared about hem online. This is particularly true when children are applying for positions after school, with many companies now conducting online searches as part of their selection process.

Malware

Malware coming from the French 'mal', meaning 'bad', relates to software that is installed on computers with adverse effects. This can include viruses, spyware, ransomware, and trojans.

Children are particularly at risk of malware if they are engaged in downloading from the internet. They should be taught to recognise files that are safe and unsafe, before downloading. Some webpages install malware through visiting them. In school, children should be protected against malware through school firewalls and filtering. At home, malware protection will vary. At school and at home, the first line of defence is children recognising the risks of visiting unsafe websites and downloading files created by unknown entities.

Technology addiction and screentime

There are addictive qualities associated with most computer games, content, and social media platforms. Addictive features keep users playing, scrolling, and viewing additional content. Children are often less experienced than adults in regulating their activity, leaving them vulnerable to using technology for extended periods.

Many parents describe screentime and technology addiction as one of the major challenges faced at home. Describing something as an 'addiction' should give a sense of the gravity of this situation. An addiction means that something has stopped being a choice and has become a need, with difficulty faced when it is withdrawn.

Children will need support managing their use of technology to counter the addictive nature of some digital tools. Signs of addiction and effects on health should be taken seriously and addressed, just as things that effected their physical health would.

Systems for ensuring E-safety in school

As we have seen, formidable challenges to children's safety exist through their use of the internet and technology. To ensure that the potential of digital technology is reached, these challenges must be addressed, prioritising children's health and well-being.

The prevalence of internet use in school and at home requires schools to adopt a proactive and coordinated approach. As we have discussed, this should be overseen by school management, but there are opportunities for other staff and even children to lead in this area.

One of the most important things that a school can do to ensure safe use of technology is to develop an **ICT acceptable use agreement**. This is a clear set of rules that children agree to follow. Children should sign this at the start of every year, either on paper or via a digital form. There can be different versions of this for older and younger children, although I would not advocate having more than two versions for a school.

The content of the agreement will be discussed and agreed by staff and management. I have found an 'I will/I will not' structure to be clearest. Key considerations should relate to children not using technology without supervision, not attempting to tamper with school systems, asking for help, following instructions, being kind and respectful and using websites that are trusted. As discussed in the previous section, the provisions of the acceptable use agreement should ensure that children's use of the internet is safe and legal, even if reference is not made to the law.

Once established, the ICT acceptable use agreement should be displayed clearly throughout the school. It should also be shared with parents, perhaps via the school website. An ICT acceptable use agreement can also contain a clause stating that cyberbullying outside of schools will be dealt with according to school policy.

Once an ICT acceptable use agreement has established conduct with school ICT, effective filtering systems and monitoring systems also need to be set up. These will help protect against external activity targeted at the school and internal activity that breaks the school ICT acceptable use agreement.

In terms of **filtering**, most academies will receive help in setting this up from their multi-academy trust (MAT). Smaller schools may have to organise their own provision, though help is usually available through the local council or local organisations.

In terms of **monitoring**, while there is no one approach that will fit all schools, schools are expected to demonstrate that they effectively monitor web activity that takes place within, whichever monitoring system they use. In 2015, **the UK Safer Internet Centre** produced a guide on effective monitoring which is available via their website[7]. This guide contains useful questions that schools can ask themselves to assess how effectively they are monitoring children's online activity.

If children know the rules, systems are in place to filter and monitor content, the other consideration is that **staff** understand what is expected of them. This includes staff following rules themselves relating to ICT use, as well as staff fulfilling their duties towards children. All staff should sign an agreement relating to their use of digital technology in school. Staff should also receive regular training about keeping children safe, which we will explore below.

Ensuring and promoting E-safety in school – a whole school approach

In chapter 8, we explored how through teaching digital literacy in computing, we can teach children ways to use technology effectively, safely, respectfully, and responsibly. Children will also receive input on using technology through relationship and health education.

To meet the threats that we discussed in the previous section, E-safety needs to be more prevalent than it would be, through teaching in computing lessons and relationship and health lessons. As with other aspects of health, a strong and proactive approach is needed to ensure that children develop the awareness and skills needed to keep themselves safe, and report instances when they experience harm.

Assemblies are a good way of promoting E-safety in school by raising the profile of the topic. Children respond well to messages form their peers and children who plan presentations on E-safety will take far greater ownership of the content. Other options for assemblies involve people from outside the school coming to talk to the children, possibly including past pupils. These can be memorable and impactful experiences.

E-safety events, such as **Safer Internet Day** offer opportunities to celebrate online safety. Safer Internet Day takes place worldwide every February, with details on the Safer Internet Day website.

Embedding E-safety into the wider curriculum is another way to raise the profile of E-safety and encourage discussion outside of computing lessons.

There is a range of literature available about topics around E-safety, catering for different year groups. **How to be More Hedgehog**,[8] by Anne-Marie Conway, is a wonderful story suitable for year 5 or 6 children. The deals with cyberbullying and could be a good option for a text which children could read and discuss a modern issue. **Penguinpig**,[9] by Stuart Spendlow, is a story that deals with unreliable information online and people who disguise their identify. **Chicken Clicking**[10] by Jeanne Wills is a story about online shopping which can form a good basis for wider discussions about E-safety.

Children could look at both fiction and non-fiction writing relating to E-safety in English, even producing their own pieces of writing, stories or films dealing with topics around E-safety.

As well as exploring E-safety through English work, children can produce artwork about matters relating to E-safety. Artwork is particularly effective if it is to be displayed. Children could produce posters, photographs, or animations about E-safety, having the chance to exhibit their work to educate the community.

In maths, children could interpret statistics relating to E-safety. This could include data about screentime, money spent online or reliability of information.

In Chapter 20, we discuss how one of the tasks of a computing coordinator might be to work with **digital leaders** – children who act as role models for other children in technology use.

An effective whole school approach makes E-safety something that children take ownership of. Through computing lessons and other lessons, they will gain a good vocabulary for talking about matters like cyberbullying, so that if problems occur, they are able to spot them and report them.

Staff training

Staff training on matters relating to E-safety is a key part of keeping children safe. Like children, staff need to possess the vocabulary to talk about E-safety in order to recognise risks of harm. Staff need to be clear as to what is expected of them in terms of helping keep children safe online and the procedures to follow if they suspect a child is at risk.

Schools can run in-house training on E-safety, led by school management and other teachers. This training should start with establishing the school's broader duties to safeguard children, under KCSIE and school policies. Training can then either focus on particular aspects of E-safety, such as cyberbullying, use of AI or contact online, or cover a broad range of topics relevant to keeping children safe online.

There are training providers that can be booked to come into school to deliver E-safety training including **South West Grid for Learning (SWGfL), UK Safer Internet Centre,** and **NSPCC Learning**. Most organisations that come into schools are happy to tailor training according to the needs of a school. Organisations such as the ones mentioned are up to date with current threats to children's online safety and can offer advice that helps protect children in their care.

SWGfL have produced a range of brilliant resources to assist school with E-safety. One of these is called **Project Evolve**,[11] which features resources for teaching children about a wide range of topics. SWGfL have also created **Project Evolve Edu**, which is aimed at professionals and can help to structure E-safety training for schools.

Another tool that SWGfL offer schools is their **360 Degree Safe Tool**. This is an audit that schools can carry out on their E-safety provision, identifying strengths and areas for improvement.

Working with parents

Parents have a key role to play in keeping their children safe online. Many schools feature information for parents about E-safety on their websites. This can be a helpful place for parents to start, particularly if this website is dynamic and updated frequently. Schools can also hold E-safety workshops for parents, although it can be difficult for working parents to attend.

National Online Safety,[12] now part of the **National College** has produced an app featuring their excellent posters about topics on E-safety, as well as other media about keeping children safe. The posters produced by this organisation are added to regularly and are a good way for adults to keep up to date with some of the risks surrounding technology that children use online.

Ultimately, schools need to find ways to engage parents on the topic of E-safety so that messages and expectations about keeping children safe online are kept high-profile and regular. It is much easier for parents to take consistent and appropriate steps if these are regularly communicated by the school. Getting children onboard through engaging E-safety education in school, and clear rules on what to do if they feel unsafe, further increases the chances of them being safe online.

Conclusions

The challenges faced by schools, parents and children online are significant. Effective E-safety provision needs to be at the centre of school safeguarding training, provided for in school policies and visible in its presence around the school. Schools need to create a culture of E-safety where children know and agree to rules, have regular opportunities to discuss E-safety and carry this attitude with them outside school.

Fortunately, the government, charities and other organisations have responded to the growing need to keep children safe with their increasing online activities. Schools should seek advice where they need to, either online or in person and ensure that E-safety is something that is regularly reviewed and improved.

Notes

1 'Keeping Children Safe in Education 2023, Statutory guidance for schools and colleges', Department for Education, 2023.
2 Generative Artificial Intelligence (AI) in Education, Department for Education, 2023.
3 https://onlinesafetydata.blog.gov.uk/about-us/.
4 https://www.nspcc.org.uk/about-us/news-opinion/2023/online-safety-advice-insights-safer-internet-day-2023/.
5 https://lgfl.net/safeguarding/resources.
6 https://www.gov.uk/government/publications/prevent-duty-guidance.
7 https://swgfl.org.uk/.
8 Conway, Anne-Marie, *How to be More Hedgehog*, UCLan Publishing, 2022.
9 Spendlow, Stuart, *Penguinpig*, Matham House, 2014.
10 Wills, Jeanne, *Chicken Clicking*, Andersen Press, 2014.
11 https://projectevolve.co.uk/.
12 https://nationalcollege.com/categories/online-safety.

References

Computing Programs of Study: key stages 1 and 2, National Curriculum of England, Department for Education, 2013.
Conway, Anne-Marie, *How to be More Hedgehog*, UCLan Publishing, 2022.
Generative Artificial Intelligence (AI) in Education, Department for Education, 2023.
Keeping Children Safe in Education 2023, statutory guidance for schools and colleges, Department for Education, 2023.
LGFL website, https://lgfl.net/safeguarding/resources
National Online Safety, https://nationalcollege.com/categories/online-safety
NSPCC Learning, https://learning.nspcc.org.uk/
NSPCC website, https://www.nspcc.org.uk/about-us/news-opinion/2023/online-safety-advice-insights-safer-internet-day-2023/
Project Evolve, https://projectevolve.co.uk/
Prevent Duty Guidance for England and Wales, https://www.gov.uk/government/publications/prevent-duty-guidance
Relationships Education, Relationships and Sex Education (RSE) and Health Education, Statutory guidance for governing bodies, proprietors, head teachers, principles, senior leadership teams, teachers, Department for Education, 2019.
South West Grid for Learning, https://swgfl.org.uk/
Spendlow, Stuart, *Penguinpig*, Matham House, 2014.
UK Government Online Safety Blog, https://onlinesafetydata.blog.gov.uk/about-us/
UK Safer Internet Centre, https://swgfl.org.uk/
Wills, Jeanne, *Chicken Clicking*, Andersen Press, 2014.

20 Leading computing and digital learning

The role of the computing coordinator

As a computing coordinator, you will oversee a subject that children love and enables them to express their ideas in new ways. You will attend CPD sessions with other educators who are looking to make lasting changes and modernise education. You will help shape teaching in a subject which is in its infancy but is likely to become a significant influence on schools and children. You will also become an expert in a field which is likely to take centre stage over the coming years and may provide career-defining opportunities.

The goal of any subject coordinator should be to make improvements that have long lasting effects, achieve agreed milestones, and show consistent progress in teaching and learning over time.

Having decided educational priorities, the discussion becomes one of whole school strategy which is best had with members of the school senior leadership team (SLT). It is then the job of the computing coordinator to suggest technologies and approaches by which these agreed goals can be reached and offer training to the school staff in using them.

Arguably the most important thing about leading computing and digital learning is to be clear about what we wish the children to be able to do, prior to any discussion about any specific technology.

PAUSE AND REFLECT...

The position of computing coordinator can be an exciting one, helping to shape a school's digital strategy.

- What should the first priorities of a new computing coordinator be?
- How can a computing coordinator ensure progression in all computing skills throughout the school?

DOI: 10.4324/9781003502555-20

Establishing priorities

The status of computing within the school will determine the priorities that the computing coordinator will agree with school leadership. In this section, we will explore some possible focuses for development of computing and strategies to address these.

Standards of work and progress

As well as overseeing long term subject-strategy, coordinators are responsible for ensuring that children's work and learning in a subject reach required standards. As discussed in Chapter 18, national curriculum objectives for computing are specified by key stage and not year group. The first task of a computing coordinator will therefore be to establish what is expected in computing in each year group. This can be done through the school interpreting the key stage computing objectives, through using a computing scheme of work, or by using the objectives in this book. Because the national curriculum does not specify year group objectives, there is plenty of score for schools to interpret the objectives according to their strengths, areas of interest and resources, as well as good practice in computing teaching.

Once standards of work have been agreed for each year group, the computing coordinator will support teachers in teaching to these objectives to ensure that children meet them. The computing coordinator should support teachers by ensuring they feel confident in preparing and teaching lessons. This is an important consideration in computing, where subject content is new for many teachers. The computing coordinator may choose to team teach some computing lessons with other teachers or teach model lessons.

Another way that the computing coordinator should support other teachers is by ensuring they have the resources needed to teach lessons. This is not just resources in terms of hardware and software (discussed below in this chapter, and throughout this book). In other subjects, teachers will have banks of materials that they can draw upon to teach lessons. In computing, teachers may be less confident knowing where to look for resources, how to make resources and how to use resources in lessons. Some schools will choose to use computing schemes of work to support teachers; the **Teach Computing** scheme is an excellent place to start in this regard. The scheme can be modified gradually depending on the needs, opportunities, and expertise in the school.

Evidencing, feedback and assessment

The computing coordinator will need access to examples of children's work to assess whether standards of work are being met in the subject. In Chapter 18, we discussed evidencing and feedback and in Chapter 19, we discussed assessment in computing. As discussed in both chapters, evidencing, feedback, and assessment in computing should be realistic and effective. It should consider the limited time children have in computing lessons and the time it can potentially take for teachers to view children's work.

Making sure that children upload examples of their work to a VLE as part of the lesson, or course of lessons is one way for evidencing in computing to be achievable. Having checklists

Leading computing and digital learning 179

where teachers can quickly assess children against agreed objectives is an achievable to monitor progress and for the computing coordinator to track this.

21st century skills

Leading computing in school goes beyond leading the teaching of one subject. The skills that children will develop through computing will enable them to work effectively using digital means in all aspects of school life, as well as outside school. There is a strong case for classifying digital literacy as a key skill, alongside reading, writing and maths.

Careful consideration must therefore be given to which digital skills children are expected to learn in each year group. Once agreed, these digital skills could form part of the school's computing objectives, in the same way that reading, speaking, and writing skills form part of the objectives for English. Since digital literacy skills are not specified by year group according to the computing national curriculum, schools have the task and the opportunity to think about what standards of digital literacy and use of ICT children should achieve each year. The computing coordinator may oversee this, but it is a discussion that is worth having with other teachers and members of school management. The progression of skills in this book may help, but schools will also wish to set their own standards according to technology that is used in school.

Enrichment of computing

An important part of the role of a subject coordinator is looking for ways to excite children about the subject and bring the subject 'alive'. This can be through organising school events, speakers, competitions, educational visits, and other initiatives. In this section, we will consider some ways to enrich computing.

Visits

School visits require planning, time, and expense. Any school visit will therefore need to be justified in terms of the educational impact and enrichment of the curriculum. Fortunately, there are exciting possibilities for potential computing visits. Much of what we teach the children in computing is centred around encouraging them to ask the question 'how do things work?' There is the potential for organising a visit to any location where staff are happy to show children examples of technology in use and ask them to think about how it works.

There are also specific venues set up for computing visits. **The National Computing Museum** at Bletchley (separate from Bletchley Park) is an amazing museum, with a host of exciting and inspirational computers to see and use. The museum also has classrooms, which teachers can book as part of their visit and staff will teach the class about an agreed aspect of computing. Situated next-door, **Bletchley Park** is also an engaging destination for children who have been learning about cryptography.

The **Science Museum** in London features several galleries about how things work, including a gallery about computer networks and a section about careers in engineering. The

180 *Leading computing and digital learning*

'Wonderlab' on the top floor is also likely to be popular with children, allowing them to take part in exciting experiments.

In Manchester, the **Museum of Science and Industry** (MOSI) features a practical experiment gallery, as well as fascinating exhibitions about the development of technology.

Other ideas for destinations include the **National Video Game Museum** in Sheffield, the **Leicester Space Centre**, or the **Legoland Discovery Centre** in Manchester. Schools could also reach out to local companies that use technology and ask if children can visit. Even visits to local supermarkets will expose children to a range of technology, from doors sensors to barcode scanners, to baking equipment. Schools can also ask companies if speakers will come to the school to talk about technology use and careers. Prior to taking children on any visit, teachers should always visit the location themselves and check whether the visit will be educationally beneficial, safe, and manageable.

School events and competitions

Whole-school events are a great way to get children excited and talking about uses of technology. Events can involve an element of competition, although any children show enter an event should receive recognition for this.

To promote digital expression, events such as **photography exhibitions**, or **student film showings** are a great way to encourage children to produce their best work and give them the opportunity to share this with an audience. Photography or films that children produce could follow a theme, promote a cause, or celebrate an aspect of their community. Schools looking to take this further could even raise money by selling children's photographs or look for external photography or animation competitions to enter children's work into.

Engineering competition can be run by the school, where children design and build devices to meet design criteria. There are organisations that run nation-wide programming and engineering competitions and events, such as the **First Lego League**. Schools can also link work done in computing lessons to events, such as asking children to 3D stadiums during sporting events. Children could also design systems to solve problems, such as monitoring energy usage or plant growth. This second project is easily achievable using simple electronics equipment, such as Crumbles kits, Microbits, or Arduinos (see Chapter 11).

Other competition relating to computing include the **BEBRAS** computational thinking challenge and the **Apps for Good** showcase (see Chapter 16).

The **Big Bang** competition runs yearly. The competition is an opportunity for children to gain recognition for things they have built to address problems. This is a great way to recognise the achievements of children with physical technology and promote computational thinking and engineering.

Extra-curricular activities

After school clubs are a great way to facilitate creative use of computers and technology, giving children the opportunity to explore technology more freely than in lessons. Running after

Leading computing and digital learning 181

school computing clubs is also a good way to make technology accessible to children who might not have access to computers and the internet at home. Possibilities for after school clubs relating to computing include coding club, STEAM club, animation club, 3D design club, Lego club, photography club, film-making club, and journalism club. All these feature exciting possibilities for technology use.

To facilitate running clubs like these, the school can make use of structured schemes of work, including courses on code.org, Lego's educational materials and Tinkercad's educational materials and tutorials. This removes some of the need to direct teaching by a teacher and gives the children opportunities to learn at their own pace.

Digital leaders

Digital leaders can be children, or staff, who are willing to lead others with technology use in school. This will include these people giving up some of their time to attend meetings and help organise technology, but should also confer benefits, such as receiving extra training, opportunities, and recognition for their work.

The best way to appoint digital leaders is to advertise the position, ensuring that responsibilities and some potential benefits are made clear, and then have children who are interested submit applications. These applications could be handwritten or digital and in them, children should explain why they would be a good candidate. Digital leader badges are available to buy online, giving children extra recognition in school. The school can decide whether children are digital leaders for a term or whole year, the benefit of having the same children for a year being that they have the time to make a real impact on technology use, as well as develop skills themselves.

Digital leaders should have regular meetings, where they provide input in technology use and suggest ideas. This can be a good opportunity for the school to hear pupil voice, especially on issues around E-safety, which teachers might not otherwise hear about. Digital leaders can visit classes and provide help where needed, organise resources, maintain systems and run events. They can be trained in using new apps and technology and might even be able to visit events or companies to learn more about technology. Digital leaders could also be given the chance to gain qualifications relating to technology use.

Staff training and CPD

To provide effective Continuous professional development (CPD) for computing, the computing coordinator should have a clear idea about how well children are meeting academic objectives and how well the school is achieving agreed milestones for the development of the subject. To have a clear idea about these things, the academic objectives and milestones must be clear and have been agreed in the first place.

Effective CPD will be followed by noticeable improvements in teaching and learning. This could be improvements in wop how computing is taught, or improvements in use of technology beyond computing lessons.

182 *Leading computing and digital learning*

CPD can take many forms. It is often delivered in staff meetings or INSET days and led by the subject coordinator. The advantages of whole school sessions include being able to deliver messages to the whole school, discuss whole school subject documents, and learning from the expertise of staff in the room. Staff leading CPD can also model technology use themselves, using technologies such as **Mentimeter** to garner opinions from the whole room. The difficulty with whole-school training is that there will be teacher from a wide variety of year groups and a range of needs present, making it challenging to deliver content that benefits everyone.

An alternative to whole school CPD sessions can be making banks of resources available for teachers to use at their own pace. This could be through posting resources on an internal blog or website, or in an environment such as Microsoft Teams or Google Classroom set up for CPD purposes.

Computing coordinators should also expect to spend individual time with teachers, talking to them about how they teach computing and finding out about how their needs can be met.

There are topics that staff should receive regular input about, including data protection and E-Safety. The computing coordinator might be involved in delivering these but should coordinate this with school management.

Possibilities for CPD in computing are discussed in more detail in **Chapter 22**.

Data protection

Like all organisations, schools have a legal responsibility to safeguard personal data. This data can relate to children, families, visitors, or staff. The computing coordinator will play a key role in ensuring that the school complies with data protection requirements.

Almost all applications and websites collect data. This data can include usage data, location data, user IP address, data entered into the application, photographs, sound recording, video, and personal data. By 'personal data', we mean any data that can be used to identify an individual child or adult. A photograph is considered personal data for this reason. A child's full name would be considered personal, as would their address. A child's date of birth should be considered personal data as although in its own, it cannot identify a child, it forms part of the identify of a child, which with other data, could be used to identify someone. School reports could be personal data, since they feature information which is unique to a child and could hence be used to identify a child.

Before sharing personal data with companies or individuals outside the school, schools have a legal responsibility to consider what is going to happen to this data. The laws relating to schools' use of personal data are set out by **the General Data Protection Requirements (GDPR)** and the **Data Protection Act 2018**. There is a useful summary of schools' responsibilities under these laws on the UK government's **Data Protection in Schools**[1] page, issued in February 2023.

The guidance issued by the government on the above website is clear and succinct and should form a good basis for schools establishing whether their use of personal data complies with the law.

Leading computing and digital learning 183

One of the ways that schools can ensure that they consider what happens to personal data is through carrying out a **data protection impact assessment (DPIA)** before sharing personal data with any external third part website or service. Schools should also ensure that their data protection policy is up to date and that staff understand and follow data protection legislation.

The computing coordinator should be aware of data protection legislation and requirements. This is because they will set up and organise many digital services provided by third parties, which may request access to children's personal data. One of the ways that a school can be compliant with data protection regulations is to maintain an up-to-date bank of data protection impact assessments (DPIAs) and the computing coordinator may help to organise this. The computing coordinator will look for ways to minimise the personal data that is shared outside the school. One way of doing this is through creating anonymised logins for children to use websites with, or by enrolling children into websites using their first name only. Subject coordinators in other subjects may also set up these logins, but it makes sense for the computing coordinator, or a member of school leadership to monitor this.

In October 2023, the UK government published a policy paper called **Generative A.I. in Education.**[2] This paper states, 'Generative A.I. stores and learns from data it is given – any data entered should not be identifiable'. Use of AI is covered in more detail in Chapter 22, but AI use in schools clearly has data protection considerations. One of the difficulties we face with using AI is that it is often not clear what happens to data that is shared with AI tools, hence the statement in the policy paper above.

I am not qualified to provide instructions for schools on being compliant with data protection regulations. Schools should ensure this through school management and external consultation where necessary. However, data protection should be a key consideration of the computing coordinator and something that they stay aware of and possibly offer training to other staff on. Managing personal data is mentioned in the National Curriculum for both key stages 1 and 2 in computing and part of the role of the computing coordinator will be ensuring that children think about who they share their data with.

ICT acceptable use

ICT acceptable use in schools includes children knowing and following school ICT rules, parents being informed about these and appropriate monitoring by school staff and management.

As with all matters concerning safeguarding, E-safety is the responsibility of all members of the school community. Ultimately, ensuring that children's use of technology is safe will be overseen by a member of school management.

E-safety is a required part of computing teaching and in computing lessons on E-safety, the class should explore ways to use ICT safely, both in and out of school. Children should have a clear understanding of the school ICT acceptable use rules and should have agreed to follow these at the start of the year, possibly through a signed agreement. ICT acceptable use should not be confined to computing lessons. These rules should be visible around the school and referred to any time children are using technology.

A good format for ICT acceptable use rules for children to follow, is an **I will always** and **I will never** format. The 'I will always' section should include provisions relating to children doing their best work, naming and organising their work, looking after equipment, telling a teacher if they feel concerned and following copyright rules. The 'I will never' section should include provisions about never sharing personal data unless instructed to, logging into someone else's account, recording someone without their permission, being unkind online, visiting websites without permission, using technology unsupervised, accessing, creating or sharing content that is likely to offend or illegal, using generative AI (see Chapter 22), or modifying the school's equipment or systems. This is a non-exhaustive list which will benefit from careful consideration and discussion by school management. A simplified list can be produced for key stage 1 children, although we should bear in mind that many of your younger children are proficient at using technology in ways that we may not expect for children of their age.

The school should also have clear rules about cyberbullying, what is meant by 'cyberbullying', what children should do if they encounter cyberbullying and how cyberbullying will be dealt with.

Resourcing and subscriptions

One of the tasks of the computing coordinator is to manage school resources relating to teaching computing, as well as often, to wider school use of ICT. As discussed at the start of this chapter, the most important thing a computing coordinator and leader of school technology use can do is to establish clear educational priorities and targets for development. This should come before any discussion of decision about purchasing resources.

Schools must manage budgets which sometimes, do not allow for large amounts of money to be spent on ICT development. School ICT spending will include purchasing hardware, software, and licences. It is also important to factor in infrastructure costs when considering expansion of ICT use and purchasing. Hardware infrastructure can include Wi-Fi provision, charging stations, storage trolleys, equipment storage, and cabling. Software infrastructure can include licences, IT support, firewalls, anti-virus services, and mobile device management (MDM) systems. Hardware and software infrastructure costs will increase as technology use increases.

Schools will need to look for cost-effective ways of meeting the educational priorities agreed. Fortunately, there are some very cost-effective options available to schools for delivering high quality computing and digital learning solutions.

Two of the main providers of virtual learning environments (VLEs), **Microsoft** and **Google**, offer free versions of their software. This comes with the caveat that some of the paid services, which might be useful for schools, require payment. However, even using the free versions of either Microsoft Education or Google Education allows schools to set up a VLE for free. Seesaw also provides a free version of its VLE aimed at schools, and particularly suitable for younger children. Other VLE platforms, while designed specifically for schools, can prove expensive when paid for as yearly subscriptions.

Leading computing and digital learning 185

Many of the software services referred to throughout this book are free of charge for schools to use. These include **Canva**, **Tinkercad**, **code.org**, **Scratch**, **Makecode**, and **Wick Editor**.

The **Apps for Good** program is a charity that offers a free course for children to complete, building an app to improve the world and working towards a showcase.

To teach touch typing, **Typing Club** offers both paid and free versions of its software. The paid version allows teachers to set up more classes and track typing progress in a much more sophisticated way and I would say is a good investment for schools wishing to develop typing skills seriously.

In terms of hardware, a recently launched **Microbit** initiative offers sets of 30 Microbits free to teachers who register, enabling a significant amount of physical computing to be done by children using Makecode. Redfern Electronics' **Crumble sets** are an affordable way of getting children engaged in designing and building physical systems, including various forms of outputs and sensors. **Arduino** sets and components are also affordable, at around £40 per starter set and offering more advanced electronics solutions (perhaps more suitable for secondary school).

Schools may decide to purchase specialist equipment for teaching ICT and this can be beneficial where possible. Beebots have been a mainstay of teaching algorithmic thinking to young children for good reasons; they are simple to sue and effective. Sets of **Beebots** (or **Bluebots** – the more modern model) are expensive, but versatile and reliable and can form a mainstay of computing teaching throughout key stage 1 and into key stage 2. The more modern Bluebots are also controllable using the Bluebot app using angles and centimetres, extending their value.

Of course, all this hardware and software requires computers to run them. It is here that schools will need to spend money and make decisions about which platform to use. One of the first decisions schools will need to make is whether to provide fixed, desktop computers, or mobile devices for children. Schools will then need to consider which software they wish to use, the main choices being between Windows and Microsoft software, cloud-based software, or Apple iOS.

There is no right answer when choosing hardware for schools and there are strong arguments for all the platforms above. We can outline the benefits and disadvantages of these.

First, the question of whether to use desktop or mobile devices in schools. Desktop computers offer greater screen space, at the cost of fixing and area for a purpose. Desktop computers also eliminate battery charging requirements which can present problems in schools. Laptops offer greater room flexibility, particularly when working with physical equipment, robotics, or other devices. However, laptop batteries need to be charged and battery charge often degrades. Laptop screens are often smaller than desktop equivalents.

As with all technology discussed in this book, the decision of which to use should stem from the learning needs and accordingly, the projects and work to be done.

In terms of which software platform to use, the discussion is similarly open.

Schools looking to purchase Windows PC's or laptops will do so knowing that they have complete customisability over their devices. Almost every aspect of a Windows device can be customised according to the needs and preference of the user. All educational software will run on a Windows device, unless it has been specifically built for another platform, such as Apple iOS. Windows devices very hugely in price and specifications, ranging from basic laptops and PCs to touchscreen PC, tablets, and high-end computers. Windows software should run on PCs for many years unless it is particularly resource intensive.

Chromebooks are computers that run Google Chrome OS. They are able to run a limited amount of software from the device, but are mainly used for running web-based software or 'web-apps'. Much of the software covered in this book runs online, including Canva, Tinekrcad, code.org, Scratch, and Microsoft Office. Chromebooks, while limited in terms of the software that can be installed on the device, can be cheaper than Windows laptops, due to the low hardware requirements of Chrome OS.

iPads are tablets made by Apple that in many ways are well-suited for schools. iPads are quick to boot up, reliable and easy to use for children. They contain in-built cameras, making them ideal for combining photo and video media with typed work. They also run a wide range of apps, many with free versions and built for children to use. The touch-screen interface suits children well. iPads connect easily to a range of devices, from Sparkvue sensors to Lego Spike devices. Some of the apps designed for iOS are a joy to use, including Keynote and Garageband. iPads also allow children to experience and even create in Augmented reality, using apps such as AR Makr or Reality Composer. There is an enthusiastic Apple Education community that supports teachers with qualifications such as 'Apple Teacher'.

One of the main drawbacks of iPads is that as iOS updates, older iPad models will not be able to easily run some apps if they do not run the latest version of iOS.

Conclusion

It is hard to state definitively which hardware is best for primary schools. In truth, it will depend on the resources and space that the school has available, as well as the educational priorities for the school.

A mixture of hardware is not necessarily a bad thing. iPads have advantages, as do PCs for certain types of work. The most important thing is that a school plans in terms of its educational priorities and goals before deciding on which hardware will best achieve this with the money available. Reading this book should help teachers to decide on what they wish to achieve with computing and ICT prior to deciding on purchasing resources.

Notes

1 https://www.gov.uk/guidance/data-protection-in-schools.
2 https://www.gov.uk/government/publications/generative-artificial-intelligence-in-education/generative-artificial-intelligence-ai-in-education#knowledge-and-skills-for-the-future.

References

Apps for Good, https://www.appsforgood.org/
Bebras, https://www.bebras.uk/
Computing Programs of Study: key stages 1 and 2, National Curriculum of England, Department for Education, 2013.
First Lego League, https://education.theiet.org/first-lego-league-programme

Mentimeter, https://www.mentimeter.com/
Teach Computing curriculum, https://teachcomputing.org/curriculum
Typing Club, https://www.typingclub.com/
UK Government – 'Data Protection in Schools.' https://www.gov.uk/guidance/
data-protection-in-schools
UK Government – 'Generative A.I. in Education.' https://www.gov.uk/government/publications/
generative-artificial-intelligence-in-education/generative-artificial-intelligence-ai-in-education
#knowledge-and-skills-for-the-future

21 Artificial intelligence

Defining AI

In this chapter, we will consider how the rapidly development field of artificial intelligence (AI) is developing and its impact on primary schools.

It is useful to be clear about what is meant by the term 'AI'. In the first part of this chapter, we will explore some of the terms used when talking about AI.

Artificial intelligence

Artificial intelligence is the manifestation of intelligent behaviour using technology. What constitutes intelligent behaviour and how much intelligent behaviour is required for artificial intelligence are deeper questions that cannot be explored properly in this book! However, for very readable texts introducing concepts around artificial intelligence, I would recommend two books: 'Life 3.0', by Max Tegmark, professor at Massachusetts Institute for Technology (MIT), and 'Superintelligence', by Nick Bostrom, professor at Oxford University.

Machine learning

Machine learning is a field within the study of artificial intelligence. The term 'machine learning' was first used in 1959 by Arthur Samuel and at the time was used synonymously with the term 'self-teaching computers'. The idea of machine learning is that computers gradually improve their accuracy at tasks through using data and algorithms, simulating aspects of how humans learn. (IBM). There are some fascinating resources and activities that let children explore and understand machine learning, which we will discuss in this chapter.

Deep learning

Deep learning is in fact a branch of neural networks, and neural networks are a branch of machine learning. Neural networks simulate the way that neurons work in the brain, passing information between nodes when they are activated. Deep learning features an additional layer of nodes over a neural network. Neural networks offer exciting possibilities for computing due to their potential to automate information access and processing, as well as their potential for the speed of accessing information.

DOI: 10.4324/9781003502555-21

Artificial intelligence 189

Strong AI and weak AI

The AI tools we are used to using for entertainment purposes, playing games, internet searching, spellchecks, and other purposes are very good at performing one type of task. As we have seen with the development of chess computers, in most cases, AI can outperform humans at a task. AI that can perform one task, or one type of task is referred to as 'narrow AI', or Artificial narrow intelligence (ANI), or 'weak AI'.

AI that could carry out a range of tasks that is comparable to a human is referred to as 'strong AI', or sometimes 'Artificial General Intelligence' (AGI). No instances of strong AI exist yet.

AI that could theoretically outperform humans in all tasks would be referred to as 'super-intelligent' AI, or 'Artificial superintelligent AI' (ASI). Scientists debate when, if ever superin-telligent AI will be developed. The development of superintelligent AI is often described as a 'singularity', meaning a 'point of no return'.

Generative AI

Generative AI is a type of AI that can produce entirely new media, including text, photo-graphs, video or music, or programming. A high-profile example of current generative AI is Chat GPT, a 'chat bot' which can generate letters, computer programs, essays, and a range of other content. Chat GPT was launched in November 2022, with the most recent version, Chat GPT4 being even more advanced.

Other examples of generative AI include Midjourney, which generates images, Bard, and Dall-E.

Impact of AI

AI may impact the world in many positive ways. AI tools are already benefitting fields includ-ing science and medicine, helping solve problems, including identifying and fighting diseases. AI is used in food production to grow crops in environmentally friendly and efficient ways. In learning and entertainment, AI algorithms personalise content, offering suggestions for content that is personalised and relevant to users' interests.

When we think about the effects of AI on education, we can look at another transforma-tive technology, the internet. One of the effects of the internet has been that is has vastly increased the resources children around the world can access. Children can access free learn-ing tools as often as they like. They can use tools creatively allowing them to express their ideas in ways that would have seemed inconceivable 20 years ago. Of course, children are required to navigate the risks involved in using the internet, which as we explored in Chapter 20, can be significant.

The impact of AI on education might equal, or even exceed that of the internet. AI tools enable the creation of materials that are tailored to the needs of individuals and situations, working at speeds previously impossible.

It was only in November of 2022 that Chat GPT was released for use by the public. Since then, AI tools have developed at a fast pace. It is difficult to predict exactly how the world will

190　*Artificial intelligence*

be affected in the next few years and decades, but one thing is for sure, our children will live in a world in which AI will be a big part of their lives and society.

Addressing risks

The primary responsibility of educators is the safety and well-being of children. Any tool that we use in school must be used safely. This means that risks have been considered, discussed with staff (and where appropriate, children) and evaluated. Where it is deemed that a risk is necessary and that it can be managed, appropriate safety measures should have been put in place to minimise the likeliness and effects of any risk.

Other school activities feature elements of risk. Physical, sporting activities contains risk, as do scientific experiments and school visits. As we discussed Chapter 20, use of the internet poses significant risk to children and schools put robust measures in place to manage these risks. Removing any of the above activities would be almost indefensible, hindering children's growth, development, and preparedness for the world around them.

Alongside any consideration of the benefits of activities or tools, including AI, awareness needs to be in place of the risks involved. If risks are deemed too great, the educational potential is irrelevant.

An example here is with generative AI. Most generative AI tools include in their terms of use that users must be over 13, and that users between 13 and 18 must be supervised by a responsible adult. This means that while the creative potential of generative AI tools is significant, creative use of generative AI tools might not be suitable for primary-aged children.

In Chapter 22, we discussed five areas of risk relating to use of AI. These are:

- **Respecting copyright and ownership.** It is very hard for children to know which content they are allowed to access and use online. Children at primary level should have an awareness that digital content is owned, that in some cases permission is given for use and that in some cases it has not been. Asking children to get images from sources that include permission gives them a good grounding for further discussion about ownership and AI. In secondary school.
- **Protection of personal data and information.** In many cases, with many AI tools, it is far from clear how securely they use and store data. It is for this reason that the 2023 government publication, **Generative Artificial Intelligence in Education** states that, "Any data entered should not be identifiable". Teachers should not enter children's names, photographs, email addresses, or other personal data into generative AI tools.
- **Recognising where information created by AI tools is false, unreliable, or biased.** As we have discussed throughout this book, children have not yet acquired the life experiences, knowledge, and critical capacity needed to balance the persuasive nature of information that is presented to them. Children who are chatting to an AI chatbot might not realise that it is a chatbot, or might not know how to react to its answers. (Primary children should not have unsupervised access to AI chatbots and use of this technology with primary children should be well-considered, if used.) Children may come into contact with AI generated content online, including films, images and news. Recognising bias is very hard for children, but they can be taught to understand that everything online has a point of view and that some sources of information are more reliable.

Artificial intelligence 191

- **Knowing when AI should and should not be used as a substitute for human work.** Part of being at school is learning the skills needed for self-expression and expression of creativity. The introduction of calculators has not had a negative effect on mathematics. The introduction of chess computers has not stopped people from learning to play chess. In fact, both examples have arguably enhanced their connected disciplines – calculators allow mathematicians to spend their time on deeper thinking rather than mundane tasks, making the results more accurate. Chess computers allow for analysis of games and improvement of strategy. AI is broader in scope than either of these examples.
- **Being aware of ethical and legal use of AI tools.** Teaching children to use technology according to the same principles of 'right and wrong' that we follow in life is one of the most important aspects of teaching them about technology use at primary level. Ultimately, children should be taught to draw parallels between their behaviour online and how they act offline. They should be taught to follow rules, they should develop the vocabulary to talk about online behaviour and they should be clear on how to report issues.

The 2023 government publication, **Generative Artificial Intelligence in Education** contains clear and useful information relating to some of the risks of using AI tools in education. It is recommended that all educational professionals read this and use this as a basis for incorporating AI into school policy, considering the goals of AI use and considering the risks and how they are addressed.

Opportunities from AI

As we have seen, AI is already impacting fields including medicine, science, entertainment, and learning. The reasons that AI is likely to revolutionise these fields also apply to education.

As with the example of calculators in maths, AI tools have the potential to allow teachers to use their time, experience and creativity in meaningful ways. Teachers can use generative AI tools to help them create worksheets, learning aids, presentations, and reading material. These creations can be tailored to the children who need them and the context of the activity. In creating these types of resources, AI operates alongside the teacher, who knows the needs of the school and class of children. The use of AI to help create is a field that will likely develop significantly, incorporating new ways to interact with the technology such as voice commands. Standard English is already used by many chatbots which operate almost as seamlessly as a human colleague would.

Assessment can be one of the most time-consuming aspects of teaching, yet accurate assessment is crucial for giving children the challenges and support that they need. Assessment is another aspect of teaching with potential to benefit from AI tools. It is not inconceivable to imagine a time when AI tools are able to quickly analyse student work, provide feedback and set work that enables children to progress with their learning.

AI is built into many applications that already exist. Platforms use AI as children answer on-screen questions, setting questions that offer appropriate challenge and support. AI is built into word processing tools, search engines and other platforms for digital creativity. This use of AI can help more children to be creative and overcome barriers and needs.

192 *Artificial intelligence*

> **PAUSE AND REFLECT...**
>
> AI is likely to impact all areas of society, including education.
>
> - Which AI tools will have the biggest impact on primary schools?
> - How might AI affect the teacher's role in school?

Conclusion

The next decade is going to witness technological developments that we might not currently be able to predict or imagine. This is both exciting and challenging for schools. It will be fantastic to be able to offer more children more help with their learning. It will also be exciting to prepare them for the quickly developing world around them by laying the groundwork for some of the technology that they will grow up using.

As we have seen in this chapter, and throughout this book, new technologies bring new challenges, as pupils and staff learn to use them effectively and safely. Schools are rightly careful about adopting new technology, as this usually involves time and expense.

To cope with the changes that AI will bring, schools should establish their ideology and look for technologies that allow them to achieve this. In all cases, this will involve safety and well-being of children. All schools will want children's learning to develop, and this is where some schools might choose to make use of AI tools. From there, schools will consider other strengths, needs and opportunities and select tools that achieve them.

References

Bostrom, Nick, Superintelligence: Paths, Dangers, Strategies, Oxford University Press Oxford, 2014
Tegmark, Max, Life 3.0, Allen Lane, 1st Edition 2017.
Computing Programs of Study: Key stages 1 and 2, National Curriculum of England, Department for Education, 2013.
Generative Artificial Intelligence (AI) in Education, Department for Education, 2023.

22 Computing CPD

Developing subject knowledge

This chapter is about ways that teachers of computing can develop their own subject knowledge. Computing teachers and subject coordinators will share this knowledge with colleagues and children where appropriate and beneficial.

Part of the role of the computing coordinator involves offering CPD to the whole school, to develop teaching in computing and promote developments in the field.

X, formerly known as Twitter

X, formerly known as Twitter, is a valuable tool for computing teachers looking to keep up to date with developments, share ideas and projects and communicate with other teachers involved in computing teaching. X lets users follow people they are interested in, generating a customisable feed of idea, thoughts, and opinions. Users can also see who follows other users, or see who users follow and follow them, quickly creating a useful web of potential information.

There is a huge range of experts to follow in terms of teaching computing. Users can also follow organisations. Some good organisations to start by following include STEM Learning, Hello World Magazine, Code.org, The National Centre for Computing Education, The Department for Education, Computing at School (CAS), Safer Internet Day, and South West Grid for Learning (SWGfL).

Networking and forums

Computing at School (CAS) is an organisation that promotes computing teaching across the UK and aims to support teachers through communities. Teachers who register on the **CAS website** can join **local communities** and more recently, **thematic communities**. These communities run virtual and in person workshops and allow teachers to network and share ideas. Teachers who wish to can apply to lead communities and help run events. Teachers can join as many communities as they wish and register for events, which show up in a feed and generate notifications.

The Computing at School website also features an online **forum**, where members can ask questions and share advice and experiences.

DOI: 10.4324/9781003502555-22

194 *Computing CPD*

STEM Community also host an online forum where members can reach out for advice and share ideas and experiences. Through participating in the STEM Community forums, members can earn badges which can be used towards the 'Teach Primary Computing' certificate, discussed below.

Other ways of networking exist, especially if a school is part of a chain of schools, trust, or another wider organisation. Reaching out to even one other school to share ideas about teaching Computing can yield great results, providing ideas and inspiration for things to try when teaching computing.

Publications

Hello World is a magazine published three times per year and delivered for free to practising teachers. Back issues can also be downloaded as PDFs from the Hello World website. There are also two fantastic, feature length books available in either print or PDF download, one about computing pedagogy and one about subject knowledge. Each issue of Hello World magazine has a particular focus, making it easy to explore themes in depth. The standard of writing and editing is superb, with articles that are succinct and accompanied by photographs and examples of work.

Courses and qualifications

As well as training and development organised by teachers themselves, there are courses that teachers of computing can complete. These have the benefits of providing a structured course to follow, access to educational materials and provides certifications or qualifications upon completing the course. Below are outlined some courses below that teachers of computing, computing coordinators, or staff interested in technology might wish to complete.

The **National Centre for Computing Education (NCCE)**, in conjunction with **STEM Learning**, run a wide range of courses for teachers of both primary and secondary computing. This range allows teachers to choose courses that develop areas that they are interested in or wish to focus on.

Courses run by the NCCE can lead to teachers achieving the **Teach Primary/Secondary Computing certificate** which is awarded by the British Computer Society (BCS), the Chartered Institute of IT.

Courses run by the NCCE are a mixture of self-study courses, remote sessions and in person events. This means that by participating in NCCE courses, teachers of computing also can make links with other practitioners in the field.

PAUSE AND REFLECT...

Computing CPD can involve both in-house and external CPD. Signing up to Computing at School and STEM Community are good first steps.

- What CPD would be a good next step for your development?
- Which areas of computing in your school would benefit from staff CPD?

Apple Education run courses that enable teachers to gain three levels or accreditation: Apple Teacher, Apple Teacher Portfolio, and Apple Distinguished Educator (ADE). The Apple Teacher features online materials and a multiple-choice quiz for each unit. The units of work are each about an aspect of using iOS effectively, such as using Garageband or Pages. The Apple Teacher Portfolio requires teachers to upload examples of use of Apple technologies in education. The Apple Distinguished Educator certification requires that teachers demonstrate innovative use of Apple products in education, as well as leading others in this use.

Any teachers who use Apple products in education will benefit from completing the Apple Teacher certification, which is free and a recognised certification in the field of education. Schools that have committed to using Apple products in lessons may consider whether to assist all staff in achieving this certification, although this decision should be made with consideration of how Apple technologies such as Pages, Keynote and GarageBand are to be used in school.

Google education

Google run their own course for educators who wish to learn about and demonstrate effective use of Google products in education. Teachers can achieve the **Google Educator Level 1 and Level 2 certifications**, before progressing to become certified Google Trainers, Coaches, and Innovators.

The level 1 and level 2 courses require a small fee and are valid for a set number of years. Schools that were planning to use Google products with children would benefit from helping teachers to achieve these qualifications, boosting effectiveness of Google technologies and helping staff with their own development.

Microsoft education

Microsoft have developed a comprehensive education environment in the Microsoft Education website. This features materials and links to enable teachers to learn about Microsoft technologies, blended learning, STEM, AI, and other aspects of using technology in school.

The **Microsoft Educator Centre** also features a wide range of courses that can be completed, including courses tailored to using technology in schools. As an example, the 'Empower Every Student with an Inclusive Classroom' course is tailored towards schools focusing on improving inclusivity through use of technology.

Microsoft also offer professional qualifications that teachers can complete, earning four levels of accreditation. These are **Microsoft Educator**, 'Microsoft Advanced Educator', 'Microsoft Educator Trainer', and 'Microsoft Innovative Educator Expert'. These courses would be useful for schools that are committed to using Microsoft as a means for teaching, class organisation and children's work.

Conclusion

Although computing is a new subject, passionate and proactive communities have grown to develop the subject and teachers. Joining a local computing hub allows for sharing of ideas and meeting other professionals with similar interest in technology.

196 *Computing CPD*

References

Apple Education, https://www.apple.com/uk/education/

Computing Programs of Study: Key stages 1 and 2, National Curriculum of England, Department for Education, 2013.

Computing at School, https://www.computingatschool.org.uk/

Google Education, https://edu.google.com/

Hello World, Raspberry Pi Foundation, https://www.raspberrypi.org/helloworld

Microsoft Education, https://www.microsoft.com/en-gb/education

National Centre for Computing Education (NCCE), https://teachcomputing.org/

Stem Learning, https://www.stem.org.uk/

X, https://twitter.com/

23 Computing and other subjects

Rationale for applying computing skills in other lessons

In this chapter, we consider how other subjects can be enhanced through application of skills taught in computing. We also discover how computing teaching can be enhanced through providing context for application of the skills taught.

To be clear, skills from computing and other subjects still need to be taught in isolation. A lesson where children are required to learn computing skills, in addition to maths skills will likely suffer, as children experience the increased cognitive load of too many new concepts. However, once children have learned to use technology in computing lessons, giving them the chance to apply these skills through work in other subjects can have positive benefits, as long as the teaching of the other subjects is not affected. There may be some instances where children can quickly learn to use a new piece of technology as part of a lesson in another subject - teachers will recognise where this is feasible.

Planning for effective use of computing skills in other subjects requires careful planning, both of computing objectives and of lessons in other subjects. A good approach is to structure the computing curriculum so that children learn the skills they will need prior to using them in other subjects. Children could, for example, learn to use spreadsheets in computing lessons prior to using a spreadsheet to collect data in science. They could learn about animation or filming techniques in computing, prior to using these techniques to record a film in another subject.

My advice to any teachers wishing to structure teaching in this way would be to start with one or two simple applications of computing in another subject before evaluating the effectiveness of this on learning for both computing skills and knowledge from another subject.

PAUSE AND REFLECT...

Incorporating computing skills into other subjects can benefit both computing and the other subject.

- Which subject have obvious links with skills taught in computing?
- How does using computing skills in other lesson benefit computing?

DOI: 10.4324/9781003502555-23

198   *Computing and other subjects*

Computing in maths

Due to the need to control computers with precision, the application of maths skills is a required part of many computing lessons. Computers also provide ways for children to use maths to quickly and accurately generate exciting results that inspire them to investigate further.

As an example, at key stage 1, through programming Beebots, children will develop the ability to count accurately, use quarter and half turns and estimate (or measure) the length of the Beebot. With the newer Bluebot robots, using the iPad app, children can extend this by using degrees and centimetres to program the robot.

As another example, at key stage 2, while programming in Scratch, children will apply their knowledge of coordinates, negative and positive numbers, and degrees of turns. Children can also apply their knowledge of multiplication and division while using repetition to create shapes and patterns.

Maths objective	Digital activity	Computing objective
Year 1 Maths, (position and direction) - "Describe position, direction and movement, including whole, half, quarter and three quarter turns".	Children create instructions (algorithms) for **Beebots** to navigate mazes, maps or reach a destination. Create a dance routine for Beebots Children program each other, then create algorithms for the robot in the **A.L.E.X.** iPad app.	Key stage 1 - "Create and debug simple programs".

Maths objective	Digital activity	Computing objective
Year 3 Maths (measurement) - "Compare the durations of events".	Children use digital timers, including on devices such as iPads, to measure the duration of everyday events, experiments, or sports events.	**KS2** - "Collect, analyse, evaluate and present data and information".

Maths objective	Digital activity	Computing objective
Year 5 Maths (multiplication and division) - "Identify multiples and factors, including finding all factor pairs of a number".	Children create a variable using **Scratch**. They program the variable to change by a multiple, i.e. by 8. Children could also create a list and add this number to a list.	**KS2** - "Design and create a range of programs, systems and content that accomplish specific goals".

Computing and other subjects 199

Maths objective	Digital activity	Computing objective
Year 5 Maths (properties of shapes) - "know angles and measured in degrees: estimate and compare acute, obtuse and reflex angles".	Children are taught that regular shapes can be drawn by knowing the exterior angles, i.e., the exterior angles for a triangle are 360° ÷ 3 = 120°. Children program a sprite using **Scratch** to draw shapes using the pen tool and turning the exterior angles. Children can repeat shapes to create patterns. Children could extend this by programming simulations of robots **in VEXcode VR,** or physical robots such as **Spheros.**	**KS2** - "Design and create a range of programs, systems and content that accomplish specific goals". **KS2** - "Use sequence, selection and repetition on programs".

Maths objective	Digital activity	Computing objective
Year 5 Maths (measurement) - "Estimate volume"	Children use **Minecraft** to build structures, estimating or calculating the volume of the structures that they build in units cubed. This could be linked to history, science, or geography, depending on the structures that the children build.	**KS2** - "Select, use and combine a variety of software (including internet services) on a range of digital devices to design and create a range of programs, systems and content that accomplish given goals, including analysing, evaluating, and presenting data and information".

Maths objective	Digital activity	Computing objective
Year 5 Maths (statistics) - "Solve comparison, sum and difference problems using information presented in a line graph".	Children record data using a spreadsheet and generate different types of graphs about this. Children make use of tools that generate graphs, such as Sphero robots, and draw conclusions from this. Children use data loggers, including iPad apps such as **Phyphox**, **Wind Tunnel**, or **Sparkvue** data loggers.	**KS2** - "Collect, analyse, evaluate and present data and information".

Maths objective	Digital activity	Computing objective
Year 6 Maths (algebra) - "Use simple formulae. Express missing number problems algebraically".	Children use **Minecraft** to represent algebraic problems visually. For example, 10x = 8x + 14 can be rearranged as blocks of 10x - 8x = 14, so 2x = 14, so x = 2.	**KS2** - "Collect, analyse, evaluate and present data and information".

200 *Computing and other subjects*

Maths objective	Digital activity	Computing objective
Year 6 Maths (statistics) - "Interpret and construct pie charts and line graphs and use these to solve problems".	Children collect data and record this using a spreadsheet. They use **Google Sheets** or **Microsoft Excel** to generate and draw conclusions about pie charts. These could be, for example, about class preferences on a subject.	**KS2** - "Collect, analyse, evaluate and present data and information".

Maths objective	Digital activity	Computing objective
Year 6 Maths (statistics) - "Calculate and interpret the mean as an average".	Children collect data using a spreadsheet. They write simple formulae to generate a mean average, i.e., =average a4:d4	**KS2** - "Collect, analyse, evaluate and present data and information".

Computing in English

English covers the skills of reading, writing, speaking, and grammar, including spelling. As stated in the national curriculum, English aims to develop children's ability to express their ideas to an audience, including through making presentations, participating in debate, and writing in a style that is appropriate for a given audience. Children should also develop an appreciation for texts appropriate to them, and texts that help them to understand their culture and heritage.

Projects and work with links to computing offer some excellent opportunities to facilitate and enrich English, meeting the aims stated above. Some of the best English work I have done with children has been work where they are writing for a real purpose, including having a real audience. Use of ICT skills taught in computing can facilitate this sense of purpose and audience, as exemplified below. English can also benefit computing, providing children with the opportunity to read about, discuss and debate topics covered in computing, to assess positive and negative aspects of technology and to learn to use the vocabulary necessary to fluently talk about technology.

English objective	Digital activity	Computing objective
Year 1-6 (spoken language) - "Participate in discussions, presentations, performances, role play, improvisations and debates".	Children set up a debate and film this, using different camera angles, before editing this together, watching, and evaluating each other's input. Children turn their writing into short films, which they record using different camera angles. Children perform their writing to accompany animation, or other short films that they make. These could be fictional, instructional, or other genres. Children vocalise their ideas as an audio or video recording, such as a video blog, tv, or radio show.	**KS2** - "Select, use and combine a variety of software (including internet services) on a range of digital devices to design and create a range of programs, systems, and content that accomplish given goals, including analysing, evaluating, and presenting data and information".

Computing and other subjects 201

English objective	Digital activity	Computing objective
Year 1 (writing, composition) - "Write sentences by saying out loud what they are going to write about, composing a sentence orally before writing it".	Children use apps such as **Chatterpix** or **Toontastic** to record characters, or photographs of characters speaking. Children could also use an app like **iMovie** to add their voice recording to pictures of characters.	**KS1** - "Use technology purposefully to create, organise, store, manipulate and retrieve digital content".

English objective	Digital activity	Computing objective
Year 3 & 4 (writing, composition) - "draft and write by composing and rehearsing sentences orally".	Children use technology to record their ideas, practising their speaking and improving their content.	**KS2** - "Select, use and combine a variety of software (including internet services) on a range of digital devices to design and create a range of programs, systems and content that accomplish given goals, including analysing, evaluating and presenting data and information".

English objective	Digital activity	Computing objective
Year 3 & 4 (writing, composition) - "Edit and evaluate by assessing the effectiveness of their own and other's writing".	Children create a shared class space, such as a blog or wiki using a website such as **Google Sites**. They post constructive and positive feedback about photographs of writing uploaded here.	**KS2** - "Select, use and combine a variety of software (including internet services) on a range of digital devices to design and create a range of programs, systems and content that accomplish given goals, including analysing, evaluating and presenting data and information".

English objective	Digital activity	Computing objective
Year 5 & 6 (reading, comprehension) - "Preparing poems and play scripts to read aloud and perform, showing understanding through intonation tone, volume and action".	Children can record themselves reading poems aloud, possibly combining these voice or video recordings with digital imagery using software such as **iMovie**. Children could film themselves using green screen backgrounds.	**KS2** - "Select, use and combine a variety of software (including internet services) on a range of digital devices to design and create a range of programs, systems and content that accomplish given goals, including analysing, evaluating and presenting data and information".

202   *Computing and other subjects*

English objective	Digital activities	Computing objective
Year 5 & 6 (reading, comprehension) - "Drawing inferences such as inferring characters' feelings, thoughts and motives from their actions, justifying inferences with evidence".	Children could use apps such as **Chatterpix** to create 'interview' style videos with characters from history or literature. Children could use AR apps such as **AR Makr or Reality Composer** to create AR scenes of characters expressing their views.	**KS2** - "Select, use and combine a variety of software (including internet services) on a range of digital devices to design and create a range of programs, systems and content that accomplish given goals, including analysing, evaluating and presenting data and information".

English objective	Digital activity	Computing objective
Year 5 & 6 (writing, composition) - "Draft and write by composing and rehearsing sentences orally".	Children use technology to record their ideas, practising their speaking and improving their content.	**KS2** - "Select, use and combine a variety of software (including internet services) on a range of digital devices to design and create a range of programs, systems and content that accomplish given goals, including analysing, evaluating and presenting data and information".

English objective	Digital activity	Computing objective
Year 5 & 6 (writing, composition) - "In narrative writing, create characters, settings and plot".	Children use digital software, such as **Minecraft** or **Wonderdraft** to create settings for stories.	**KS2** - "Select, use and combine a variety of software (including internet services) on a range of digital devices to design and create a range of programs, systems and content that accomplish given goals, including analysing, evaluating and presenting data and information".

English objective	Digital activity	Computing objective
Year 5 & 6 (writing, composition) - "Read aloud their own writing, to a group or to the whole class, using appropriate intonation and controlling the tone and volume so the meaning is clear".	Children use video editing software to create videos of them reading their writing aloud. This could be in the form of a news report, interview, video advertisement, or recording of their story writing with appropriately chosen imagery.	**KS2** - "Select, use and combine a variety of software (including internet services) on a range of digital devices to design and create a range of programs, systems and content that accomplish given goals, including analysing, evaluating and presenting data and information".

Computing and other subjects 203

Computing in science

Science has been transformed through developments in digital technology. New types of experiments are possible and existing experiments have been made more accurate through the ability to collect data precisely.

Science in schools can benefit from use of technology in similar ways. Children can perform experiments and simulations of experiments using technology. Children can collect data about their experiments, leading to further questions and tests. Children can use technology to explore scientific concepts using computer models and simulations.

Science objective	Digital activity	Computing objective
Year 1 (plants) – "Identify and describe the basic structure of a variety of common flowering plants, including trees".	Children take photographs of trees and plants, zooming in and focusing to observe small details.	KS1 – "Use technology purposefully to create, organise, store, manipulate and retrieve digital content".

Science objective	Digital activity	Computing objective
Year 1 (animals, including humans) – "Identify, name, draw and label the basic parts of the human body".	Children take photographs of each other, insert these photographs into apps and label their photographs. Children use apps such as **Luke AR** to create images and videos where they explain the parts of the human body.	KS1 – "Use technology purposefully to create, organise, store, manipulate and retrieve digital content".

Science objective	Digital activity	Computing objective
Year 1 (seasonal changes) – "Observe changes across the four seasons".	Children take photographs of things particular to a season. These could include setting up time lapse photographs to record longer-term changes.	KS1 – "Use technology purposefully to create, organise, store, manipulate and retrieve digital content".

Science objective	Digital activity	Computing objective
Year 2 (plants) – "Observe and describe how seeds and bulbs grow into mature plants".	Children set up time lapse photography to capture the growth of plants. Children learn about photography and apply these skills to taking photographs of plants growing, including editing and displaying their photographs.	KS1 – "Use technology purposefully to create, organise, store, manipulate and retrieve digital content".

204   *Computing and other subjects*

Science objective	Digital activity	Computing objective
Year 3 & 4 (working scientifically) - "Making systematic and careful observations, and, where appropriate, taking accurate measurements using standard units, using a rage of equipment, including thermometers and data loggers".	Children use data collection apps, such as **Phyphox** and **Arduino Science Journal** to take readings relating to experiments they do. Children use data loggers, such as **Sparkvue data loggers**, to capture accurate readings.	**KS2** - "Collect, analyse, evaluate and present data and information".

Science objective	Digital activity	Computing objective
Year 3 & 4 (working scientifically) - "Reporting on findings from enquiries, including oral and written explanations, displays or presentations of results and conclusions".	Children use digital science journals, such as **Arduino Science Journal** or **Phyphox** to record oral observations of experiments they are doing. Children create video logs of experiments they are doing.	**KS2** - "Collect, analyse, evaluate and present data and information".

Science objective	Digital activity	Computing objective
Year 3 (animals including humans) - "Identify that humans and some other animals have skeletons and muscles for support, protection and movement".	Children use iPad apps such as **Luke AR** or **Skeleton 3D** anatomy to view features of the skeleton and make videos.	**KS2** - "Collect, analyse, evaluate and present data and information".

Science objective	Digital activity	Computing objective
Year 3 (rocks) - "Describe in simple terms how fossils are formed when things that have lived are trapped within rock".	Children use stop motion animation to create short films showing the process of fossil formation. This could be physical animation, or digital animation using websites such as **Wick Editor**.	**KS2** - "Select, use and combine a variety of software (including internet services) on a range of digital devices to design and create a range of programs, systems and content that accomplish given goals, including analysing, evaluating and presenting data and information".

Computing and other subjects 205

Science objective	Digital activity	Computing objective
Year 4 (living things and their habitats) – "Explore and use classification keys to help group, identify and name a variety of living things in their local and wider environment".	Children use Scratch to make a program that identified living things based on questions asked. (This is a challenging activity that will require use of a branching conditional structure. Children should start with a simple example, using 3 or 4 things).	**KS2** – "Use sequence, selection and repetition on programs". **KS2** – "Use logical reasoning to predict how some simple algorithms work and detect and correct errors in algorithms and programs".

Science objective	Digital activity	Computing objective
Year 4 (states of matter) – "Identify the part played by evaporation and condensation in the water cycle and associate the rate of evaporation with temperature".	Children create a time lapse video to show evaporation or condensation happening, possible in conjunction with an experiment such as creating evaporation and condensation in a jar. Children use Scratch. Or other tools, to create annotated animated explanations of the water cycle.	**KS2** – "Select, use and combine a variety of software (including internet services) on a range of digital devices to design and create a range of programs, systems and content that accomplish given goals, including analysing, evaluating and presenting data and information".

Science objective	Digital activity	Computing objective
Year 4 (electricity) – "Identify whether a lamp will light or not in a simple series circuit".	Children use **Tinkercad** to create and test simulations of circuits.	**KS2** – "Design and create a range of programs, systems and content that accomplish specific goals, including controlling or simulating physical systems".

Science objective	Digital activity	Computing objective
Year 5&6 (working scientifically) – "Taking measurements using a range of scientific equipment, with increasing accuracy and precision, taking repeat readings where appropriate".	Children use data logging equipment to make data gathered in experiments accurate. This could include data collection apps, such as **Arduino Science Journal** or **Phyphox, Sparkvue data loggers**, or **Sphero** robots which collect and record data.	**KS2** – "Collect, analyse, evaluate and present data and information".

206   *Computing and other subjects*

Science objective	Digital activity	Computing objective
Year 5 (Earth and space) – "Describe the movement of the Earth and other planets in relation to the Sun in the solar system".	Children use AR tools, such as **CoSpaces**, **AR Makr** or **Reality Composer** to create AR videos of the planets in the solar system. Children use the physics tools **Tinkercad** to create simulations of the orbit of the planets. Children use **Scratch** to program orbit of the planets, using trial and error for program each planet.	**KS2** – "Select, use and combine a variety of software (including internet services) on a range of digital devices to design and create a range of programs, systems and content that accomplish given goals, including analysing, evaluating and presenting data and information".

Science objective	Digital activity	Computing objective
Year 5 (forces) – "Recognise that some mechanisms, including levers, pulleys and gears, allow a smaller force to have a greater effect".	Children use simulation of physical systems, such as **Tinkercad** or **Contraption Maker** to experiment with physical systems. Children use **Lego Spike** systems to construct and test physical systems.	**KS2** – "Design and create a range of programs, systems and content that accomplish specific goals, including controlling or simulating physical systems".

Science objective	Digital activity	Computing objective
Year 5 (forces) – "Identify the effects of air resistance, water resistance and friction, that act between moving surfaces".	Children use the **Wind Tunnel Free** iPad app to test the effects of different shapes on air resistance and downforce. Children could use these results to design 3d models, such as cars or aeroplanes.	**KS2** – "Design and create a range of programs, systems and content that accomplish specific goals, including controlling or simulating physical systems".

Science objective	Digital activity	Computing objective
Year 6 (evolution) – "Identify how animals and plants are adapted to suit their environment in different ways and that adaption may lead to evolution".	Children use simulations of evolution, such as Evolution Simulator, to replicate and observe the process where evolution occurs over generations.	**KS2** – "Design and create a range of programs, systems and content that accomplish specific goals, including controlling or simulating physical systems".

Computing and other subjects   207

Computing in art and design

The national curriculum states that children should,

> Become proficient in drawing, painting, sculpture and other art, craft and design techniques.

It also states that children should be equipped with the skills to,

> Experiment, invent and create their own works of art.

Digital forms of art are not mentioned by the national curriculum, while physical forms of art including drawing, painting and sculpture are required. However, digital forms of art can be taught alongside their physical counterparts, reflecting the modern world in which digital art, such as animation, forms such a large part of our culture.

Another use for digital technology in art is form displaying and enhancing children's physical artwork. Children can upload pictures of their artwork online for a real audience, or create digital portfolios of their art. They can also use apps to bring alive parts of their artwork and the work of others.

As well as the requirements for creating art, the national curriculum states that children should,

> Know about great artists, craft makers and designers, and understand the historical and cultural development of their art forms.

As we will see with the key stage objectives below, there is scope to use some of the digital tools available to children to help them explore and learn about the work of artists and its historical significance.

Art objective	Digital activity	Computing objective
Key stage 1- "Pupils should be taught to use drawing, painting and sculpture to develop and share their ideas, experiences and imagination".	Children use digital tools to bring their drawings to life, including **Chatterpix** and apps that animate parts of still pictures.	**KS1**- "Use technology purposefully to create, organise, store, manipulate and retrieve digital content".

Art objective	Digital activity	Computing objective
Key stage 1- "Pupils should be taught about the work of artists, craft makers and designers, describing the differences and similarities between different practices and disciplines".	Children use the **Google Arts and Culture** app to experience work by different artists and experiment with their style.	**KS1**- "Use technology purposefully to create, organise, store, manipulate and retrieve digital content". **KS1**- "Recognise common uses of technology beyond school".

208 *Computing and other subjects*

Art objective	Digital activity	Computing objective
Key stage 2 - "Pupils should be taught to improve their mastery of art and design techniques, including drawing, painting and sculpture with a range of materials".	Children use digital drawing apps and tools, such as **Procreate, Tayasui Sketches,** and **Wick Editor** to create digital artwork, including animation. Children learn to express their ideas through photography and photo editing. Children use digital methods to display their physical art work, including AR apps such as **AR Makr** and **Reality Composer**. Children use Tinkercad to create sculptures, which can be 3D printed using 3D printers.	**KS2** - "Select, use and combine a variety of software (including internet services) on a range of digital devices to design and create a range of programs, systems and content that accomplish given goals, including analysing, evaluating and presenting data and information".

Computing in PE

PE is a subject in which we hope that children will have a break from screens, focusing on physical skills, fitness, coordination and sporting attitude.

However, as we see with professional athletes, there is huge potential for technology to improve sporting performance. This can include children simply recording themselves to watch back and evaluate their performance and collecting data to drive improvement. Below, are examples of how skills taught in computing lessons have a place in PE lessons, benefitting both subjects.

PE objective	Digital activity	Computing objective
Key stage 1 - "Master basic movements including running, jumping, throwing and catching...and begin to apply these in a range of activities".	Children use an iPad camera to film each other performing movements and sequences. They watch these back for evaluation and improvement.	**KS1** - "Use technology purposefully to create, organise, store, manipulate and retrieve digital content". **KS1** - "Recognise common uses of technology beyond school".

PE objective	Digital activity	Computing objective
Key stage 1 - "Perform dances using simple movement patterns".	Children create algorithms to perform dance routines. They identify patterns of movements and state where patterns can be repeated.	**KS1** - "Understand what algorithms are".

Computing and other subjects 209

PE objective	Digital activity	Computing objective
Key stage 2 - "Play competitive games...and apply basic principles suitable for attacking and defending".	Children play algorithms for attacking and defensive plays. They associate these patterns of movement with functions in computing.	**KS2** - "Use logical reasoning to predict how some simple algorithms work and detect and correct errors in algorithms and programs".

PE objective	Digital activity	Computing objective
Key stage 2 - "Compare their performances with previous ones and demonstrate improvement to achieve their personal best".	Children record their technique in sporting activities, including filming each other using a slow-motion camera. Children watch these videos back and identify areas for improvement. Children create algorithms for sporting activities and movements, such as 'taking a penalty'.	**KS2** - "Collect, analyse, evaluate and present data and information".

Computing in history

As stated in the national curriculum, history teaching aims to "help children gain a coherent knowledge and understanding of Britain's past and that of the wider world". As stated in the aims of the national curriculum, this includes children:

- Gaining understanding of a consistent chronological narrative
- Knowing the history of aspects of the wider world, including ancient civilisations and non-European societies
- Understanding historical concepts, such as change cause and consequence
- Understanding methods of historical enquiry
- Understanding connections between local, regional, national, and international history, as well as cultural, economic, military, and other contexts

Some of the skills taught through computing can offer children useful ways to meet history objectives. These can include children expressing historical ideas using skills taught in computing, as well as using technology to enhance historical enquiry and investigation.

History objective	Digital activity	Computing objective
Key stage 1 - "Pupils should be taught about the lives of significant individuals in the past who have contributed to national and international achievements".	Children use apps such as **Chatterpix** to bring pictures of historical characters to life, thinking about what they might say.	**KS1** - "Use technology purposefully to create, organise, store, manipulate and retrieve digital content".

210   *Computing and other subjects*

History objective	Digital activity	Computing objective
Key stage 2 - "Pupils should be taught about the Roman Empire and its impact on Britain".	Children use **Geacron** to explore how empires and civilisations have changed through history. They could record themselves in front of a greenscreen and combine their own explanations with use of digital maps.	**KS2** - "Select, use and combine a variety of software (including internet services) on a range of digital devices to design and create a range of programs, systems and content that accomplish given goals, including analysing, evaluating and presenting data and information".

History objective	Digital activity	Computing objective
Key stage 2 - "Pupils should be taught about a local history study".	Children use digital maps, such as **Google Maps** or **Google Earth** to explore local sites. Children use **Google Earth** to create a tour of a local area.	**KS2** - "Select, use and combine a variety of software (including internet services) on a range of digital devices to design and create a range of programs, systems and content that accomplish given goals, including analysing, evaluating and presenting data and information".

History objective	Digital activity	Computing objective
Key stage 2 - "Pupils should be taught a significant turning point in British history, for example, the first railways or the Battle of Britain".	Children create video explanations of significant turning points in history. These could be live recordings, interviews or include animations of significant events.	**KS2** - "Select, use and combine a variety of software (including internet services) on a range of digital devices to design and create a range of programs, systems and content that accomplish given goals, including analysing, evaluating and presenting data and information".

History objective	Digital activity	Computing objective
Key stage 2 - "Pupils should be taught about the achievements of the earliest civilizations".	Children use **Google Earth** to explore famous historical sites. They create tours of sites using **Google Earth** tours. Children use apps such as **Google Arts and Culture** to explore and experience cultural artefacts.	**KS2** - "Select, use and combine a variety of software (including internet services) on a range of digital devices to design and create a range of programs, systems and content that accomplish given goals, including analysing, evaluating and presenting data and information".

Computing and other subjects 211

Computing in geography

Geography, as outlined by the national curriculum, bears resemblances to science, as it fosters curiosity, observation, and measurement.

The national curriculum for geography states:

> A high-quality geography education should inspire in pupils a curiosity and fascination about the world and its people that will remain with them for the rest of their lives.

As such, there are powerful opportunities for using technology to enhance outcomes in geography, while at the same time giving children opportunities for applying skills taught in computing.

In the national curriculum, the aims for geography at key stages 1 and 2 are given as:

- Developing knowledge of places, as well as their defining physical and human characteristics
- Understanding the processes that create both physical and human features of the world.
- Collecting data gathered through fieldwork.
- Interpreting geographical information, including maps, diagrams and aerial photographs, and Geographical Information Systems.
- Communicating geographical information, including through maps, writing, and numerical/quantitative skills.

We will now explore some examples of how digital technology can be used to achieve outcomes for both geography and computing.

Geography objective	Digital activity	Computing objective
Key stage 1–"Use world maps, atlases and globes to identify the United Kingdom and its countries, as well as the countries, continents and oceans studied at this key stage".	Children use the **Google Earth** website and app to explore the countries and oceans studies. Children use **Google Maps** to learn about the geography of countries and oceans studies.	**KS1**–"Use technology purposefully to create, organise, store, manipulate and retrieve digital content". **KS1**–"Recognise common uses of technology beyond school".

Geography objective	Digital activity	Computing objective
Key stage 1–"Use aerial photographs and plan perspectives to recognise landmarks and basic human and physical features".	Children use **Google Earth** and maps to learn about the features of human settlements.	**KS1**–"Use technology purposefully to create, organise, store, manipulate and retrieve digital content". **KS1**–"Recognise common uses of technology beyond school".

212   *Computing and other subjects*

Geography objective	Digital activity	Computing objective
Key stage 2 - "Locate the world's countries, using maps to focus on Europe (including the location of Russia), and North and South America, concentrating on their environmental regions, key physical and human characteristics, countries and major cities".	Children use **Google Earth** to explore locations studied and locate features. Children create tours of places studied by creating tours in **Google Earth**.	**KS2** - "Collect, analyse, evaluate and present data and information".

Geography objective	Digital activity	Computing objective
Key stage 2 - "Describe and understand key aspects of physical geography, including climate zones, biomes and vegetation belts".	Children use **Google Earth Timelapse** to explore how locations have changed over the last decades.	**KS2** - "Collect, analyse, evaluate and present data and information".

Geography objective	Digital activity	Computing objective
Key stage 2 - "Describe and understand key aspects of human geography, including types of settlement and land use".	Children use **Google Earth Timelapse** to explore how settlements have changed over the last decades.	**KS2** - "Collect, analyse, evaluate and present data and information".

Geography objective	Digital activity	Computing objective
Key stage 2 - "Use fieldwork to observe, measure, record and present the human and physical features in the local area using a range of methods, including sketch maps, plans and graphs, and digital technologies".	Children collect data using spreadsheets, generating and interpreting graphs. Children use data logging equipment, including apps such as Phyphox, Arduino Science Journal, and Sparkvue data loggers to record data about locations studied. Children use digital tools, such as **Google Earth**, **Google Earth Timelapse**, and **Microsoft Flight Simulator** to explore locations studied for fieldwork. Children create videos, including timelapse videos and videos using drones to help them study locations for fieldwork.	**KS2** - "Collect, analyse, evaluate and present data and information".

Computing and other subjects 213

Computing in design and technology

Of all subjects required by the national curriculum, design and technology perhaps has the strongest links to computing.

As stated in the introduction to design and technology in the national curriculum:

> Using creativity and imagination, pupils design and make products that solve real and relevant problems within a variety of contexts... They acquire a broad range of subject knowledge and draw on disciplines such as mathematics, science, engineering, computing and art.

For key stage 2, it is stated that pupils should,

> Apply their knowledge form computing to program, monitor and control their products.

In design and technology, there is a requirement for children to use practical tools and develop their physical skills. At key stage 1, the national curriculum states that pupils should:

> Select and use a range of tools and equipment to perform practical tasks (for example, cutting, shaping, joining and finishing).

At key stage 2, it is stated that pupils should:

> Select from and use a wider range of tools and equipment to perform practical tasks (for example, cutting, shaping joining and finishing) accurately.

Many of the other objectives for design and technology relate to the engineering process, which has been discussed in this book. Broadly, this is the process of identifying a need, designing a solution, testing it and improving it. Both physical elements of design, as well as digital, electronic elements, including program, may well be part of the solutions that children think of to problems. We will look at examples of work that meets design and technology objectives. Further examples are given in this book in the chapters on engineering and physical computing.

Design and technology objective	Digital activity	Computing objective
Key stage 1 - "Generate, develop, model and communicate their ideas through talking, drawing, templates, mock-ups and where appropriate, information and communication technology".	Children communicate and collaborate via a shared document, using apps such as **Google docs**, **Jamboard**, or **Google Sites** to contribute ideas.	**KS1** - "Use technology purposefully to create, organise, store, manipulate and retrieve digital content".

Design and technology objective	Digital activity	Computing objective
Key stage 1 - "Explore and use mechanisms (for example, levers, sliders, wheels and axels) in their products.	Children use apps such as **Crazy Gears** or **Simple Machines by Tinybop** to experience and experiment with mechanisms. Children create simple mechanisms using **Lego Spike** systems.	**KS1** - "Use technology purposefully to create, organise, store, manipulate and retrieve digital content".

214 *Computing and other subjects*

Design and technology objective	Digital activity	Computing objective
Key stage 2-"Generate, develop, model and communicate their ideas through discussion, annotated sketches, cross sectional and exploded diagrams, prototypes, pattern pieces and computer aided design".	Children use **Tinkercad** to create 3d designs for a product. This can include physics simulations and simulations of circuits.	**KS2**-"Design and create a range of programs, systems and content that accomplish specific goals, including controlling or simulating physical systems".

Design and technology objective	Digital activity	Computing objective
Key stage 2 -"Apply their knowledge form computing to program, monitor and control their products".	Children use **Tinkercad** to program elements of a circuit for a 3D design (**Arduino** or **Microbit**). Children use the **Crumble** software to program elements for a Crumble physical system.	**KS2** -"Design and create a range of programs, systems and content that accomplish specific goals, including controlling or simulating physical systems".

Computing in music

Music, as outlined by the national curriculum, aims to develop children's appreciation and understanding of existing music, their ability to sing and play instruments and their creativity in expressing their own ideas through music. As stated in the aims of the national curriculum for music, there is also a requirement that pupils start to understand the technical aspects of music, including patterns, musical structure, pitch, dynamics, and tempo.

Most professional musicians and composers will use digital technology to experience music, improve their own performance of music, and compose their own music. The national curriculum requires that children develop their physical musical skills and abilities to play instruments. Digital technology should not therefore, replace playing of instruments and performing, but operate alongside the skills outlined above to enhance children's appreciation and understanding of music and their potential for musical creativity.

We will now explore some of the ways in which digital technology can be used to enhance music and consider which computing objectives are met.

Music objective	Digital activity	Computing objective
Key stage 1-"Experiment with, create, select and combine sounds using the inter-related dimensions of music".	Children use age-appropriate software to experiment with different sounds. This could include **Sketch a Song**, **Garageband**, **Blog Opera** (part of **Google Arts and Culture**).	**KS1**-"Use technology purposefully to create, organise, store, manipulate and retrieve digital content".

Computing and other subjects   215

Music objective	Digital activity	Computing objective
Key stage 2 – "Improvise and compose music for a range of purposes using the inter-related dimensions of music".	Children use digital tools to compose music. These tools could include the tools mentioned for key stage 1, as well as more sophisticated music apps such as **Beatonal** and **Polyphonic**. Children use **Scratch** to program tunes through creating patterns of notes.	**KS2** – "Select, use and combine a variety of software (including internet services) on a range of digital devices to design and create a range of programs, systems and content that accomplish given goals, including analysing, evaluating and presenting data and information".

Computing in relationships education and health education

According to the 'Relationships Education, Relationships and Sex Education and Health Education' guidance[1] published by the Department of Education in 2019, relationships education is compulsory in all primary schools, and health education is compulsory in all state-funded primary schools.

Relationships education, as explained in the guidance, specifically mentions objectives relating to computing, in relation to online safety. Mental well-being is also covered as part of Health Education and with young people being exposed to a growing range of technology, safe and positive use of technology plays a part in children's mental well-being.

We will explore some of the objectives from relationships education and health education and consider links that can be made with computing objectives.

It is worth considering that for both relationships education and health education, that the objectives given in the guidance are for primary children and not broken down by year group. As we discussed in Chapter 18 on assessment and progression, what is taught and expected in should vary between year groups. Teachers will need to either select key stage objectives appropriate to their year group or teach key stage objectives at a level appropriate to their year group.

The same can be said of objectives relating to E-safety required by relationships education and health education. Teachers will either select objectives appropriate for year groups or teach all objectives at a level that is appropriate to the children of that age.

In the 2019 'Relationships Education, Relationships and Sex Education and Health Education' guidance, there is an entire section in the relationships education guidance entitled, 'Online relationships'. This section contains five areas that children should know about in order to ensure that they are safe online. All five of these areas are important, and all have links to E-Safety taught in computing. Below, we will consider two of these areas and make links to content taught in computing.

216   *Computing and other subjects*

Relationships education objective	Digital activity	Computing objective
Primary level - "Pupils should know that people sometime behave differently online, including pretending to be somebody that they are not".	Children engage in discussion about how people act online, using resources from websites such as **Think You Know**.	**KS1** - "Use technology safely and respectfully, keeping personal information private; identify where to go for help or support when they have concerns about content or contact on the internet or other online technologies". **KS2** - "Use technology safely, respectfully and responsibly".

Relationships education objective	Digital activity	Computing objective
Primary level - "Pupils should be taught how to critically consider their online friendships and sources of information including awareness of the risks associated with people they have never met".	Children engage in discussion and role play, using resources from websites such as **Think you Know**.	**KS1** - "Use technology safely and respectfully, keeping personal information private; identify where to go for help or support when they have concerns about content or contact on the internet or other online technologies". **KS2** - "Use technology safely, respectfully and responsibly".

Relationships education objective	Computing activity	Computing objective
Primary level - "Pupils should be taught how information and data is shared and used online".	Children use online resources from websites such as **Think you Know**, **Childnet** and **NSPCC** to support in-class discussion and create their own guides for keeping information safe online.	**KS1** - "Use technology safely and respectfully, keeping personal information private; identify where to go for help or support when they have concerns about content or contact on the internet or other online technologies". **KS2** - "Use technology safely, respectfully and responsibly".

In the 2019 'Relationships Education, Relationships and Sex Education and Health Education' guidance, there is a section in Health Education entitled 'Internet Safety and Harms', containing seven areas that children should learn about. Below, we will consider some of the objectives from this section, making links between health education and computing. Teachers should read this section of health education objectives carefully, as all the objectives relating to online safety are important and should be taught to all primary children.

Computing and other subjects 217

Health education objective	Digital activity	Computing objective
Primary level - "Pupils should be taught about the benefits of rationing time spend online and the risk of excessive use of electronic devices. In primary school, pupils should be taught why social media, computer games and online gaming have age restrictions and should be equipped to manage common difficulties encountered online".	Children use the internet to research the age restrictions for online tools and social media. This should form the basis of discussion and debate in class. Use the tools from websites such as **Think you Know**, **Childnet** and **NSPCC** to support in class discussion about age-appropriate content.	**KS1** - "Use technology safely and respectfully". **KS2** - "Use technology safely, respectfully and responsibly".

Health education objective	Digital activity	Computing objective
Key stage 2 - "That the internet can also be a negative place where online abuse, trolling, bullying, and harassment can take place, which can have a negative impact on mental health".	Children take part in anonymous surveys and polls in class, using websites such as **Kahoot**, **Poll Everywhere** and **Mentimeter**, where they share experiences and facts about things that have happened online.	**KS2** - "Use technology safely, respectfully and responsibly". **KS2** - "Use search appreciate effectively; understand how results are selected and ranked and be discerning in evaluating digital content".

Computing in foreign languages

Under the national curriculum, learning a foreign language, either ancient or modern, is compulsory from key stage 2.

As the national curriculum states,

The focus of study in modern foreign languages will be on practical communication.

The national curriculum mentions all four skills: reading, listening, speaking and writing in the key stage 2 modern foreign language objectives, while children that study ancient languages will focus more on reading the language and learning about the culture the produced the language.

We will now consider how skills and objectives from computing can link to teaching of foreign languages and the benefits to both subjects where these links are made.

Languages objective	Digital activity	Computing objective
Key stage 2 - "Listen attentively to spoken language and show understanding by joining in and responding".	Children use video conferencing tools to communicate with children in other countries (such meetings should be set up by the school!)	**KS2** - "Use technology safely, respectfully and responsibly".

218 *Computing and other subjects*

Languages objective	Digital activity	Computing objective
Key stage 2 - "Present ideas and information orally to a range of audiences".	Children video themselves talking in the target language about a topic of their choice.	**KS2** - "Collect, analyse, evaluate and present data and information".

Languages objective	Digital activity	Computing objective
Key stage 2 - "Describe people, places, things and actions orally and in writing".	Children use **Google Earth Tours** to create a tour in the target language about a location from the country they are learning about.	**KS2** - "Collect, analyse, evaluate and present data and information".

Languages objective	Digital activity	Computing objective
Key stage 2 - "Engage in conversations; ask and answer questions; express opinions and respond to those of others; seek clarification and help".	Children communicate with children from other counties by video conference or email.	**KS2** - "Use technology safely, respectfully and responsibly".

Conclusion

We have explored how computing objectives can be achieved alongside objectives from other subjects. In some cases, this will mean teaching children computing skills outside computing lessons. However, as we have seen, applying computing skills outside computing lessons has the potential to deepen understanding in both computing and other subjects.

As stated at the start of this chapter, teachers are concerned with ensuring that children achieve learn effectively and produce work to the highest possible standard. Careful consideration must be given before using digital technology, as to whether learning is being enhanced and whether use of technology is both necessary and beneficial.

Note

1 'Relationships, Education, Relationships and Sex Education, (RSE) and Health Education, Statutory guidance for governing bodies, head teachers, principles, senior leadership teams, teachers,' Department for Education, 2019

References

Computing Programs of Study: key stages 1 and 2, National Curriculum of England, Department for Education, 2013.
Relationships, Education, Relationships and Sex Education, (RSE) and Health Education, Statutory guidance for governing bodies, head teachers, principals, senior leadership teams, teachers,' Department for Education, 2019
Childnet, https://www.childnet.com/
Google Earth, https://earth.google.com/

Google Sites, https://sites.google.com/
Kahoot, https://kahoot.com/
Mentimeter, https://www.mentimeter.com/
NSPCC, https://www.nspcc.org.uk/
Poll Everywhere, https://www.polleverywhere.com/
Scratch, https://scratch.mit.edu/
Think you Know, https://www.ceopeducation.co.uk/
Tinkercad, https://www.tinkercad.com/
Vexcode VR, https://vr.vex.com/
Wick Editor, https://www.wickeditor.com/
Wonderdraft, https://www.wonderdraft.net/

24 The future of computing

Digital developments in education and society

There have been several recent developments that highlight the importance of teaching children to use technology effectively.

In March 2023, the government published a document called **The UK's International Technology Strategy**.[1] This document states the aim of making the UK a 'technology super-power by 2030'. Developing use of UK technology is not just concerned with developing UK influence and economy, but with helping to shape a world where technology is used according to values we aspire to in Britian.

This strategy is backed by investment and actions, as developments like the opening of the **National Quantum Computer Centre** in 2022 demonstrate.

More immediately connected to education, in 2023, the Assessment and Qualifications Alliance (AQA) announced the **introduction of digital exams**.[2]

Accordingly, from 2026, children will take some exams digitally, with the scope of this likely to increase after that.

It is not just through exams that children will express themselves increasingly digitally. Coursework is likely to be done in digital format, through methods including typing filming, programming and 3D design.

Preparing children for this future begins now, in primary education, where children should begin learning the digital literacy skills that they will need at secondary level and beyond.

The future of computing as a subject

The objectives laid out in the computing national curriculum ensure that every child has access to teaching about the fundamental skills relating to technology. Thanks to the introduction of computing as a subject, children have had the opportunity to develop their interests in coding, networks, forms of digital expression, digital citizenship, and other fields that help them understand the changing world around them.

One of the greatest benefits of computing teaching is that children become creators of technology, thinking about the needs in the world around them and thinking of their own solutions. Children become discerning about the technology they encounter and use their

DOI: 10.4324/9781003502555-24

The future of computing 221

creativity and ingenuity to suggest and develop their own solutions. This is how pioneers and entrepreneurs are born.

It may be that we now need to further define the digital skills that we expect children to achieve in each year of primary school and by the time they are ready to enter secondary school. Schemes of work, as well as Chapter 18 of this book offer a path to this, interpreting the objectives of the national curriculum by year group. Perhaps it is time to codify this, with expectations that all children gain particular skills and knowledge, for example, learning to touch type.

In Chapter 23, we explored how digital skills taught in computing are also required in some other subjects. This reflects the opportunities and needs of the increasingly digital world around us.

Relationships and health education specifically mention aspects relating to E-safety and the need for teaching this in relationship to children's health. Design and technology mentions use of digital tools, as does geography. Any development to the curriculum is sure to include further requirements for children to use digital technology to express their ideas.

It is great that good teaching in other subjects requires the skills taught in computing. As we saw in Chapter 23, this not only enhances other subjects, but also deepens children's understanding of skills taught in computing lessons. Good planning would match up the skills needed in other subjects to teaching in computing lessons.

Overall, it is likely that digital skills will become increasingly valued by schools. Digital expression may eventually come to be regarded as a 'core subject', alongside English and maths. There is certainly a strong case that children's digital literacy impacts all areas of their study, as well as life outside school.

Developments, opportunities, and challenges in educational technology

Cloud computing

Cloud computing refers to services, data and programs being hosted on computers that are elsewhere, outside school or home.

This presents opportunities for schools. Many programs can now be accessed via the internet browser, without the need to install programs on computers in school. Children in school can use **Google Docs**, **Slides**, **Sheets**, or **Microsoft Word**, **PowerPoint** all online, without any software having to be installed and maintained on school computers. Other services such as **Scratch**, **Tinkercad**, **VexcodeVR** offer similar, cloud-based use of software without local installation.

Another benefit of cloud computing is cloud storage. Many online platforms now save work after every change that is made. It might be that we look back with some astonishment from the future at a time when we had to press the 'save' button every ten minutes.

Since programs that use cloud computing are hosted outside school, on computers much more powerful, schools potentially have access to programs that would have required fast, modern computers to run. One example of this is computer games. Although many teachers are careful about using computer games in school, some games have real educational potential.

222 *The future of computing*

Microsoft Flight Simulator allows users to pilot aircraft and explore cities and geography around the world. Due to the high computer running requirements, its use in schools is likely limited. However, if, or when, it is possible to access this software via cloud computing, the experience of flying over the Grand Canyon, or the city of Rome with children will be magical.

Universe Sandbox is a beautiful, 3D physics simulation of bodies in space. Children can observe how planets and stars behave near each other, understand how orbits work and view the comparative sizes of stars and planets. They can also add a helpful black hole when they are finished to tidy everything up. Again, this program requires a fairly powerful computer to run, but cloud computing might offer a way for children to access services like this.

We have already discussed **Kerbal Space Program**, the last 'game' to be mentioned at this point. The original Kerbal Space Program has significantly lower system requirements than the sequel and can be used in schools to teach about engineering and coding.

Cloud computing also presents challenges. Since software and data is stored outside of the school, schools need to be confident that data is being stored securely, particularly if it is of a personal nature. It is now common practice to use cloud-based services for school data, but schools must make sure that use of these services adheres to the school data protection policy.

Subscriptions are also a consideration for cloud-based services. Almost all cloud-based services require subscription payments for usage, rather than one-off purchase. Over long periods of time, this can amount to significant amounts of money being paid without actually owning any software.

Virtual reality

With virtual reality (VR), we have the capacity to experience locations as if we were there. This is not limited to locations on Earth, it is possible to visit fictional locations and places on other planets! This kind of experience can have a profound impact on children and adults alike.

VR is already being used in some industries to enable trainees to practice skills in simulations of their jobs. What kind of effects can we expect VR to have on computing education and digital learning?

Use of VR in schools presents unique challenges. First, good quality VR headsets are expensive. It is likely that a class set of VR headsets would be outside the budget of most schools, or that schools would rather invest this money elsewhere. Second, use of VR headsets can cause symptoms similar to motion sickness for some users. Just as with motion sickness, different users can experience a range of different reactions. Teachers might also be cautious about letting children look at screens, close to their eyes, for long periods of time.

It will be interesting to see how use of VR develops over the next few years and what opportunities it presents education with for skills development, creativity, and communication, in addition to the experiences it can offer.

The future of computing 223

Augmented reality

Augmented reality (AR) is a term used for the superimposing of digital images on views of the real world. Augmented reality is achievable with non-specialised equipment, such as iPads or phones.

AR can be used for experiences and gaining knowledge, and for creativity. **Luke AR** is an app that allows children to experience the systems of the human body using AR. **Apollo Moonshot** allows children to witness rockets launching and standing on the Moon in AR. **JigSpace** is a library of AR experiences covering many areas of the curriculum and helping children to understand and collect information about physical processes.

For children to be creative, express their ideas, and create AR content, they can use apps such as **AR Makr**, **Reality Composer,** and **Jig Workshop**. All of these allow children to create AR scenes, which they can even film themselves in. **CoSpaces** is a website that allows children to build and program AR scenes which can be a powerful means of digital expression and useable across the curriculum once learned.

Communication and collaboration

Technology allows us to communicate with people around the world, instantly and easily. While teachers are rightly cautious about letting children communicate online, guided, supervised, and safe communication can be powerful.

Children can now easily communicate with each other and share ideas, creating blogs and wikis, as discussed in Chapter 7. Schools can arrange video calls and email exchanges so that children can communicate with other children around the world. This can help children see the value in global citizenship, learning languages and being accepting and tolerant of different cultures.

Redefinition

Some of the technology covered in this book, taught in computing lesson and other subjects, has the potential to redefine outcomes and learning. New tasks become conceivable, offering children new ways to express their ideas and creativity. The **'SAMR' Model**, proposed by **Dr Reuben R. Puentedura**, explains a continuum of technology use, moving from technology that merely substitutes for, or augments traditional methods, to technology that modifies, or even redefines outcomes.

Tasks should reflect the opportunities of the wider world beyond school. As new forms of creative expression appear in society, these should be reflected by the opportunities for digital expression we give children in school. This include, but is not limited to expression through engineering, robotics, filmmaking, animation, programming, and use of augmented reality.

Futureproofing

How do we plan ahead in computing teaching, with technology developing quickly and opportunities, challenges and changes on the horizon?

224 *The future of computing*

The answer is that schools should establish educational priorities and then look for technology that facilitate these. Educational priorities should be agreed in consultation with school management and other staff in the school, as well as in consultation with governors and the wider school community.

Educational priorities that have been well considered will not change drastically, even though the technology available to achieve them might. Some priorities linked to use of technology that schools might consider include:

- Problem-solving
- Physical computing and engineering
- Entrepreneurship
- Sustainability
- Communication and collaboration
- Digital citizenship, including responsible use of technology such as AI
- Touch typing
- Graphic design
- Animation
- Film making
- Data collection, presentation, and analysis

Once educational priorities have been selected, the decision about which technology or services to use to accomplish them will be one that teachers of computing are well placed to make.

Conclusion

Technology is developing at a rapid pace, presenting new opportunities for schools, children, and their learning. Children can now express their ideas in new ways, access resources independently and collaborate instantly and seamlessly.

This book has presented some of the most effective platforms for using technology to facilitate learning, in computing and across the curriculum.

For example, children who design apps in the **code.org 'App Lab'** have access to a powerful form of digital self-expression, particularly when this is coupled with the excellent **'Apps for Good'** project.

Children who learn to make films, animation or take photos to express their ideas about a theme are learning to use digital technology to convey their ideas to an audience.

Children who collect data about a problem, before designing and building solutions using **Lego**, **Crumble**, or **Arduino** equipment are engaging in the type of engineering that will one day allow them to solve real-world problems.

It is difficult for schools to predict the type of technology that will be available to them in five or ten years. Schools can, however, plan to develop their learning philosophy, learning goals and accordingly, curriculum and teaching. Once these have become established, the technological needs will become clear.

Notes

1 https://www.gov.uk/government/publications/uk-international-technology-strategy/the-uks-international-technology-strategy.
2 https://www.aqa.org.uk/digital-exams.

References

AQA – 'Digital Exams.' https://www.aqa.org.uk/digital-exams
'The UK's International Technology Strategy', Department for Science, Innovation and Technology, 2023.Apps for Good, https://www.appsforgood.org/
Code.org, https://code.org/

Index

Note: **Bold** page numbers refer to tables and *italic* page numbers refer to figures.

abstraction 6, 8, 43, 128
accuracy score 40
Across Asia Youth Film Festival (AAYFF) 90
advanced robotics systems 58
advanced robots 45, 128
advertising boards 123
after-school computer clubs 140
alarm system 70-71
A.L.E.X. 56, 107, 109
algorithms 1, 7, 10, 18, 42, 52-53, 65-66, 118;
    design 6, 79; features of 52; tools for teaching
    children to use 53-66; 'unplugged' 65-66
Android devices 39, 55, 108
animation 33, 35, 45, 61, 85, 91-92, 109, 207;
    animated film 35, 109; animated videos 91
anthropomorphic robotic devices 64, 65
Apollo Moonshot AR 87, 223
App Lab 16-17, 53, 56, 77, 137, 138, 146, 152, 224
Apple 85, 111
Apple Distinguished Educator (ADE) 195
Apple Education 195
Apple iOS 185, 186
Apple Teacher 186, 195
Apple Teacher Portfolio 195
apps 39, 107
Apps for Good project 17, 53, 57, 146-148, 180,
    185, 224
Arduino 35, 113, 115, 119, 121, 124, 143, 185, 224
Arduino IDE 121, 123
Arduino projects 123-124; plant watering system
    123-124; self-driving cars 124
Arduino Science Journal 86, 148

AR Makr 87, 186, 223
art and design, computing in 207-208
Artificial General Intelligence (AGI) *see* strong AI
artificial intelligence (AI) 33, 103; deep learning
    188; definition 188; and E-safety 167; generative
    189; impact 189-190; machine learning 188;
    opportunities from 191-192; risks 190-191; strong
    189; weak 189
artificial narrow intelligence (ANI) *see* weak AI
Artificial superintelligent AI (ASI) 189
assemblies 174
assessment 155-156; in computing 156; in
    teaching 191; types 155-156
Assessment and Qualifications Alliance (AQA)
    220
assessment for learning (AFL) *see* formative
    assessment
assignment quizzes 41
attention deficit hyperactive disorder (ADHD)
    136-138
augmented reality (AR) 33, 87, 186, 223
autistic spectrum disorder (ASD)/autistic
    spectrum condition (ASC) 136, 137
automatic doors 59, 68
axis 18

Babbage, Charles 140
Bagge, Phill 66
BBC website 148
BEBRAS 139-140, 180
Beebot app 118
Beebots 45-47, 54-55, 72, 106, 107, 109, 113, 118,

228 *Index*

119, 128, 185, 198; creative tasks 55; emulators 118; navigating path 55; stopping at destination 54-55

Beetleblocks 74

Berners-Lee, Tim 78, 140

bias recognition 190

Big Bang competition 180

blended learning 49

Bletchley Park 179

block-based coding 113, 126

block-based programming 16, 17, 21, 54, 64, 69, 73, 77, 87, 114, 115

Blockly games 27, 39, 137

blogs 100, 149

Bluebots 54-55, 72, 113, 185

Bluetooth 54, 64, 86

Book Creator 85, 154

Boole, George 20

Boolean logic 12, 20, 21

Boolean statement 20-21

Bostrom, Nick 188; Superintelligence 188

branching/nested conditionals 12

British Computer Society (BCS) 194

British Dyslexia Foundation website 138

broadcasts 15, 16

brute force approach 8

bullying, definition 102, 168

C (programming language) 10

C++ 121

'calling' a function 15, 61

camera shots 89, 90

Canva 85-87, 103, 185

Capek, Karel 112; *Rossovoni's Universal Robots* 112

Cargobot 39-40, 77, 134

CAS website 193

Chat GPT 103, 167, 189

Chat GPT4 189

Chatterpix 106

chess 7, 130

chess computers 189, 191

Chicken Clicking (Wills) 98, 109, 174

Childline 103, 168

'chroma key' features 91

Chrome 25

Chromebooks 186

class blog 86, 148, 151

Class Notebook 151

Class Teams 154

close up shots 90

cloud-based data 79

cloud/cloud-based computing 24, 79, 221-222

cloud storage 221

Code Lab 152

code.org 13, 15, 16, 27, 28, 39, 44, 52, 53, 56-57, 72, 77, 79, 128, 134, 136-141, 146-148, 152, 181, 185, 193, 224

coding commands 65

coding logic 59

cognitive abilities 48

cognitive load theory 27-28, 37, 47-48, 77, 82, 122, 134, 137

colour sensors 63, 115, 117

communication: and collaboration 28, 52, 223; skills 45

comparison operators 21

computational power 24

computational thinking 1, 22, 42-44, 51, 79, 107, 129, 130, 145; definition 6-7; teaching 7-8

computer: definition 19-20; games 59, 69, 74, 89, 100, 129; licence 38, 84; programs 1, 10-11, 19-20, 52, 57, 65

computer-assisted assessment tools 155-156

computer networks 23-24, 52, 78-79; definition 78-79; teaching children about 79

computer science 1, 2, **2**, **3**, 32, 51-79, 81, 96; algorithms 52-53; concept of variables 75-76; definition 51-52; functions and procedures 76-77; networks 78-79; tools to use algorithms **53**, 53-66; using repetition 71-74; using selection 67-71, *68*; using sequence 66-67

computing: curriculum 1, 8, 33, 34, 39; education 1, 5, 6, 42, 51, 145; by key stage 3-4; licence 82; logic of 52; objectives 2-3, **3**; strands of 1-2; as subject 220-221; vocabulary of 10

Computing at School (CAS) 193

computing coordinator 35-36; 21st century skills 179; data protection 182-183; enrichment of computing 179-181; evidencing, feedback and assessment 178; ICT acceptable use in schools 183-184; resourcing and subscriptions 184-186; role of 177; staff training and CPD 181-182; standards of work and progress 178

computing enrichment 179-181; digital leaders

Index 229

181; extra-curricular activities 180-181; school events and competitions 180; school visits 179-180

computing exercise books 27, 41, 152

computing schemes of work 31-36; appropriate level of challenge 34; assessment opportunities 35; balance between skills-based lessons *vs.* project-based lessons 32-33; curriculum 33; exciting and purposeful outcomes 34; importance 31-32; linking to school strengths, celebrations, themes, and values 34-35; skills-based approach 32; spiral approach 33

computing skills 4, 32-34, 39, 143, 156

computing skills in other subjects 197-218; art and design 207-208; design and technology 213-214; English 200-202; foreign languages 217-218; geography 211-212; history 209-210; maths 198-200; music 214-215; PE 208-209; relationships education and health education 215-217; science 203-206

computing teaching 37-49; basic skills 37-38; benefits of 220-221; blended learning 49; cognitive load theory 47-48; examples **46**, 46-47; extending learners 45; independence and problem-solving 42-44; independent starter activities 39-41; intangible 'buzz' 49; lesson structure and routines 37; paired programming 44-45; PRIMM 44; start of lessons 38-39; supporting learners 47; virtual learning environment (VLE) 41-42

conditional logic *12*, 70

conditional statements 69

conditions 28

continuous professional development (CPD) 193-195; courses and qualifications 194-195; developing subject knowledge 193; networking and forums 193-194; publications 194; staff training and 181-182; X 193

Conway, Anne-Marie 103, 174; How to be More Hedgehog 103

cookies 101

copyright and ownership 99-101, 147, 190

CoSpaces 87, 223

Costal Climate Central 147

Counter Terrorism and Security Act (2015) 170

course plotting challenges 116

Creative Commons licence 100

creative process 7

creativity 1, 7, 42, 51

cross-curricular approach 86

cross-curricular project 12, 123, 144

Crumble 113, 115, 118-120, 123, 124, 185, 224

Crumble kits 35, 120

Crumble project 123; advertising boards 123

cryptography 179

cutaway shots 90

cyberbullying 102-103, 168-169, 175, 184

Daisy the Dinosaur 56

dance routines 127-128

data centres 23, 24, 78

data collection 32, 64

data loggers 35

data protection 182-183, 222

Data Protection Act (2018) 182

data protection impact assessment (DPIA) 183

Data Protection in Schools page 182

debugging 6, 7, 22-23, 27, 118, 130-135; need to teach 131; patterns spotting 134; process 133; progression of skills **132**, 132-133; resilience and growth mindset 134-135; way to practise 134

decision trees 69, 70

decomposing 6-8, 11, 59-60, **60**, 62, 114

'deep fake' pornography 166

deep learning 188

'defining' a function 15, 61

Department for Education (DfE) 31, 193, 215

design and technology, computing in 213-214

designated safeguarding lead(s) (DSL) 164, 166, 170

desktop computers 185

desktop publishing suites 85

digital: art 92, 108, 207; camera 106, 110; citizenship 101-102 *see also* E-safety; content 2, 35, 81, 82, 92, 93, 95, 100, 142, 149, 164, 190; developments in education and society 220; devices 28, 40, 42, 51, 53, 68, 71, 81, 86, 90, 96, 108; documents 151; drawings 85, 92, 108, 111; exams 220; feedback 154; footprint 101, 172; leaders 174; media 33; portfolios 207; safety 96 *see also* E-safety; skills 152, 179, 221; systems 51; technology 84, 96, 105, 144, 152, 173, 207; tools 82, 138; watches 20; writing 108

230 *Index*

digital literacy 1, **2**, **3**, 32, 81, 111, 179; artificial intelligence 103; being kind 97; copyright and ownership 100; cyberbullying 102-103; definition 2, 95-96; digital citizenship 101-102; digital footprint 101; following rules 96, 99; inappropriate content management 97-98, 100; privacy 97; reporting concerns 98, 103; resources for teaching 96; sources of information 97, 99-100
digital/online activity 166
Dinosaur Train 83
'disk mover'/'disk transport' challenges 117
distance sensor 23, 28, 63, 67, 70
doubling programs 21
'Do Your Bit' website 148-149
dragging blocks of code, concept of 146
Draw and Tell HD 108, 109
drone: deliveries 113; security 113
Duplo Coding Express 11, 16, 54, 106, 107
dyscalculia 137, 138
dyslexia 137, 138

early years area of learning 105-111; communication and language 106; expressive arts and design 111; information and communication technology (ICT) 105; literacy 108-109; mathematics 109-110; personal, social, and emotional development 107; physical development 107-108; understanding world 110
early years foundation stage (EYFS) framework 105
eating disorders 166, 171
eBooks 85
EdClub 153
Edison, Thomas 22, 122
editing process 90
educational priorities 224
electronic devices 108
email 102, 149, 223
engineering 33, 37, 148-149; process 28-29, 122; skills 35
English, computing in 200-202
English as an additional language (EAL) 140
Enroads 148
environmental problems 149
E-safety 29, 33, 40, 41, 96-100, 103-104, 109, 164-176, 183, 215, 221; adult content 171;

and artificial intelligence 167; commercial activity 169-170; contact and grooming 170; cyberbullying 168-169; digital footprint 172; ensuring and promoting in school 173-174; illegal behaviour 171; importance of teaching 168; malware 172; mental health and body image 170-171; misinformation 169; objectives 4, 164, 166; personal information 171-172; radicalisation 170; requirements for teaching 164-167; staff training 175; technology addiction and screentime 172; violent movies and gaming 169; working with parents 175
E-safety week 104
ethical and legal use, of AI tools 191
EV3 set 115
event 16-17, 23
evidencing and feedback 150-154; in computing 150; computing exercise books 152; external websites 152-153; providing feedback 153-154; using VLE for 150-152
exclusion 102
exterior angle 60-61

face-to-face communication 98, 106, 165
facial expressions 65, 114, 128
fibre optics 24
filmmaking 33, 35, 89-90
filtering systems and monitoring systems 173
Firefox 25
First Lego League competition 57, 115, 139-140, 180
flaming 102
Flashforge 88
Flash Player 57
flip books 91
flow charts 10, 42, 69, 74
Flowol 4 11, 15, 17, 63, 67, 68, 77, 137
foreign languages, computing in 217-218
'forever if' logic 74
formative assessment 155
functions and procedures 52, 57, 61, 66, 76-77, 127, 128; at key stage 2 76-77; text-based programming 77

Game Lab 137
Garageband 33, 186
Gearsbot 14, 18, 40, 63-64, 70, 117

General Data Protection Requirements (GDPR) 182
generalisation 6, 64
generative AI 189, 191
Generative A.I. in Education 183
Generative Artificial Intelligence in Education 167, 190, 191
geography, computing in 211-212
Google 151, 184
Google apps 151
Google Chrome OS 186
Google Classroom 25, 38, 41, 42, 87, 102, 141, 150, 151, 154, 156, 182
Google Docs 33, 84, 102, 221
Google Drive 90
Google Earth app 110
Google Earth Engine 147
Google Education 184, 195
Google Educator Level 1 certification 195
Google Educator Level 2 certification 195
Google Forms 39, 156
Google Sheets 221
Google Sites 86, 149
Google Slides 85, 102, 221
Google Translate 140
graphical effects 61
graphic design 34, 59
graphs 41
green initiatives 149
greenscreen 90-91, 147
green technology 145-149; Apps for Good 146-147; children using technology 145; computing and 145-146; data collection, analysis, evaluation, and presentation 147-148; photography 149; physical computing and engineering 148-149; writing, blogging and communicating 149
green thinking 145
Grover, Lov 140
growth mindset 7, 22, 29, 43, 90, 134-135

Hamilton, Margaret 140
handwriting skills 83
harassment 102, 165, 168
hardware 79
health education 164, 165, 168, 215; primary 171
Hello World (magazine) 193, 194
Hello World website 194
history, computing in 209-210

Hopper, Grace 22, 140
Hopscotch 56
How to be More Hedgehog (Conway) 103, 174

I Can Animate app 91
ICT acceptable use agreement 101, 173
ICT acceptable use in schools 183-184
'if/else' structures 12, 52, 61, 67, 75
illegal content 166, 171
iMovie 90, 91
impersonating 102
inclusion 136-141; able pupils 139-140; attention deficit hyperactive disorder 137-138; autistic spectrum disorder 137; in computing 136; diverse range of backgrounds 140; dyscalculia 138; dyslexia 138; economic background 140-141; English as an additional language 140; physical disabilities 138-139; special education needs and disabilities provision, purpose of 136-137
independent starter activities 39-41; lesson preparation 40-41; problem-solving 39-40; typing practice 40
infographics 85
information and communication technology (ICT) 2, 35, 96, 110, 111, 171, 184
information technology (IT) 1, 2, **2**, **3**, 32, 81-93; 3D design 87-89; animation 91-92; augmented reality 87; collaboration 86-87; data collection, organisation, analysis, storage, and presentation 86; definition 1-2, 81-82; digital art 92; filmmaking 89-90; greenscreen 90-91; keyboard skills 82-84; mouse skills 82, 83; photography and photo editing 92; presentations 84-86; programming 93; skills and tools 82; tablet skills 82, 84; word processing 84
inputs 19, 23, 71, 115
interior angle 60, 61
internet 23, 24, 33, 52, 78, 83, 96, 98, 100, 101
internet services 81
'Intro to App Design' course 146, 147
iPad apps 55, 72, 111
iPad cameras 110
IP address 23, 25, 78-79
iPads 20, 26, 35, 39, 55, 86, 87, 90, 91, 92, 106-108, 110, 152, 186

232　*Index*

Iron Man 113
iteration 12-14

Jamboard/Microsoft Whiteboard 40, 87
Java 10, 146
JavaScript 77
jigsaw puzzles 107
JigSpace 223
JigWorkshop 87, 223
Jobs, Steve 140
Johnson, Katherine 140

Kahoot 39, 41, 156
Keeping Children Safe in Education (KCSIE) 166,
　168, 175
Kerbal Space Program 222
keyboard skills 83-84
Keynote 85, 91, 186
King, Zack 89
knowledge and debugging 132
Kodables 11, 56
Kodu 18, 65, 69, 70, 75

language skills 106
laptops 28, 32, 84, 120, 121, 185, 186
Lazy Teacher's Handbook (Smith) 133
Lego 44, 71, 91, 118, 143, 181, 224
Lego Education systems 57
Legoland Discovery Centre, Manchester 180
Lego Mindstorms/EV3/Spike Prime 18
Lego Robotics 27
Lego Spike 57-58
Lego Spike Prime 27, 35, 45, 57, 70, 113, 115-116,
　124
Lego Spike robots 128
Leicester Space Centre 180
LGFL website 168
Li, Robin 140
Life 3.0 (Tegmark) 188
Lightbot 39, 57, 77
line following challenges 116
listening skills 106
logical approach 35
logical operators 21
logical reasoning 42, 51, 131
logical thinking 42
Logo 10

long shots 89-90
loops 12-14, 17, 28, 66, 72, 81, 126, 128, 134, 157
Lovelace, Ada 140
Luke AR 87, 223
lunchtime computer club 140

machine learning 188
Magic Studio 86
Magic Tools 103
Makecode 120, 185
making a function 14
malware 172
masquerading 102
Massachusetts Institute of Technology (MIT) 58
mathematical operators 21
mathematical quizzes 21
maths, computing in 198-200
mazes 11, 14, 55, 60, 63, 64, 70, 114, 116, 117
mental health 171; and body image 170-171;
　cyberbullying on 102; education 100, 102
Mentimeter 39, 87, 100, 182
meta learning 29
meta-thinking 6, 7, 25, 55, 122, 129
Microbit initiative 185
Microbits 22, 120, 148-149
'Microbits for UK teachers' 148
Micromouse challenge 116
Microsoft 151, 184
Microsoft Advanced Educator 195
Microsoft apps 151
Microsoft Class Teams 38, 41, 150, 151, 156
Microsoft Education 184, 195
Microsoft Educator 195
Microsoft Educator Centre 195
Microsoft Educator Trainer 195
Microsoft Flight Simulator 222
Microsoft Forms 39, 156
Microsoft Innovative Educator Expert 195
Microsoft's Immersive Reader 138
Microsoft Teams 102, 182
Microsoft Word 84, 221
Midjourney 103, 189
mimics 64
Mindstorms series 115
Minecraft 88-89
Miro 87
Miyamoto, Shigeru 140

MLC Maths apps 109
MLC website 109
mobile devices 35, 54, 57, 64, 84, 91, 98, 140
'mod' operator 21
modularising 11
moisture sensors 123, 143
Monkeytype.com 40
Monster Park AR 87
Moodle 150
Moore's law 20
motion photographs 92
motor skills and coordination 107, 108, 138
mouse skills 83
movement/turning commands 76
multi-academy trust (MAT) 173
muscle memory 84
Museum of Science and Industry (MOSI) 180
music, computing in 214-215
musical scores 66
musical sequences 73

National Centre for Computing Education (NCCE) 31, 96, 193, 194
National College 175
The National Computing Museum, Bletchley 179
National Online Safety 175
National Quantum Computer Centre 220
National Video Game Museum, Sheffield 180
nature cams 110
nested loops 13, 61, 66, 73, 74, *74*, 76, 157
neural networks 188
NHS website 138
NSPCC Learning 175
NSPCC website 168
NXT sets 115

object retrieval challenges 116
obstacle avoidance challenges 116
offline behaviour 97, 101
Ohbots 114-115; robotic heads 45, 64-65, 70, 128
on event block 146
'onion skinning' tool 91
online abuse 166, 168
online behaviour 97, 101
online bullying *see* cyberbullying
online creative tools 96
online platforms 153, 166

online relationships 164-165
online safety 81, 166, 168
Online Safety Act (2023) 166, 169, 171
Online Safety Data Blog 168
online shopping 97, 170
online software 83
online technology 86, 95
on-screen coding 120
on-screen programming 16, 18, 21-22, 45, 107, 119
on-screen robotics environments 70
on-screen technologies 148
operators and expressions 21; comparison 21; logical 21; mathematical 21
outing 102
outputs 19, 23, 71, 115

packets 24, 78, 79
Padlet 87, 97, 100
'painting with light' technique 92
paired programming 28, 44-45; in classroom 28
'palm rejection' feature 108
Parson, Dale 127
Parson's problems 25, 26
Parson's puzzles 59, 67, 73, 127
pattern recognition 114
pattern spotting 6, 7, 13, 18, 43, 129, 130, 134
PBS Games 83
PE, computing in 208-209
peer assessment 155
'pen' commands 60, 76
Penguinpig (Spendlow) 174
persevering 6
personal data and information 167, 171-172, 190
'person' graphic 85
Photobooth app 111
photocopying 152
photo editing 92
photo editing apps 149
photography 35, 92, 111, 149; exhibitions 180
Phyphox 86, 148
physical animation 91
physical bullying 168
physical computing 119-125, 148-149, 152; Arduino projects 123-124; benefits 119-120; definition 119; electronics sets 120-121; engineering process 122; example 122-123
physical disabilities 137-139

234   *Index*

physical robotics problems 64
physical robots 63
picture blocks 115
Pixabay 100, 147
pixel 21-22
plant watering system 123-124
plasticine 91
Poisson Rouge 83
Poll Everywhere 41
pornography 166
PowerPoint Slides 85, 221
Predict, Run, Investigate, Modify, Make (PRIMM) 25-27, 44, 127; 'Investigate' 26, 44; in lessons 26-27; 'Make' 26, 44; 'Modify' 26, 44; 'Predict' 25, 44; 'Run' 26, 44
pre-made sequences of instructions 77
President Obama's Computer Science for All initiative 136
Prevent duty guidance: for England and Wales 170
privacy 97
problem-solving 7, 32, 33, 34, 37, 39-40, 42-44, 57, 64, 106, 129, 145; skills 107
problem-solving in computing lessons 43-44; materials to support 43; raising profile of thinking 43-44; use of computational thinking 43
programming 93
progression, in computing 156-163, **157-163**
Project Evolve 96, 175
Project Evolve Edu 175
pseudo-code 10, 18, 62, **62**, 127, 152
Puentedura, Reuben R. 223
Puppet Pals 106
Puppet Pals (with Director's Pass) 108
Python 10, 16, 18, 57, 115, 117, 127, 134

QR code 151, 152
quantum computing 20
quiz game 12, *12*, 69, *70*, 75
quizzes 61, 69, 156
Quizziz 39, 156

radicalisation 170
Raspberry Pi Foundation 25, 44
Reality Composer 87, 186, 223
real-time quizzes 41
Redfern Electronics 35, 120, 185

relationships education 164, 215
'Relationships Education, Relationships and Sex Education and Health Education' guidance 165, 215, 216
relationships education and health education, computing in 215-217
relay switches 124
repetition 12-14, 71-74, *73*, 81, 127; nested loops 74, *74*
resilience 37, 44, 57, 107, 134-135
resources sharing 28
robot emulators 118
robotics/robots 14, 33, 35, 40, 45, 70, 112-118; Beebot emulators 118; Beebots and Bluebots 113; chess set 113; in context 112; devices 112; in education 112; Lego Spike Prime 115-116; motors 116; nurses 113; Ohbots 114-115; problems 63; simulations of 116-117; Sphero robot 114; systems 35; teachers 113; teaching children about 113
role models 140
Rossovoni's Universal Robots (Capek) 112
routers 24, 79
routines 96
rubric tool 151, 156
'rule of three' 92, 149

Safer Internet Day 174, 193
'SAMR' Model 223
scaffolding 7, 8, 18, 25, 26, 47, 54
school computing clubs 181
school special educational needs coordinator (SENCO) 138
science, computing in 203-206
science, technology, engineering, and maths (STEM) 142
Science Museum, London 179
score, concept of 75
Scratch 4, *4*, 10-12, *12*, 14, 15, 17, *19*, *20*, 22, 25, 26, 33, 44, 57-62, 67, 70, *73*, 74, 76, 114, 115, 120, 127, 134, 185, 221; art and patterns 60-61; creating shapes in 14; creating simulations using 62; game design using 59-60, **60**; principles of using 59; user interfaces in 61
Scratch Junior 10, 13, 16, 25, 26, 55-57, 107, 108, 115, 134
screen animation 91

Index   235

screen recording 90
scripts 11, 17
search engines 2, 165, 191
Seesaw 38, 41, 150-152, 154, 184
selection (condition) 11-12, 67-71, *68*
selection logic 71
self-assessment 155
self-driving cars 124
self-teaching computers 188
senior leadership team (SLT) 177
sensors 32, 58, 86, 113, 115, 117, 123
Sentance, Sue 25, 44
sequence 17, 66-67, 126, 128
servers 23, 24, 78
Sesame Street 83
set screen block 146
sex education 164
'shared iPad' tool 152
shopping websites 169
singularity 189
Sketches 91
Sketchup 88
skills-based approach 32
skills-based lessons *vs.* project-based lessons 32-33
Smith, Jim 133; *Lazy Teacher's Handbook* 133
Snap 10
social media 101; platforms 167
software 69, 79, 81, 82
solar system programming **62**
South West Grid for Learning (SWGfL) 175, 193
Sparkvue apps 86, 148
Sparkvue sensors 148
speaking skills 106
special education needs and disabilities (SEND) provision 136-137
Spendlow, Stuart 174; *Penguinpig* 174
Sphero app 114
Sphero Bolt 114
Sphero robots 18, 35, 45, 64, 86, 114
Spike Essentials 57, 115
Spike Prime 33
spiral approach 4, 31, 33, 93, 156
spiral curriculum 31, 33, 75, 82
spreadsheets 86
Standard English 191
STEAM (science, technology, engineering, art

and maths) 124, 136, 142-144; and computing 142-144, **144**; definition 142; incorporating into primary curriculum 143
STEM Community 194
STEM Learning 193, 194
STL file 88
Stop Motion Animator app 91
straw tower 8
Streetview 110
strong AI 189
student film showings 180
styluses 90, 92, 108, 109
subroutines 14-15, *15*, 76, 77; function 14, 15; parameter 14, 15; procedure 14, 15
summative assessment 155
Superintelligence (Bostrom) 188
superintelligent AI *see* Artificial superintelligent AI (ASI)
switches 79
syntax 11, 77
syntax error 11

Tayasui Sketches 92, 108, 111
Teach Computing curriculum 31, 96
Teach Computing scheme 178
teacher assessment 156
teacher-created rubrics 42
teacher modelling of computational thinking 7
Teach Primary/Secondary Computing certificate 194
technology addiction and screentime 172
Tegmark, Max 188; *Life 3.0* 188
temperature sensor 86
terrorism 166, 170
text-based coding 127
text-based programming 12, 18, 77
thinking stations 6
3D design 87-89, 153
3D environments 65, 69
3D games 69
3D models 87, 88
3D printer/printing 88
360 Degree Safe Tool 175
'ticking clock' project 58
time lapse cameras 110
timelapse videos 148
'times table practise' programs 21

236 *Index*

Tinkercad 87, 88, 102, 121, 139, 141, 153, 181, 185, 221
tinkering 6, 27
tinytap.com 83
Toontastic 108
touch sensors 63
touch typing 40, 84, 139, 153
Trimble 88
trolling 165, 170
Turing, Alan 140
Twitter *see* X
2D pictures 91
Typing Club 40, 83, 137, 153, 156, 185
typing practice 40

UK Safer Internet Centre 173, 175
The UK's International Technology Strategy 220
uniform resource locator (URL) 25, 83, 97
Universe Sandbox 222
unplugged activities 65-66, 126-130; chess and
    football 130; in computing lessons 126-127;
    dance routines 127-128; definition 126; 'fakebot'
    exercises 128; marshmallow tower/weight
    bridge 129-130; Parson's puzzles 127; physical
    copies of games 129
unreliability 96
UN Sustainable Development goals 148
user interfaces 61

variables 16, 75-76, 127; children's understanding
    of 75-76; concept of 75
verbal feedback 154
verbalising and planning ideas 28
VexcodeVR 14, 18, 40, 63-64, 70, 117, 124, 128, 134,
    221
violent movies and gaming 169
virtual learning environment (VLE) 25, 33, 38, 39,
    41-42, 49, 56, 59, 60, 76, 101, 102, 133, 134, 139,
    141, 184; using for evidencing 150-152
virtual reality (VR) 222
virtual robots 124
visual effects 90, 91
vocabulary 10, 29, 52, 98, 100, 102, 103, 106
voice calls 102, 149, 223
voice commands 191

voice narration 109
voice recognition 114
VR headsets 222
Vygotsky's zone of proximal development 26,
    155

WALT ('We are learning to') 37
waqi.info 147
water cycle programming **62**
weak AI 189
web address *see* uniform resource locator (URL)
web-apps 186
web-based software 186
web browser 25, 99
webcams 114
webpages 24, 25, 38, 78
web search 74, 100
web services 100
websites 41, 96, 99-101, 103, 107, 120
WhatsApp 167
whiteboard.fi 40
Wick Editor 91, 185
Wikipedia 86, 100
wikis 86, 100
WILF ('What I'm looking for') 37
Wills, Jeanne 174; *Chicken Clicking* 98, 109, 174
Windows File Explorer 120
WindTunnel Free 86
wired networks 23, 78
wireless networks 23, 78
word blocks 115
word per minute (WPM) score 40
word processing 84
wordwalls 41
workplane tool 88
World Weather Map 148
World Wide Web 24, 52, 78
written feedback 154

X 120, 193

YouTube 101, 113, 120

zero-tolerance policy 103

Printed in the United States
by Baker & Taylor Publisher Services